AN ACT OF IMMORALITY

AN ACT OF IMMORALITY

John Carr

Hodder & Stoughton

LONDON SYDNEY AUCKLAND TORONTO

British Library Cataloguing in Publication Data

Carr, John
  An act of immorality.
  1. Blacks – South Africa – Segregation
  2. South Africa – Race relations
  I. Title
  305.8'00968   DT763

  ISBN 0-340-39956-2

CONTENTS

Prologue   9
1   The Meeting   11
2   The Cottage   46
3   The Watcher   69
4   The Pregnancy   98
5   The Hatful of Christmas Cheer   106
6   The Two Worlds   126
7   The First Move   137
8   The Police Raid   160
9   The Letter   187
10 The Baby   213
11 The Living Nightmare   235
12 The Earthquake   256
13 The Bid for Freedom   276
14 The Voyage   297
Epilogue   303

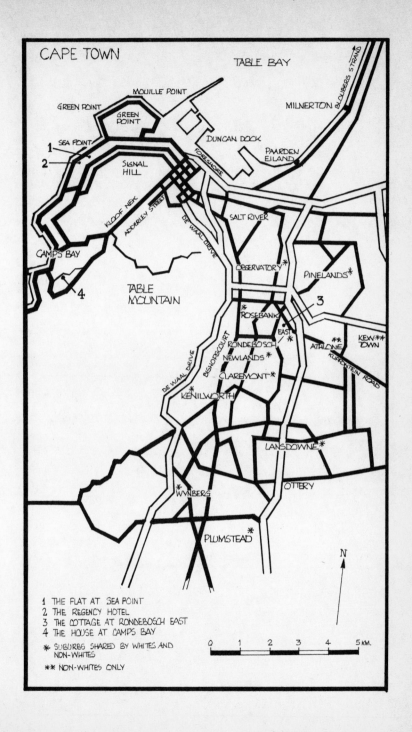

CAPE TOWN

TABLE BAY

BLOUBERG STRAND

MOUILLE POINT

GREEN POINT

GREEN POINT

MILNERTON

DUNCAN DOCK

1 SEA POINT

FORESHORE

PAARDEN EILAND

2

SIGNAL HILL

KLOOF NEK

ADDERLEY STREET

DE WAAL DRIVE

SALT RIVER

CAMPS BAY

OBSERVATORY *

PINELANDS *

4

TABLE MOUNTAIN

3

ROSEBANK *

EAST

RONDEBOSCH

ATHLONE **

KEW TOWN **

DE WAAL DRIVE

BISHOPSCOURT

NEWLANDS *

KLIPFONTEIN ROAD

CLAREMONT *

KENILWORTH *

LANSDOWNE *

WYNBERG *

OTTERY

PLUMSTEAD *

N

1 THE FLAT AT SEA POINT
2 THE REGENCY HOTEL
3 THE COTTAGE AT RONDEBOSCH EAST
4 THE HOUSE AT CAMPS BAY

✳ SUBURBS SHARED BY WHITES AND
  NON-WHITES

✳✳ NON-WHITES ONLY

0   1   2   3   4   5 KM.

PROLOGUE

This is an account of certain events which took place in and around Cape Town, South Africa, in the 1960s.

Although the notorious Immorality Act was repealed in 1985, at the time these events took place it was considered by the South African authorities to be a very serious criminal offence for whites and non-whites to fraternise in any way. Even a private social gathering at which people of different races were present, was then illegal. 'Mixed' couples suspected of enjoying each other's company or – in the eyes of South Africa's Vice Squads – even worse, could find themselves subjected to house- and body-searches and remorseless interrogation, not to mention national press coverage of the offence. As often as not the law handed out harsh sentences to such people for the 'crime' of being in love with one another.

Despite the threat to personal freedom and the insult to human dignity implicit in the implementation of the Immorality Act, people still tended to be people, but on average, illicit relationships between couples of different ethnic groups lasted only a short time, often ending with long prison sentences of hard labour, or suicide.

The author managed to maintain a close, loving relationship with the young woman who eventually became his wife, for a period of two and a half years. How he was able to do this – and the price they paid – is the sum total of this story. Although the events described actually took place, the names and some of the descriptions and activities of people mentioned in the story have been changed, for obvious reasons.

THE MEETING

The view from the office window looked like something out of a travel brochure. In the foreground lay Cape Town docks with the harbour beyond. In front of a customs shed an elderly steam locomotive hauled a long train of wagons. In the sparkling harbour a pair of tugs assisted a stately Union Castle mailboat as she made her way towards the harbour mouth and the freedom of Table Bay. One of the tugs was an old coal-burner; a great stream of thick black smoke billowing from her yellow and green smokestack contrasted vividly with the creamy-white wake boiling around her broad stern. Out in the blue serenity of Table Bay were a number of vessels of all shapes and sizes. One of them was a Korean whaler, riding at anchor with its conspicuously high bow nosing into the wind. I half expected to see a whale blowing; not an uncommon sight in the bay.

The coastline swept around and away to the right in a long curving arc. On and beyond the power station at Paarden Eiland I could just make out the smudgy outline of Blouberg Strand, a tiny hamlet perched on the edge of the bay and a favourite family picnic rendezvous on Sunday afternoons.

I looked across to the extreme left of the panoramic view and my eyes stopped to focus on the hump of Robben Island, South Africa's penal colony and at that time home of Nelson Mandela and other political dissidents imprisoned on the grim-looking rock. The island, from which no one has ever escaped, is surrounded by a maelstrom of treacherous currents and icy cold water, impossible to swim through. Rumour had it that a few desperate prisoners had tried but had perished in their attempts. What would the prisoners be doing at this time, I wondered. Breaking rocks perhaps? Performing mundane and soul-destroying tasks prescribed by a vindictive state, or simply sitting and staring at the walls?

I felt pity for them and it occurred to me that they would be able to see Cape Town just as clearly as I could see Robben Island. How must they have felt about the people walking freely in the city streets? Were they thinking of their families and friends? It was depressing to consider such things.

It was early summer and outside the building it would be uncomfortably hot but inside my office it was a cool, air-conditioned sixty-five degrees F. The building itself was, at that time, the tallest in Cape Town. Being the tallest it was also the most prestigious, a multi-million-rand steel, concrete and glass structure standing seventeen storeys high. With its high-speed elevators, mosaic-tiled reception area containing a fountain, a post office, a bank, a complex of high-priced shops, hairdressing salons and a superb penthouse restaurant, the building provided luxury accommodation for many South African companies and organisations, including one government department.

The tall green building stands near the Cape Town foreshore at the beginning of an imposing highway known as Die Heerengracht – Gentlemen's Walk – which leads almost from the harbour directly into the heart of the Republic's oldest and certainly most beautiful city at the foot of magnificent Table Mountain. A wide expanse of immaculate green lawn shaded by palm trees divides the Heerengracht's twin traffic lanes. The whole area is a delightful place to earn one's living and at that time I was making mine as a copywriter for an advertising agency.

It was not such a long time previously that I had been working in London, but the problems of trying to cope with the rat-race of living and working there, combined with the dreadful climate, had resulted in my packing my bags and heading south early in 1962, like the swallows I suppose. I had no regrets although there were many things about England that I missed. So here I was without a care in the world, living a very pleasant life with no idea of what lay in store for me.

I returned my attention to my immediate task. I had been briefed to write a hundred or so words to promote a new product for one of the agency's principle clients, a local manufacturing chemist with a nice line in proprietory branded products which were popular throughout South Africa. Not satisfied with the success of his established range of pharmaceutical dispensations and potions, our ambitious client was constantly striving to reach his own personal El Dorado in the form of the 'ultimate' product.

It is a well-known fact that over the centuries Man has made almost desperate attempts to discover a cure for that condition that most men fear – baldness – a sad reflection on Man's vanity and avarice. It is also a well-known fact that so far Man has failed.

The client and I were on John-and-Hymie terms and I couldn't help admiring his single-mindedness. He had already attempted to launch a 'cure' for baldness but his efforts had been thwarted by the South African Newspaper Proprietors Association which disagreed with the claims made in his press advertisements. One of these showed an unhappy-looking gentleman with a splendid head of skin and in the same ad the same gent appeared with a splendid head of hair. The typical 'before and after' technique. The chap in the ad told how he had recovered his hair after regularly using Hymie's product. What he didn't mention was that his baldness had been due to alopecia, and I suspected that he had recovered his hair through the vigorous brushing and stimulation recommended in Hymie's literature rather than Hymie's product.

Needless to say the watchdogs of South Africa's press and other media would not allow the luckless Hymie to claim his 'cure' for baldness. Despite this minor setback our worthy and irrepressible client was poised on the brink of launching news of a major breakthrough towards yet another of mankind's cherished dreams – a genuine aphrodisiac – and I had been chosen as the lucky person to help Hymie promote and market his remarkable new product.

I remember the product clearly. It was a perfectly spherical pill with a metallic-looking silver finish to it, and if it hadn't been for its weight I would have sworn that it was a ball-bearing. It laid claim to containing practically every vitamin known to man plus a few that I had never heard of, but its most fascinating ingredient, if that is the right word, was 'an extract removed from particularly sensitive organs of a Balkan bull'. I had to hand it to Hymie: if he had thought that one up he should have been sitting behind my typewriter.

Despite my warnings that he didn't stand a snowflake's chance in Hell of getting any of my copy past the SANPA he told me to shut up and get on with it. My brief was a simple one: 'Write something that will imply that the product is a genuine aphrodisiac without actually saying so.' I started off with a few inane captions just to limber up, to get into the swing of it. 'Could this be the answer to a maiden's prayer?' didn't seem right, somehow. I ended up with: 'When did you last give your wife that special look?' This seemed promising and just as I was rubbing my hands together in gleeful anticipation of what was to follow, the telephone on my desk buzzed.

It was Basil Keller, a close friend of mine. We had first met some years earlier in London when I was running a small advertising and public relations company. He had walked in out of the blue carrying a very impressive portfolio of graphic artwork. I liked him and his work and we became friends. Basil was a South African and had been born in the Orange Free State, but had spent much of his working life in different parts of the world including Australia and the USA. He had married Brenda, herself a talented sculptress from England, and the pair of them were beginning to build up a good reputation for themselves in the galleries of the Republic.

Basil wanted to know if I could get away for a few minutes to join him for coffee in a café a few floors up from my office. I was OK for time and after telling the receptionist where I would be I made my way towards the elevators.

As I walked out of the lift, directly into the café, Basil was reading a newspaper at a window table nearby. He looked up and smiled and I sat down opposite him. 'OK, Basil, what's happening?' I knew that there must be a good reason for him calling around at this time of the day and I could tell by the way his fingers drummed impatiently on the table that coffee was not uppermost in his mind.

He waited patiently for the Cape Coloured waitress to finish pouring the coffee before speaking. When she left he leaned forward conspiratorially and said quietly, 'Brenda and I have been invited to a multi-racial party tonight and we wondered whether you might like to come along with us.' My reaction must have showed clearly on my face because he laughed and said, 'Christ, man! Don't look so shocked.'

'I'm not shocked, just a bit surprised, that's all. It's not every day of the week that I'm invited to participate in serious criminal activity; in fact I think this is actually the first time. Where is it being held, or is that hush-hush at the moment?'

Basil glanced round to make sure no one was taking any interest in our conversation. 'Not all that far from where you're living.'

At that time my home was in a suburb of Cape Town known as Rondebosch East, a quiet and pleasant neighbourhood not more than twenty minutes or so from the city, fifteen if there were no traffic cops about. 'Tell me more,' I said, and ordered two more cups of coffee.

He told me that a select group of mixed non-white intellectuals was holding a social evening in a 'safe' flat and it would be strictly a few drinks and polite conversation, no funny stuff or blue movies and suchlike. Multi-racial parties were not all that uncommon among the young intellectuals of the Republic and I had to admit to myself that the idea of attending one appealed to me.

Basil was a well balanced individual and was pretty shrewd. I knew that if he intended taking Brenda along, the chances of anything nasty happening or the *polisie* arriving uninvited would be highly unlikely.

'Well . . . the idea appeals to me but the prospects of ending up over there don't.' I nodded in the direction of Robben Island which seemed more sinister than ever at that moment.

Basil looked over his shoulder. 'There's no chance of that happening, man, unless you're a blood-red commie planning mayhem and destruction, and if that were the case you wouldn't be here now . . .'

'Absolutely right,' I interrupted. 'I'd probably be sitting in some cellar in Pretoria wired up for sound.'

Basil assured me that the worst that could happen if the police did roll up at the festivities would be that we would spend an uncomfortable night in a police station and would receive a right royal rollicking from some huge Afrikaner police sergeant advising us not to do it again.

'OK,' I said. 'What's the drill?'

It was arranged that I would meet them at their Sea Point flat for drinks at seven-thirty and from there we would make our way to the venue which was in a suburb called Wynberg (pronounced Wineburg). In addition to the rented cottage at Rondebosch where I spent most of my time, I had been lucky enough to find a very small flat at Sea Point which I used at weekends, so I headed there directly after work.

The flat had at one time been used as servants' living quarters and was at the back of a block of flats, which proved to be a blessing later on. Sea Point was at that time, and probably still is, an exclusive white residential area in Cape Town where rents are astronomical. Because my flat was behind the main block and was too small for a family I was able to rent it for twenty rand a month, then the equivalent of ten pounds sterling. The flat was ideally situated. At the top end of the side-street adjacent to it was Regent Road, with its many shops and restaurants, and at the opposite end lay Beach Road and Sea Point's magnificent open-air swimming pool, the Pavilion.

Two short flights of stone steps led to the entrance from an access walkway at the rear of the building. This walkway connected with the side-street. The one and only door to the flat opened into a living-room which was just thirteen feet square. The windows were about two feet high and just below ceiling level, which also proved to be advantageous later. From the living-room, a door to the left opened into a small but well-planned kitchenette, another door in the kitchenette led into an equally small bathroom containing a handbasin, a toilet and a shower cubicle with plastic curtain. Immediately above the toilet unit there was a casement-type window with a hinged portion at the top for ventilation.

The flat had presented a number of problems, the main one being the limited size of the living-room which had to double as a bedroom as well as a dining-room. I set about trying to make it appear as spacious as funds and my interior-design capabilities would permit. I placed my wardrobe at right angles to the wall immediately to the right of the front door, so that on entering the flat the wardrobe created the illusion of a small inner hall. My single bed fitted neatly behind the wardrobe, leaving enough room for a small bedside cabinet.

I acquired a crate complete with stencil marks all over it. I took it carefully to pieces, and after sanding the surfaces of the wood to remove some of the roughness and dirt, I built from it a small double-doored cupboard and combined bookcase-cum-cocktail cabinet. The still visible stencil marks – THIS WAY UP, etc. – added a very trendy air to this magnificent piece of modern furniture. Several coats of hard, glossy varnish transformed it into what could only be described as a conversation-making object.

My masterpiece was a cunningly conceived and craftily constructed item which was a combined dressing-table with mirror and two drawers, and dining-table. This had pride of place at the foot of the bed so that when the hybrid was being used as a dining-table the bed became a comfortable dining-chair, for one person, that is. The smooth wooden floor tiles received a couple of coats of varnish and a reasonable reproduction of a Persian carpet purchased from Woolworths for a few rands.

My kindly Jewish landlady paid me an unexpected visit and after eyeing my frugal furnishings she sighed and disappeared, to return shortly afterwards with an old but serviceable dining-chair. I gave it a new lease of life by stripping it, painting it glossy white and embellishing it with a few gilt adornments purchased from a nearby DIY store. After introducing this exquisite piece to my collection, plus a couple of offbeat paintings which I hastily produced, the small flat developed quite a bit of character and I was extraordinarily pleased with the results of my efforts.

The kitchen had a useful work-top and was well equipped with built-in cupboards. All that was needed, apart from the usual odds and ends, were a small gas cooker, a stool and a fridge. A contact of mine bought a second-hand refrigerator on my behalf and paid twenty rand for it. It was fairly large and I wondered why it was so cheap. On inspecting it I could find no sign of an electric motor or any other power source and fumed as I realised that my well-meaning contact had been seen coming by some smart operator.

Nevertheless, always an optimist, I loaded it with butter, meat, milk and so on, plugged it into the wall socket and switched it on, half expecting an explosion. Nothing happened and not a whisper of sound came from the unit. It sat there impassively without a tremor disturbing its infuriating equanimity. I glared at it for a few moments, shrugged and went out for a drink, and forgot about the fridge as soon as I closed my front door behind me.

When I returned to the flat some hours later I opened the fridge door to get some milk and found that everything had frozen solid. I was astonished. That old fridge gave me almost three years of loyal service and when I finally parted with it I sold it for twice as much as I had paid for it. My one regret is that I cannot remember the maker's name as I would have been only too happy to recommend his products.

The bedside clock showed that it was getting on for seven and I would soon have to leave for Basil's place. Casual dress was obviously the order of the day and taking into account that I might be called upon to do a quick bunk, should the fuzz arrive, I decided that I would be less conspicuous wearing dark gear. I chose a pair of navy-blue lightweight beach trousers with a matching shirt. A pair of dark-blue canvas beach shoes with rope soles would be just the thing for silent, speedy sprinting if called for, I thought with a grin. After slipping them on I mixed myself a hefty Hollands gin and tonic – nothing like a bit of Dutch courage to get the evening off to a flying start, I mused, as I gulped it down with one eye on the clock.

It was a beautiful evening and the remains of what had been a magnificent sunset still lingered above the horizon against the darkness of the ocean as I parked my Beetle near the block of flats in which Basil and Brenda lived. It was a small, square block faced with light stone; Basil's flat was situated at the top of the building and had a splendid balcony which was ideal for consuming sundowners or holding cocktail parties. Moments after locking the car door I was enjoying another large gin and tonic and the view from the balcony.

Brenda looked great in a simple black cocktail dress while Basil lay back on a sunbed decked out in a pair of white trousers, a dark-blue shirt and a white casual jacket – and white shoes. He couldn't have looked more conspicuous if he had wanted to.

I looked down at him and said, 'Has it occurred to you that if we have to do a swift bunk from the scene of the crime you are going to stick out like the proverbial sore thumb?'

With a wave of a hand he dismissed this. 'If I thought we would have to resort to that sort of caper we wouldn't be going.'

Brenda laughed, and nudged me, saying, 'You're scared stiff, aren't you, John?'

I took a gulp from my glass. 'Well, not scared exactly but certainly a bit apprehensive. I mean, for Christ's sake, I've never done anything along these lines before and being a law-abiding citizen by nature it is rubbing against the grain a bit. But at the same time, I must admit I am rather excited about the evening ahead.'

Basil appeared to be quite blasé about the whole business, as if he did this sort of thing every day of the week. He told me not to expect too much. 'It'll be a bit like an English piss-up but in technicolour.'

I grinned and looked across at Brenda who was freshening up our glasses. She was a remarkable woman, not beautiful in the classic sense of the word but with something indefinable about her. She hardly ever bothered with more than a touch of make-up but always managed to look strikingly attractive. Her long, naturally raven-black hair contrasted vividly with the pallor of her skin and in the subdued lighting of the balcony her face appeared to be almost chalk-white. She was a very forceful woman without actually appearing so, and there was no doubt in my mind that Basil owed to her much of his success as a designer. Basil was inclined to be a dreamer by nature, when allowed to be by Brenda. She would make either a millionaire of him – or a nervous wreck.

She looked at both of us. 'Well, it's dark enough and it's also about time we were on our way.'

I finished my drink and suddenly realised that I had that funny feeling like when I first went swimming with the school. I felt as though my stomach had dropped about an inch. We left the flat and went to our respective cars. It was agreed that I would follow their tail-lights. Basil had decided to take the

De Waal Drive route to Wynberg. At that time it was Cape Town's super highway and the panoramic views from this superb piece of civil engineering were breathtakingly lovely.

In the 1960s many of the suburbs towards which we were heading were populated predominantly by whites, but there were still some parts inhabited by non-white families. When I say non-white families I mean Cape Coloureds or Asians; Bantus were not allowed to live in or near to white-populated areas. Africans, who were compelled by law to carry pass books, were severely limited in their movements whereas Cape Coloured people had identity cards as did the whites. Cape Coloured folk had considerable freedom of movement but despite this they were very much restricted in other ways by apartheid. Post offices had separate entrances for whites and non-whites, and park benches were clearly signed 'Blankes' for the use of whites only or 'Nie Blankes' for non-whites only. In the Cape the beaches were segregated as well. The whites had the best beaches and the unfortunate coloured people had the second-best, which were often quite dangerous for swimming.

The fact that Wynberg had a mixture of whites and non-whites was in our favour, as no one would take the slightest notice of us if we happened to be seen driving along a road lived in by non-whites. On the other hand, only simple-minded or drunken white people would drive around a restricted non-white area or township alone at night. In the first place it was strictly against the law and secondly such a person would be taking dreadful risks with his life. Under the circumstances that existed at that time one could hardly blame non-white people for feeling bitter or vindictive towards whites.

As we left De Waal Drive and made our way to the main road and on into Wynberg, I kept an eagle eye on Basil's tail-lights which suddenly brightened as he slowed to make a turn. I followed his car down a quiet side-road. After a hundred yards or so he pulled into the kerb and stopped. I also stopped behind him, switched off the motor and lights as he had done, and climbing out of the car I walked over to him.

'We go on foot from here.' His thin face was a waxy blue in the street lights. 'It's not far.'

I returned to my own car and locked the doors and windows

before joining them on the pavement. We walked to the end of the road and turned at a T-junction into a busier road with a few shops. Basil steered us into another quiet side-road and after about fifty yards we stopped outside a block of flats which stood back quite a way from the road. They appeared to have been built from reinforced concrete and three ill-lit alleyways subdivided the frontage. Each one had a name above it. Basil stared up at the name above the first alleyway, mumbled something and moved on. At the third one he turned and said, 'This is it. Let's go.'

We followed him into a courtyard beyond the alley and made our way up a flight of stone steps until we came out onto a balcony that ran around the inner courtyard of the flats. There were numerous doors and windows around this balcony and a few coloured people watched our progress from some of them as we made our way along. I felt a bit conspicuous and also tense and hoped that none of them were police informers. They didn't appear to be overexcited at the sight of strange white faces appearing in their domain.

Music drifted towards us as we approached a corner flat and I guessed, correctly, that this was our destination. Basil pressed an illuminated bell push beside the door and almost immediately the door was opened by an attractive young Cape Coloured woman who, we discovered later, was a staff nurse at the Red Cross Memorial Hospital in Rondebosch East.

'Hello there!' she said with a warm smile. 'I don't know who you are but please do come in.'

She led us along a carpeted hall and opened a door which led into a surprisingly large L-shaped living-room in which about a dozen people were gathered in three groups. The music was loud and lively and one or two couples began dancing. They were a mixed bunch and they were obviously happy and relaxed. I felt myself unwinding and I was glad that I had decided to accept Basil's invitation. The atmosphere was so friendly that I could not help but feel at ease.

The room was pleasantly decorated and comfortably furnished. One complete wall at the end of the room was fitted with shelves which extended from floor to almost ceiling height. They were filled with books. A tall, dignified, Cape Coloured man with greying hair walked over to us, and we were introduced to him and his kindly wife, who also came over and joined our little group. He was our host, the headmaster of a school for non-white children in the Cape Town area, and he proved to be the most charming and erudite of people. He seemed pleased to welcome us to his home and if he feared any calls by the police he certainly did not show it.

It wasn't easy to hold a conversation against the loud beat of the music and we seemed to be in the way of the dancers. The host's wife led Brenda away to a group in one of the corners while Basil and I were conducted to the kitchen where a makeshift bar had been set up. This was obviously where the action was. It was almost packed with people, most of whom were non-white, and soon we were involved in earnest discussion about the state of affairs in the Republic, with much speculation as to the future.

One of the guests, a likeable Asian of Indian origin, grinned at me and thrust a well-filled tumbler of good South African brandy into my hand. I raised it, and thanking him with a smile said 'Geshondeid!', and took a large swig. My new-found friend laughed at my peculiar pronunciation of the Afrikaans word which is the equivalent of 'Good health'.

The brandy seemed to be particularly strong and for safety's sake I wedged myself between the gas cooker and the fridge. There was a flash of teeth in the dark, friendly face. 'I believe you are from overseas?' my friend asked. The word 'overseas' to most South Africans usually means Britain. I nodded and he went on to tell me his name was Younnuss and that he was a Muslim. Not a very orthodox one, I thought, eyeing the half-filled tumbler of brandy he was using to punctuate his speech. At first our conversation was a bit stilted but two brandies cured that problem and we were soon chatting animatedly.

The South African political system took an awful hammering that night, but everybody was good natured and there appeared to be no bitterness or animosity in the non-white ranks. As I tried to listen, despite the dreadful background noise, to Younnuss who was now in full cry, I suddenly became aware that I had shaken hands with a non-white person for the first time since I had arrived in the Republic, and this was certainly

the first time that I had shared a social drink with a non-white.
It occurred to me that I had become aware of my colour – for
the first time in my life. I felt uncomfortable and then angry
that I had been made conscious of such a thing because of the
ridiculous system that existed in South Africa. It was a peculiar
feeling and stayed with me for some time afterwards.

The door bell chimed above my head and brought me
down to earth. The effects of several stiff brandies seemed to
fade as I gasped, 'Christ! I bet that's the police!' No one
seemed to be perturbed and Younnuss laughed. 'The police
won't bother you here, my friend. They have more trouble-
some people than us to concern themselves with. What harm
are we doing having a drink together? We're not planning
insurrection.'

My glass was empty and as I was about to place it on the
top of the fridge an arm appeared from somewhere behind me.
Firmly clasped in the hand at the end of it was a bottle of
brandy. My glass was refilled, almost to the brim, and the
arm, complete with hand and bottle, disappeared again. 'That
was clever,' I thought, trying to swivel my neck to nod a thanks
in the direction of the benefactor's arm.

We were all making the most terrible racket in the kitchen
by this time and it was almost impossible to hold any sort
of understandable conversation. Younnuss was still gabbling
away happily and all I could do was to nod as if I could follow
him quite clearly whereas I had no idea at all what the hell
he was talking about. I was relieved when Basil's drink-flushed
face appeared around the door. His eyes were obviously searching. I waved my glass and he spotted me and beckoned wildly.
I yelled an apology into Younnuss's ear and inched my way
out of the scrum without spilling a drop of the precious brandy.
Quite an achievement under those circumstances.

Not to put too fine a point on it, Basil was quite clearly
half-pissed. He placed a brotherly hand on my shoulder and
breathing volatile fumes into my face said, 'I've been looking
all over the bloody place for you, man. Thought you'd
buggered off for a moment.'

I looked down at my glass of brandy. 'What? And leave all
this behind? You must be joking.'

He ignored that and tugged urgently at my arm. 'Come

through to the lounge for a minute. The most gorgeous female has arrived and I wouldn't want you to miss her.'

He led me away, keeping a grip on my arm to prevent my escaping. The lounge was pretty full by this time and quite a few people were trying to dance in a confined space. I noticed the gleam of flawless white teeth in a black, shining face as a tall African danced by with a blue-eyed, Scandinavian-looking blonde in his arms. I couldn't help wondering what a titanic, blue-chinned, neckless Afrikaner police sergeant would have done if he could have seen that. Wincing at the thought, I followed Basil across the room towards Brenda who was with a group in a corner. All the people in the group seemed to be talking at the same time; I wondered if anyone was listening. I recognised the host's wife, and standing next to her with her back to us was a young Cape Coloured woman dressed in a stylish turquoise-blue trouser suit.

Basil nudged me, and nodding towards the young woman said, 'Wait until she turns round.'

For a moment I thought he was kidding and I expected to see a warty nose combined with crossed eyes. When she did eventually turn I was stunned. She was so lovely I couldn't stop staring at her. She wore very little make-up and in her ears were pendant earrings like miniature chandeliers. I always remember those earrings.

I came down to earth again and noticed Brenda watching me closely. She knew very well the effect the young woman was having on me and she smiled a secret, woman's smile. Reaching out she touched her on the arm and said, 'Cynthia, I would like you to meet a friend of ours.'

The beautiful head with the neat, shortly cut hair turned towards me and the brown eyes smiled and sparkled. She too realised the effect she was having on me. Her eyes flickered quickly over me and I knew that I had been weighed up carefully.

For a man normally never short of words I was momentarily speechless. It was a bit disconcerting really, and unsettling. I had never experienced such feelings before in the presence of a woman but then again I had never met a woman like Cynthia before. I didn't realise until later that I had fallen in love from the moment I first saw her.

'Let's talk,' I said, holding out a hand, and we excused ourselves from the group and managed to find a couple of empty chairs at the other end of the room. She didn't touch alcohol so I brought her a Coke, and a brandy for myself, and we sat and talked and talked and talked. I told her quite a bit about myself, what I did for a living, where I came from and so on. Cynthia told me that she had started out as a shorthand-typist but found it difficult to hold a job, as usually within a short time of taking up a post she would be approached and propositioned, usually by the boss – white, of course. She was now working as a children's nurse and had a live-in job with a wealthy family at Camp's Bay, a very salubrious suburb beyond Sea Point. She had been brought up in an orphanage with two older sisters, who now lived in Kew Town, a Cape Coloured township in the Cape Flats area. She and her sisters were very close and she visited them regularly. She also had an aunt living at a town called Malmesbury in the Western Cape, not so very far from Cape Town. She had no idea how her parents had died.

She appeared to be a perfectly decent girl and I was very impressed with what the orphanage had done for her. She seemed to have been considerably luckier than many other Cape Coloured children left without parents to look after them. I wondered what the future would hold for a girl like Cynthia. Would she meet a decent, hard-working coloured chap who would marry her and try to give her a decent life, or would she fall into the wrong hands and possibly end up on the streets like so many unfortunate Cape Coloured girls did?

Cape Town was full of young coloured girls struggling to support some white man's bastard child. When a coloured mistress of a white man became pregnant he usually terminated the relationship, leaving the poor girl to fend for herself and her rejected baby. As often as not she would be rejected by her family too. I knew of one such unfortunate girl who spent cold winter nights sleeping in public conveniences whilst in an advanced stage of pregnancy. Needless to say the infant-mortality rate in such cases is abnormally high and in many cases the wretched mother suffers an ignominious end too. In those days a non-white woman could not file a paternity suit against a white man, at least not unless she was eager to go to prison and possibly to suffer hard labour. God alone knew what happened to the infants born to such unhappy women.

I remember asking a well-meaning Afrikaner lady why South Africa had brought in the Immorality Act, and she told me that it had been introduced to 'protect' non-white women from unscrupulous white men. She really meant what she was saying and truly believed the words she uttered. She was highly indignant and quite offended when I pointed out that it had precisely the opposite effect. I did not think it discreet to mention to her that according to statistics that had been published by a South African newspaper, the majority of men convicted of having sexual relations with non-white women were Afrikaners; possibly her husband had partaken of the odd illicit 'quickie' unbeknown to the good lady or the authorities. This sort of humbug is rampant in the Republic.

The evening drifted happily by and Cynthia and I were quite content to sit in our corner talking about all manner of things. I was surprised to discover that she had a fair know-ledge of English writers including Milton, Chaucer, Shake-speare and Charles Dickens. At last it was time to say goodnight, or would it be goodbye?

It had been a wonderful evening and I was glad now that I had taken the opportunity to spend these hours at a multi-racial party. I was quite sorry that the party was over and I said so to Cynthia. I wondered what she might say or think if I suggested that we meet again, but I decided against it as I suspected that she would think the worst, and even if she agreed it could lead to a dangerous situation for both of us, and particularly for her. I had not failed to notice when reading newspaper reports of immorality cases that quite often the white man would receive a suspended sentence but the poor coloured lass nearly always ended up doing time.

Before leaving we walked out onto the balcony to greet the early dawn and to take in a bit of fresh air. I thanked her for sharing her time with me and for giving me some very pleasant hours to remember. She seemed happy to hear this and told me that she too had enjoyed herself and that she was pleased to have met me. Impulsively I leaned forward and kissed her quickly on the cheek, then rejoined Basil and Brenda. We

chatted for a few minutes beside our cars and went our separate
ways.

It was nearly 5 a.m. when I arrived at my cottage. I set the
alarm clock for 8 a.m. and fell asleep on the bed fully clothed.

Shortly after the party Bob entered my life. I was sitting on
the bed in the little flat at Sea Point wondering whether to
have an early night or to dress and go for a walk up the road
to the Regency Hotel for a drink. Before I could make up my
mind there was a heavy double knock at the front door. When
I opened it I was confronted by a cheerful character dressed
in very English-looking baggy trousers, a paratrooper's old
jumping jacket, and a maroon shirt adorned with a Parachute
Regiment tie.

The face above all this was thin, deeply lined and waxy
white. Beneath the pointed nose lay a neatly trimmed military-
type moustache. The eyes were blue, slightly protuberant and
topped by a pair of thick, highly mobile eyebrows. My visitor's
hair was dark, neatly parted and slicked down with one lank
lock hanging untidily over one eye. There was a distinctive
look about the fellow and I knew that I was in for an interesting
evening.

I opened my mouth to speak but he beat me to it. 'You're
John, aren't you?' he barked.

For a moment I was nonplussed and I actually had to stop
to think about it for a moment before nodding a tacit yes. I
wondered who he was and where he had sprung from as I
seldom received visitors at the Sea Point flat. As I was about
to make a discreet enquiry or two he must have read my
thoughts. He told me that he had been having a drink in the
public bar at the Regency. During a conversation with Reg
the barman, Reg informed him that another Rooinek – English
settlers were usually referred to as 'rednecks' by South Africans, especially the Afrikaners – was living down the road
somewhere. Bob was acutely homesick for England and he
desperately needed another Englishman to natter to. Reg's
vague directions as to where I lived appeared to have been
enough to enable Bob to find me.

He was about to say something else but I raised a hand

quickly and stopped him. 'Don't tell me who you are,' I said, 'Let me guess. I'm good at this.'

He stared at me in open-mouthed anticipation.

'You're Adolf Hitler, aren't you?' I asked.

'Adolf fuckin' 'oo?' he squawked. 'Do I look like bleedin' Adolf fuckin' 'Itler then?'

I stood aside to allow him to enter. 'Now you mention it there is a rather striking resemblance, but you don't sound much like him.' I gestured towards the bed for him to sit down and while I poured him out a liberal glass of Oude Meester brandy he told me his name was Bob. 'Born an' bred within the sound of Bow Bells, mate.' He stared around my minuscule flat with a look of wonder on his face. 'Blimey! Is this all there is of it then?' I nodded and handed him his brandy.

We lit cigarettes and sat drinking in companionable silence for a few minutes and then he told me his little tale. He and his wife and their son of twenty-one had come out to the Republic to settle some three years previously, on the promise of a good job and accommodation waiting for them on arrival. Unfortunately for them when they duly arrived in Cape Town, the person who had made the offers had disappeared without trace, leaving the little family high and dry.

Somehow they managed to survive, but not long after they had established themselves Bob's wife had given him the order of the boot. It appeared that Bob was not one of the world's greatest providers and this, along with one or two other minor character flaws such as a tendency to forget to pay bills, rent, etc., weighed rather heavily upon his long-suffering wife. The fiasco that they walked into on first arriving in South Africa proved to be the last straw for her and that was the end of Bob's marriage.

At the time I met Bob he had more or less worked his way around most of the motor-service garages in Cape Town. According to him he was a master motor-mechanic who, by some strange quirk of fate, usually discovered after a relatively short period of employment that his employer was a four-letter man. Never Bob, of course.

It was quite plain that Bob was a bit of a misfit, one of the world's walking-wounded. Although not tough, he was aggressive by nature which was clearly his sole means of defence against the slings and arrows of outraged employers and the world in general. As I listened with interest and sympathy to the tribulations of this strange character it soon became apparent that Bob was one of those many unfortunates who, for reasons they do not appreciate, are simply unemployable and have to live by their wits. Unhappily many of them are sadly lacking in the latter. He was a bit of a mess and he needed a friend, someone to talk to but not necessarily to listen to. Eventually he proved to be almost completely unreliable, but I couldn't help liking him and our rather odd meeting was the start of a close friendship.

The highlight in Bob's sad life was when he served as a sergeant in the Parachute Regiment during World War Two. Some of the tales he spun about his exploits during his brief moment of glory were amusing, most of them unbelievable. It had been the one and only time in his life that he had achieved any sort of status and consequently he tended to live in the shadowy world of twenty-odd years previously. He was delighted to learn that I had flown with Bomber Command during the war years and in this respect we had something in common. We spent two or three happy hours of that first meeting reminiscing about our wartime adventures.

For all his faults, Bob was a true British patriot and during the time I knew him his affection for England never diminished. We both had different reasons for leaving the land of our birth. He left it for what he thought would be a better life with instant success and wealth. I left mainly because of the rotten weather.

Life slipped back into neutral again. My job at the agency presented no mind-bending problems. Hymie had been told what to do with his 'genuine' aphrodisiac and was sulking. I spent my days tapping happily away at my typewriter – all I had to do was keep up a steady flow of hard-selling copy and meet production deadlines.

I found myself thinking about Cynthia quite often and wondered if any thoughts of me ever trickled into her mind. I remembered that she worked somewhere in Camp's Bay and thought about driving around the area in the evenings on the off-chance of meeting her. Then I decided that this wasn't a very good idea as the sight of a white man driving aimlessly around such a prestigious suburb might have attracted unwanted attention.

One Sunday afternoon after returning to the Sea Point flat from a pleasant afternoon's swimming and sunbathing, I began to make a cup of tea but the sugar container was empty. Sod it! I thought, and with a shrug I set off for further supplies. The main road was only a few minutes' walk away and there was a big supermarket at the top of the side-road adjacent to the flat. It was Greek-owned as most of the supermarkets and cafés are in South Africa.

Just as I was pausing at the kerb in readiness to cross the busy main road I became aware of a person dressed in white approaching from my left. Before stepping into the road I glanced casually in that direction, and my breath caught in my throat as I recognised Cynthia. She was wearing a smart trouser suit and also a large pair of sunglasses. I was momentarily stunned. She had recognised me, I could see, but she did not show it.

If we had been living in a free society it would have been the most natural thing in the world for us to have stopped and greeted each other with a smile and a cheery word or two. This was not for us. Here we were, a black girl and a white man on a busy main road on a Sunday afternoon with numerous families taking an afternoon stroll before tea – in South Africa. If we had smiled at each other it would have aroused suspicion; for us to have been stupid enough to actually stop and talk to each other would have been an open invitation to be pounced upon by the crew of a cruising police truck.

The consequence for me was frustration. She looked absolutely fabulous in the warm sunlight and I knew that her eyes were smiling at me from behind the huge sunglasses. I had often read in novels about lovers meeting and 'their hearts leaping in their breasts' and so on. Well, it's true; that is what happened with me. I would have given anything just to be able to speak to her for a few minutes but all that I dared do under the circumstances was to mumble an almost inaudible 'Hello there.' She gave a quick little smile and was gone. As I stepped out into the road I was almost struck by a passing bus.

On reaching the other side safely I turned and stared across
to where I expected her to be and I caught sight of her as she
disappeared into a throng of people gathering at a bus stop.
Just before she did so, she also turned, and seeing me she
smiled. I felt exhilarated and depressed at the same time.
What sort of a society is this? I wondered, as I entered the
store and looked around for the sugar. What possible harm
would two people be doing to the fabric of society in South
Africa by exchanging friendly greetings and possibly enjoying
each other's company over a cup of tea? What the hell are
they so afraid of? My mind went back to some advice which
was given to me not long after I arrived in the Republic. It
had come my way while enjoying a few drinks in a hotel bar
in Johannesburg. The oracle dispensing the pearls of wisdom
had breathed them beerily into my ear.

'When you settle down here you'll like it, you'll see, but let
me give you a friendly word of advice, young fellah. In South
Africa they don't mind a spot of felony or a touch of arson;
embezzlement is routine stuff; but never – I repeat never, ever
– get caught with a leg over a kaffir woman.' 'Kaffir' is a
derogatory word to describe a black person and is the South
African equivalent of 'nigger'. I have never forgotten those
words and probably never will.

I walked slowly back to the flat and when I entered it, it
seemed very lonely. I put the sugar away and opted out of the
tea. I got a bit drunk instead. Later on I drove over to
see Basil and Brenda as I felt a need to talk to someone
understanding. Usually I was in a cheerful frame of mind but
gloom eclipsed my cheerfulness that evening. I told them what
had happened and Brenda, who was sitting beside me, put an
arm around me and said,

'John, if Cynthia means as much as this to you, let Basil
speak to someone who knows her and we can arrange for you
to see each other somewhere quiet and safe.'

Basil chipped in. 'No problem, John, if that's what you
want, but I'm not so sure that I would be doing either of you
a favour in the long run. However, it's up to you, man.'

I knew it was a non-starter and said so. 'If I meet her just
for another little chat, we all know that it won't end there,
don't we? And we all know that sooner or later either she or I

or possibly both of us would end up in Pollsmore Prison and I have no intention of putting the girl into that sort of situation or buggering up my own career in Cape Town.' So that, I thought at the time, was the end of the matter.

Not long after that meeting with Basil and Brenda I decided to take myself out for an evening and treat myself to a good seafood supper at a well-known restaurant in the city. It was an excellent meal, rock lobster as the South Africans call crayfish, with all the trimmings plus a bottle of Twee Jonge-zellen Spätlese, followed by cheese and biscuits and a couple of brandies. I sat smoking over my coffee thinking how nice it would have been if Cynthia were sitting opposite me. She had never been in such a restaurant in her young life. Would she ever do so? I began to feel a bit depressed and decided it was time to go home to write a few outstanding letters.

As a rule I would have driven back to Rondebosch East along the foreshore via the National Road, but on impulse I took the De Waal Drive route. While sitting at the robots, as traffic lights are called in South Africa, a minor drama developed which I watched with interest. A large black Mercedes was kerb-crawling and it was quite apparent that the young woman the driver was pestering wanted nothing to do with him or his overtures. When the robots changed I drove ahead slowly and eased into the kerb, curious to see what the outcome would be.

The young woman crossed the road and began walking in the opposite direction but her determined pursuer was not to be put off by this strategy. He pulled away from the kerb and executing a swift U-turn between a line of palm trees which divided the road into two lanes, he continued pestering her. Neither the pursuer nor the pursued had noticed me or my interest in the proceedings, and although it was none of my business I felt that the young lady could do with a spot of assistance. I started my Beetle and driving through the same gap that the Mercedes had used I joined in the game.

Plainclothes policemen in Cape Town favoured the use of Volkswagen Beetles. At that time in South Africa one in every ten cars was a Volkswagen Beetle and the most popular colour was cream. Police Volksies were cream and so was mine. I decided to play a little trick on the gent in the Mercedes.

Driving ahead of him, I pulled into the kerb, switched off my lights and motor and waited. I heard the click-clack of the young woman's footsteps drawing near; she was almost running and as she passed my stationary car the Mercedes passed me also. As he drew level with my open window I bawled, 'Stop, man! Polisie.'

It worked very effectively for with a shriek of tortured tyres our friend took off and in seconds his tail-lights disappeared over a rise in the road directly ahead. The girl must have heard my yell and she glanced quickly behind and hurried on, no doubt thinking, This bloody policeman is now going to try his luck. I pulled ahead of her and leaning over the front passenger seat called through the window, 'Are you OK?'

She looked more closely into the car and to my astonishment I found myself gaping into the equally surprised face of Cynthia. I opened the door and she hesitated for only a few moments, looking around to make sure no one was watching before she climbed into the back seat of the car. I pulled away from the kerb and drove on.

'I don't believe it,' she laughed. 'That loonie has been pestering me for almost half an hour and I was going to walk down to the main police station.'

I could hardly believe my luck at having found her again even though the circumstances could have been happier. 'How strange that we should meet like this,' I said. 'I have always believed in fate but this is ridiculous.' We both laughed and were obviously very happy to see each other again.

As it was dark I felt fairly relaxed. I said I would take her wherever she wanted to go and she told me that she was on her way back to Camp's Bay after visiting her sisters. I was at a loss for conversation but I felt happy just knowing that she was sitting with me in my car. The journey was over all too soon and before she opened the door to leave I managed to blurt out, 'Please don't misunderstand me, Cynthia, but I have missed you and I would love to see you again. Will you have tea with me next Sunday if you can get away?'

She looked directly at me for a moment and said, 'Yes, if that is what you want. What time and where shall we meet?'

We arranged that she would make her own way to the flat and I gave her explicit instructions on exactly how to get to my front door. The latch would be left up and all she would have to do would be to push the door open and I would be waiting inside for her. This would eliminate the need for her to knock on the door which might have attracted someone's attention. I also suggested that she should wear soft-soled shoes. She said she would be there and a moment later her slim figure hurried away into the shadow of the trees surrounding the house where she worked.

As I entered the bar of the Regency the first thing I noticed were the shoulders of Bob hunched over the bar counter. I could almost see the pall of gloom hanging silently above him. Disaster had struck in his eventful life yet again, that was fairly clear. Bracing myself for what looked like being a depressing evening, I tapped him on the shoulder and offered him a cheerful grin. It soon vanished when I saw his own bleak look. Reg, the friendly South African barman, came over and asked me what I would like. Bob's glass was almost empty and I ordered two Oude Meesters. I made the mistake of asking Bob how things were.

'Fuckin' 'orrible!' he almost yelped. 'It's that bleedin' git that I'm workin' for—or I should say *was* workin' for,' he added darkly.

Oh, Christ! I thought. He's done it again. Chucked his bloody job in. Either that or the 'bleedin' git' has slung him out. He wouldn't tell me exactly why he had left, apart from a difference of opinion about some of his own lofty ideals, but reading between the outbursts of indignant rage and four-letter words it was easy to see that Bob had been given his marching orders.

I shook my head, partly in sympathy and partly out of irritation at Bob's seeming difficulty in holding down an apparently straightforward job as a motor mechanic. Although he seemed to be running out of garages to get fired from, Bob always managed to come up with something within forty-eight hours of losing a job. He went on to tell me that he had already phoned another unsuspecting potential employer and had an appointment arranged for the morning.

I said nothing to him about my meeting with Cynthia or my arrangements for the coming Sunday, but I did drop heavy hints that I would not be around on Sunday afternoon as I had been invited elsewhere. It might have been a bit disconcerting if Bob should suddenly appear during Cynthia's visit, apart from which, Bob's thunderous knock at the flat door could easily give me a stroke as I would immediately think that the police had arrived. Under normal circumstances I might have been able to trust Bob with a revelation about Cynthia and by 'normal' I mean when he was sober. However, he had a tendency to pass his personal secrets to the nearest convenient earhole when he was in his cups. If the particular earhole had been attached to a member of the Special Branch in mufti it might have led to an embarrassing situation for me.

When Saturday arrived I decided to give the tiny flat at Sea Point a good spring cleaning, and after opening all the windows and the door I polished the wooden floor until it gleamed and did the same to my bits of furniture. By the time I had finished the place fairly shone with cleanliness. Even if Cynthia failed to turn up she had at least inspired me to give the flat a much-needed cleaning. For good measure I placed a vase of fresh flowers on my packing-case bookcase and some fancy soap in the bathroom. After this I headed for the local laun-derette with the week's dirty laundry.

Bob's flat lay hidden behind an open concrete screen immedi-ately behind the forecourt of a large petrol station not far from the Regency Hotel. His flat was large but sparsely furnished. His kitchen was bigger than my living/bedroom and it was where we spent our time during my visits. The kitchen furni-ture consisted of an old wooden table covered with old-fashioned oilcloth, a large wall cupboard above an elderly stone sink complete with brass taps, four rickety chairs, and an antique gas cooker with a detachable panel in the side in which he kept hidden a Colt .45 automatic pistol which he told me he had forgotten to hand in after his war service. How the hell he had managed to smuggle it into South Africa I don't know.

The kitchen window was fitted with cheap cotton curtains printed with a ghastly floral pattern in a combination of purple, green and pink. The curtains were permanently drawn closed.

Despite all this it was a homely spot and we shared some very enjoyable evenings and weekend afternoons there, knocking back brandy as if there were no tomorrow.

Although Bob was not exactly the most fastidious of furnishers or interior decorators his flat was always clean and tidy. This was because he employed what is euphemistically known in South Africa as a 'housegirl'. Her name was Beattie and she was a cheerful young woman of dark complexion and rather plain appearance which stood in Bob's favour. It was quite in order for a single man to employ a housegirl on a strictly living-out basis, but it was asking for trouble if the girl happened to be young and pretty. The wise bachelor would make certain that his housegirl was not over-attractive or too young. A clean-living lady with slightly wall eyes and a burgeoning hump would have gone un-noticed.

I had noticed a certain amount of free-and-easy banter between Beattie and her 'master' and suspected that a little more than bedmaking and washing up was taking place in their relationship. Good luck to them; they seemed to be happy enough. I knew that Bob would give me the whole story in due course and I remained discreetly silent on this point.

Despite Bob's sometimes irritating ways we had become good pals by this time. Our idea of bliss was to spend Saturday afternoons seated in his kitchen munching tinned-salmon-and-cucumber sandwiches washed down by large and frequent cups of hot, strong tea, while exchanging outlandish stories of our adventures during World War Two. Bob was a homely chap and his simple tastes and humble domesticity reminded me of my own early days when I shared some hard times with my brother and parents during the great depression of the Thirties.

On that particular Saturday afternoon Bob and I spent an amiable hour or two reminiscing, and we finally made our way to the bar at the Regency and got down to some serious boozing. The main bar closed at 11 p.m. but oddly the Ladies Bar remained open until midnight. As old patrons of the Regency we were allowed to transfer ourselves to the Ladies Bar which we did that night with alacrity until, somewhat the worse for wear, we parted company beneath the cold light of the sodium street lamps in the cool air and I staggered off one way leaving Bob to stagger off the other.

When I awoke the following morning I wasn't sure where I was for a moment, and wondered why I had woken with a start. A couple of loud knocks on the front door provided the answer. I practically fell out of bed, tottered around the wardrobe and opened the door to find Basil and Brenda standing there. I stepped hastily behind the door. 'Can't ask you in, I'm afraid. I'm only wearing underpants.'

'Don't worry about that; have a quick shower, you lazy sod, and come and join us for breakfast at the Pavilion Café.'

When South Africans take a liking to someone they are likely to turn up on your doorstep complete with the whole family, to haul you off for the day, either on a *braaivlei* which is Afrikaans for barbecue, or to a party of some sort, and they won't take no for an answer. I showered quickly and within a few minutes I was strolling in brilliant sunlight towards the Pavilion. It was a beautiful morning, hot but with a refreshing breeze blowing in from the sea.

As we sat around the table with a large beach umbrella rattling in the breeze above us, and the sound of the surf over the sea wall behind, I thought how nice it was to be there with two of my closest friends. The coffee was good and I had a couple of toasted cheese-and-tomato sandwiches for breakfast. There were hundreds of people around, mainly mums and dads with children all enjoying this beautiful Sunday morning. I was doubly delighted knowing that later that day I expected to see Cynthia again. I felt happy and relaxed and at that particular moment I didn't have a care in the world.

Basil wanted to tell me about an exhibition of his work that was being planned in Johannesburg and he and Brenda wanted me to visit the exhibition. It was agreed that I would drive up to Jo'burg for the weekend to join them and to have a look at Basil's work at the same time. He seemed to be doing quite well for himself and was beginning to make contact with some eminent and wealthy South Africans. He wasn't making enough to live on and earned his daily bread by acting as an agent for overseas artists.

Looking around, I couldn't help noticing how healthy and affluent most of the people looked sitting beneath their beach umbrellas. What went through the minds of the coloured waitresses as they compared their own lifestyles with ours? I began to get that uneasy feeling of guilt again and realised that I was allowing my own white skin to make me feel like a criminal. I hadn't done anything wrong to these people, so why should I feel this way?

I wondered if the South Africans themselves felt any guilt about the way they blatantly exploited their less fortunate fellow South Africans. From conversations that I had had I got the distinct impression that a number of them were very uneasy in their consciences. I remembered walking out of a top-class hotel in Cape Town where I had just indulged in a sumptuous lunch. Feeling contented and somewhat complacent, I was brought to my senses by the sight of a young coloured girl who was no more than a child; she was thin and sad-looking and was begging at the hotel door carrying a baby that she could hardly support. It probably wasn't her baby, of course, but this confrontation sickened me and I felt so bloody ashamed of myself. I gave her far more money than I should have done, I suppose, and she gave me an almost shocked look before hurrying away, as if she was afraid that I might change my mind. Up until that moment I had been having a nice day but for the rest of it I felt riddled with guilt although I knew that I had done nothing to deserve it. How long would I be able to stay in South Africa if this sort of thing was going to bug me frequently?

Brenda brought me out of my reverie by giving me a nudge with her sharp elbow. She asked me if I still thought about Cynthia at all. I wondered if they had somehow found out that Cynthia was planning to visit me later during the day. I kept quiet about our strange meeting that night in Cape Town but I did admit that I thought about her from time to time. Basil and Brenda studied me closely for a few moments before changing the subject.

After our breakfast we went for a stroll towards Green Point with the blue waters of Table Bay on our left and luxurious multi-storey apartment blocks on our right, and the soft, green grass felt good beneath me. Although I was dying to tell them about Cynthia and our forthcoming meeting I felt that the fewer people who knew about Cynthia and me, the better it would be for everyone. By telling Basil and Brenda I would be sharing my 'crime' with them. I didn't want them to be involved nor did I want them to worry unduly about me. We parted at Green Point and it was arranged that I would join them for dinner later in the week.

At two forty-five that afternoon I was pacing backwards and forwards in my small living-room; there wasn't a lot of pacing room available but I managed. The flat was gleaming, the front door was closed but the latch was fixed up, and my stomach was churning with a mixture of excitement, anticipation and a touch of apprehension. Would she come? What if her madam had unexpected visitors and had insisted on her working on? What if she wasn't well? The minutes became hours in my imagination although it was still only five minutes to three.

I looked at the drinks on my improvised bar but decided against having a quick one. I don't suppose Cynthia would have minded but I felt that breathing alcohol fumes into her face would hardly make a good impression on her. Instead, I went into the kitchen to check for the umpteenth time that everything was as it should be. The kettle was simmering on a low gas. The cream cake sat invitingly on the glass cake-stand I had bought – from my favourite store, Woolworths – cups and saucers were primed with tea bags, and a small jug of fresh milk and matching bowl of sugar stood on a tray in readiness for serving. The bathroom was spotless with fresh clean towels and a new toilet-roll. As I walked nervously back into the main room my eye spotted a brown-paper parcel parked on top of the wardrobe. I took it down and opened it. Inside were three bright orange velvet cushions I had bought especially for the occasion as I felt that they would help to brighten up the little room. I had forgotten all about them and I placed them in what I considered to be strategic positions.

It was now almost ten minutes past three and I was finding it hard not to grab the brandy bottle. I stood back to admire the cushions when I felt a light draught of cool air against my neck. I spun round and she was there, looking so very lovely I was speechless with joy and wonder. Bless her beautiful heart, she hadn't failed me after all.

'Well, aren't you going to invite me to sit down?' she asked with a smile.

'Er, please do,' I stammered. I looked round frantically. 'Sorry it's such a small place. Er, you sit on the bed, it's more comfy, and I'll sit on the chair.' I drew forward the one and only chair and excused myself to go and make the tea.

I served the tea and cake and asked her what she thought of my little pad. She looked around and told me that she hadn't expected it to be so small but she very much admired it, especially my weird pieces of furniture. After she had finished her tea I took her on a conducted mini-tour of the flat and she was clearly taken with what she saw.

'It's so clean! Who does the cleaning?'

When I pointed towards myself her eyes opened in surprise. 'Don't you have a housegirl to keep it clean for you?'

I shook my head. 'I prefer to look after the place myself, to be frank with you.'

She seemed to be quite impressed by this revelation.

We spent almost three hours talking to each other and I found it fascinating. Time flew by. During our conversation Cynthia told me quite a lot about her sisters. She also told me that she had recently celebrated her eighteenth birthday. Her upbringing at the orphanage had been strict and her first language was Afrikaans but she spoke English excellently and had a wide vocabulary.

The impression that she made on me that first afternoon was that of a well-brought-up, kind-hearted young woman, and I wondered what she thought of me. I was a bit embarrassed when I considered the age gap between us, but when I casually mentioned this she said, 'So what, you're a nice person and I'm glad I came to see you.' I decided that we had better not meet again otherwise the whole thing might get out of hand, and I didn't want to be responsible for putting this nice kid into a dangerous position.

She insisted on doing the washing up and tidying around after our informal tea, and I sat smoking a cigarette and just thinking and enjoying the bit of fuss she was making of me. She certainly was a beautiful young woman and I well remember what she wore on that first visit. She had on a slim-fitting navy-blue skirt and she wore it with a jersey with wide lateral blue and white stripes. I called it her pirate jersey. She also wore matt grey stockings which showed off her lovely, long legs admirably. She was above average height for a woman and her soft, curly, blue-black hair was cut almost in a boyish style. She would have made a fortune for any fashion house in London or Paris.

I watched her busily washing the cups and saucers in the tiny sink and she was humming happily with her young head bowed in concentration. How vulnerable she looks, I thought. It was almost time for her to leave as she was expected back for evening duty by her madam.

She turned to me. 'Thank you, John, for a lovely afternoon. I have never enjoyed anything so much for such a long time. I hope I haven't bored you.'

I laughed. 'Bored me? I have been worried in case I bored you.'

She smiled and dried her hands. 'Far from it, John, I really meant what I said just now.'

I felt happy to hear her say this and as we walked into the living-room she said, 'Will we be seeing each other again, John?'

I lit a cigarette before answering. 'If I had any sense, Cynthia, I would tell you to run for your life and never come here again. Unfortunately I haven't got much sense and I would love to see you again.' I fiddled with the cigarette packet, having got that off my chest.

'We would have to be very careful, wouldn't we?' she said quietly.

'You can say that again, love,' I replied and continued, 'We must get one thing perfectly clear right now at this stage. Under no circumstances should we tell anyone, anyone at all, about our relationship. This will be our safest form of protection. Today's friend can often be tomorrow's enemy,' I warned, looking directly into her brown eyes. Her expression was thoughtful.

As I opened the door quietly to check that it was safe for her to leave she stood close to me and I could smell her perfume. On impulse I kissed her quickly on the cheek and whispered, 'Same time next week?' She blushed and nodded and she was gone. After she left I felt like an adolescent after his first date. I knew that my life would never be the same again. I didn't realise that for the next two and a half years I would be living in two different worlds, almost as two different people.

A foretaste of what was to come took place some weeks later. Cynthia and I had developed a pleasant little routine with our Sunday-afternoon teas and chats. We were easier in each other's company by this time but not yet lovers, although I knew that I was hopelessly in love with her. I didn't want to frighten her away or give her the impression that I was only interested in her for her body. I sensed that she trusted me and had warm feelings for me too, and I was happy in this knowledge.

During our talks I stressed the importance of not revealing anything to any of her friends as it could be a very dangerous thing to do. I explained that her friends could become jealous of her relationship and might give her away to the police on the simple basis of: If I can't have a rich, white boyfriend, why should she? Not that I was rich by any means but I had discovered that most non-white people automatically assume that all white people are rich, though South Africa has its fair share of poor whites.

One Wednesday evening I was padding around my little Sea Point flat in my customary underpants clutching a glass of brandy. It was about nine-thirty and I was toying with the idea of dressing and walking up to the Regency to see if Bob might be there. There was a light knock at the door. I stopped and cocked my head inquisitively. This was a new knock. It wasn't Bob, it wasn't Basil and it certainly wasn't the rozzers – so, who the hell was it? I stepped around the wardrobe and opened the front door a few inches as I wasn't dressed for visitors. To my astonishment it was Cynthia and to my horror she had with her another young Cape Coloured woman who was eyeing me speculatively. It was no time for dawdling or dithering so I stepped back and opened the door, nodding them to enter quickly.

I was furiously angry with Cynthia after all I had told her about never bringing any other girl to the flat, but I managed to control my anger. After all, she was only young and I dare say the temptation to show off her English boyfriend had proved too much for her. Nevertheless I decided that they would have to leave quickly for my sixth sense – which has never failed me – warned me that something was wrong somewhere. Cynthia could tell that I was far from pleased about her calling out of the blue with another girl, and she said, 'I hope you don't mind about me bringing Priscilla over with me.'

'We can talk about it some other time,' I said, and told them that it would be dangerous for them to stay as anyone might call on me and it would be very embarrassing for us all. 'I'll get you a couple of Cokes and you had better drink them quickly and leave. I'm sorry, but I feel nervous at the moment.'

They sat on the bed behind the wardrobe and sipped their drinks while I fidgeted nervously and lit one cigarette after another and gulped away at my glass of brandy. My stomach was churning madly and my sixth sense was silently screaming for them to leave at once, danger is on the way.

I nearly dropped my glass with sheer fright when a wardrobe-rattling and thunderous knocking at the front door almost paralysed me. Cynthia and Priscilla froze and I whispered, 'For God's sake don't move or talk. I know that is the police. What did I tell you?' I walked across to the door on legs made of rubber and with a trembling hand I opened it. The glass of brandy still clutched in my left hand nearly slid through my fingers when I found myself looking up at the largest South African policeman I had ever seen. He was a sergeant and the heavy gold stripes on his sleeve seemed to grow bigger and bigger as I gaped at them. I desperately wanted to swallow the contents of my glass but I was so scared I was afraid that I might twitch and fling the contents at his face. Huddled next to him was a small Cape Coloured, a slimy-looking little man who resembled a beady-eyed ferret. So this is what a coloured police informer looks like, I thought. No wonder they get short shrift from their own kind when detected. The beady eyes took me in and were attempting to leave their sockets to go on a walkabout around my flat.

The police sergeant was polite enough. 'Sorry to trouble you, sir, but is this flat a servant's quarters?'

The perverse humour of the situation saved me. A great calm descended on me and holding the glass of brandy up I said in my most affected English accent, 'Sergeant, if this was a servant's quarters do you honestly think that I would be standing here in my bloody underpants boozing?' I shook my head and took a sip from the glass. 'I know we English have a reputation for being a bit eccentric but this is taking it to the bounds of lunacy.'

Trying to act as nonchalantly as possible – which is no easy thing to do when being questioned by the police in your underpants and scared stiff – I raised my glass and finished off the fiery liquid. I then pointed to a lighted window the other side of the area outside my front door and said, 'The owner of the block of flats lives there. You can check with her if you like. I have been her tenant for some months and she will be happy to confirm what I have just said.'

This seemed to satisfy the sergeant who looked a bit puzzled and said something to the ferret-faced individual who made as if to step inside the flat.

'Sergeant!' I said forcefully, 'if this weasel as much as sets one foot inside my flat without my permission, I shall kick him in the nuts.'

I thought I heard a faint snigger from behind the wardrobe.

The sergeant spoke again to Ferret-face who turned and disappeared down the steps rather quickly. The sergeant apologised for having interrupted my privacy, wished me goodnight and left.

After I closed the door the reaction was so devastating that I almost fainted with relief. I rallied when I heard Cynthia tittering nervously behind the wardrobe. I was furious and I walked around to them and told her and her friend that nothing funny had happened and it was only by the grace of God that we were not on our way to Sea Point police station in the back of a police truck. Neither of them said a word. I think they were too scared to speak – scared of me, that is.

I told them that it would not be safe for them to leave the flat for at least half an hour. I suspected that Ferret-face was still hanging around hoping to make a name for himself. He already had as far as I was concerned and it wasn't Ferret-face.

With the light off in the bathroom I climbed quietly onto

the toilet seat and listened carefully through the partly open ventilation window. I stayed there for at least five minutes and all was quiet and still. I went back to the living-room and dressed quickly in beach pants, tee-shirt and flip-flops. 'I'm going to create a diversion and I want you girls to listen carefully to what I'm going to say.' They looked at me and I could see that the experience had scared them. Good! I thought, they won't be so bloody silly in future.

The diversion was simplicity itself. If Ferret-face was hanging around he would be somewhere at the back of the building. It would be easy for the girls to leave the building through the front entrance by using a service door on the landing outside the flat which led to the main stairs and elevators. It was agreed that I would put the lights out and leave the flat in my customary manner, down the back steps and not in a stealthy way. At the same time the girls would go through the service door and make their way out of the building into Beach Road via the front entrance.

As I walked away from the flats I felt eyes boring into my back. Perhaps it was my imagination overactivated by recent events. In due course, this sixth sense of mine was going to save Cynthia and me from numerous disasters.

THE COTTAGE

Cynthia had become a regular visitor to the flat and our relationship had changed to something more than just a casual friendship. In quiet moments alone I wondered where the hell it was all going to lead to.

I analysed my feelings as objectively as love would allow, and I knew that I cared very much about this young woman who had come so strangely into my life. I cared about her safety and well-being in the situation we were in, and I cared about her future. She had become dependent on me and obviously trusted me and my judgement.

I suppose that in some ways I had become dependent on her as well, but the responsibility for the immediate future lay fairly and squarely on my shoulders. I was acutely aware of the potentially dangerous situation I had allowed to develop and I knew without any shadow of doubt that I would have to take unusual precautions to prevent something unthinkable taking place. From this point on my life would change dramatically.

One of the first things I had to do was to decide whether or not it would be safe to continue using the flat at Sea Point or if we should start meeting at my cottage in Rondebosch. I was not too happy about the latter idea. First of all there were too many neighbours around and secondly, it would not be easy for Cynthia to enter the cottage because there was a tall sodium street-light almost directly opposite the house and extremely nosey neighbours living across what was not a particularly wide road.

My cottage was semi-detached and the one adjoining it was identical in appearance. There was nothing pretentious about either of them. They were typical South African bungalows which South Africans like to call 'cottages'. Mine had a traditional corrugated-iron roof painted with aluminium paint, a stoep at the front – a verandah, that is – white-painted outside walls and a small front garden complete with path and wrought-iron gate. Immediately beyond the low front-garden wall was a grass verge about ten feet deep which sloped gently down to the pavement edge.

The cottage contained two bedrooms. The main one was at the front of the house and overlooked the road, the second bedroom was next to the fairly large lounge. In addition there was a roomy kitchen and a combined bathroom and toilet. The cottage was neatly but sparsely furnished and it suited my requirements adequately. The kitchen was fitted with a large wooden table with a plastic top, an old chest-of-drawers doubling up as a kitchen cabinet, an old-fashioned stone sink, and a wooden worktop above some cupboards with shelves.

The one thing that bothered me slightly was the garden at the back. It was large, but had no dividing fence or hedge, so that it was shared with my immediate neighbours who, as it happened, were also my landlord and landlady. There would be no privacy in the garden if Cynthia visited the cottage, and we would also have to make sure that we kept the back door bolted during her visits just in case the landlady, a friendly soul, decided to pay an unexpected call.

On the other side of my cottage stood a small corrugated-iron chapel belonging to some offshoot of the Episcopalian Church. Its members were all Cape Coloured folk and on Sunday mornings I and everyone else within a radius of about half a mile shared their uninhibited and joyous singing, accompanied by a rather flat and wheezy organ. Actually I rather enjoyed it. Although I was not on chatting terms with the resident preacher and his wife, we were on cordial nodding terms.

Their religious fervour was a sight to behold. It was quite physical and on certain occasions the congregation would gather in the garden at the rear of the chapel where a special service would be conducted which included all manner of gyrations, including a few handstands. I'm sure that the Good Lord found this as entertaining as I did.

Although the front garden was neat and well looked after, the garden behind the chapel was a tangle of weeds and there

47

was a veritable thicket of large shrubs at the further end. This was to play a significant role in the future. Backing onto the end wall of the rear garden of the chapel was a small yard which lay immediately behind a Cape Coloured shebeen, an illicit drinking establishment which the police knew about but turned a blind eye to for reasons best known to themselves.

My landlord and his wife were extremely nice people. Dan was a Hollander, as Afrikaners call Dutch people, and Marie, his wife, an Afrikaner. Dan made a living as an organ technician and travelled around the Western Cape visiting interesting old chapels and churches to repair or carry out maintenance on equally interesting old organs. They were good neighbours, friendly and kind, but neither of them poked their noses into my private affairs nor did they ask searching questions. They had a small son and a boisterous Dalmatian called Spot and I got along well with them both. Many a pleasant evening or Sunday afternoon I had spent sitting in Dan and Marie's kitchen drinking Dan's brandy and trying to solve some of South Africa's problems in friendly conversation. We had some good laughs together and we became firm friends.

Amongst the cottage's plus-factors the main one lay in its location: its proximity to the non-white chapel and the fact that several non-white families still lived in the neighbourhood, although the authorities were gradually moving them out to inhospitable townships which the non-white people strongly objected to. No one would take too much notice if a non-white woman was seen walking through the neighbourhood should it become necessary for Cynthia to do so. On the other hand, if someone as attractive as Cynthia should be seen entering the home of a known bachelor one could hardly have blamed the observer for assuming that she was not handing out religious tracts or carrying out palm-reading. Certainly not if the bachelor were white.

After giving the matter a great deal of thought I decided that we might manage the occasional meeting at the cottage providing extraordinary care were taken at all times. Cynthia and I talked about the prospects and it was agreed that under no circumstances should she ever come to the cottage on her own. There would be no daylight visits for obvious reasons.

No one must ever find out about her visits and we should always be alert in our clandestine activities to make sure that we never made the mistake of establishing dangerously regular patterns of movement. Her visiting times would always vary and so would the days. Her departure times from the cottage would also be irregular.

I had heard that the police, when raiding a house or flat where it was suspected that a white and a non-white were indulging in 'immoral activities', would go through a ridiculous but no doubt effective routine to obtain evidence that sexual intercourse might have taken place. This consisted of searching toilet bowls, baths, wash-basins and shower cubicles for signs of negroid-type hair. Beds would be carefully stripped and searched and closely examined with torch and magnifying glass for any signs of sexual activity or any indication that the suspects had shared the bed. According to newspaper reports describing cases involving immorality, much useful evidence was obtained by the use of these somewhat un-savoury methods of detection.

In fairness to the police involved in such cases, many of the officers objected to and refused to carry out such duties, but the law was the law and had to be obeyed.

We decided to try a dummy run and Cynthia was excited about the prospects of seeing the cottage at Rondebosch. It was agreed that she would wait in the shadows of a quiet road not far from the flat at eight-thirty one night where I would pick her up. If anyone happened to be walking along the road I would drive on and do a circuit around the block and try again until the coast was clear. The pick-up went smoothly and Cynthia lay down in the back of the car; not very comfortable, I thought, but far more so than a cell at Sea Point police station.

This lying-down on the back seat of the car was fine until I found myself parked next to a bus on one later occasion when the lights were at red, and streams of perspiration poured down my face at the thought of astonished passengers looking down and seeing Cynthia trying to hide. I made sure that situation never arose again.

While we were on our way to Rondebosch I explained to Cynthia the rather undignified method she would have to adopt to enter the cottage without being seen by anyone. I felt lousy about her having to go through such humiliating antics but what could we do?

The drill was that I would approach the cottage from a direction where the left-hand side of the Beetle would be nearest the side of the road on which the cottage stood. I would then drive up onto the grass verge and stop as near to the garden wall as possible, but leaving enough room for the passenger door to be opened. I would have my briefcase on the passenger seat so that after stopping the car and switching off the motor, the briefcase would be my excuse to walk around to the passenger side and open the door, so giving Cynthia an opportunity to scramble out. I would then open the front gate and make my way to the front door while poor Cynthia made her uncomfortable and undignified journey on her hands and knees.

On opening the front door of the cottage I would not switch on any lights until she was safely inside and in the lounge, because the front door was glazed with frosted glass and she might have been seen. On leaving, unless it was in the early hours of the morning, the procedure was reversed.

The first visit went as smoothly as circumstances would permit and after recovering from the indignity of her entrance, Cynthia happily went around the cottage on stockinged feet to explore. She quite liked the house and what I had done to make it as presentable as possible.

Cynthia visited me at the cottage two or three times a week from then on and we enjoyed many happy hours there, making plans, getting to know each other better, fantasising, cooking and so on. Under normal circumstances we would have been blissfully happy together but all the time I was on edge wondering whether someone might have seen us entering the house, and I found that I was beginning to drink more alcohol than I usually did. I took little notice of it at first but gradually I realised that I was finding it easier to cope with the unusual lifestyle I had adopted after topping myself up with a few large brandies. I never went too far, of course, as I had to drive Cynthia and couldn't afford to be stopped by the police for erratic driving, or worse. Nevertheless I grew a bit concerned about my increasing input of alcohol.

Despite the stresses and strains we both had to suffer we managed to live a reasonably normal existence and had moments of great happiness. We never relaxed in our 'safety procedures' as I called them, and I became almost obsessively vigilant. I realised later that it was this obsessiveness that saved us from joining the sad statistics which appeared so regularly in the columns of the daily and weekend newspapers. There were many cases of suicide due to people being arrested for so-called acts of immorality. That a human being should be driven to taking his or her own life for loving someone was hard for me to understand at times, but it was part of everyday life in the Republic and one had to take it in one's stride.

We had plenty of time on our hands during Cynthia's illicit visits, and when she said that much could be done to make the house even more comfortable, I readily agreed. Armed with a list of things to buy, many of which were at Cynthia's suggestion, I set about purchasing tins of paint, cheerfully coloured cushions, some prints of London rather attractively framed, and a standard lamp. When I returned with my purchases I stored them carefully in the spare bedroom, as I had promised Cynthia that she would be the one to decide where the various items should go. We were like a couple of newly-weds setting up home and when she paid her next visit she was very happy with the things I had bought. After we had spent some time distributing them around the place we were delighted with the improved appearance of the lounge. The kitchen needed redecorating and as Cynthia intended being away the coming weekend on a visit to her aunt at Malmesbury, I said I would keep myself out of mischief by painting it so that it would look nice for her during her next visit.

It had been some time since I had visited Bob because of my DIY activities at the cottage – and Cynthia of course. So, after spending a busy day stripping old paint in readiness for new paint on the Sunday, I had a hot bath and drove off to the Regency at Sea Point with the hope that he might be there.

He was. He was perched in his usual place in the public bar, his old Parachute Regiment jumping jacket dangling around the bar stool on which he was sitting.

When I made my presence known he swung round and was obviously pleased to see me. I received a characteristic welcome: 'Where the fuckin' 'ell 'ave you been then?' This was affection indeed from Bob and I grinned. I had to admire his directness and brevity of speech. He always got to the nub of things without any preamble. I apologised for my recent absence and said that I had been tarting up the cottage a bit in readiness for the not-too-distant Christmas. When I had finished the work he would be invited to a small but select housewarming.

Standing next to us and chatting animatedly with the bar-man was an elegantly dressed, middle-aged man who had been talking to Bob when I had first entered. He turned towards us and leaned nonchalantly against the bar, eyeing me and obviously waiting to be introduced. A quick glance had already told me a lot about him. He had the florid face and rheumy eyes of the professional boozer – not that I was in a position to criticise him the way I was going. He had a glassy stare, and a nose you could have squeezed a double out of. His immaculate, dark-blue blazer complete with six highly polished brass buttons and RAF squadron badge told me the rest. I prepared myself for a long and possibly boring session. He appeared to be an English-speaking South African who would no doubt impress me with his war record, his connections in high places in the Republic and, of course, his family tree would go back to the Domesday Book. As it happened I was right on all counts apart from the fact that he was UK-born and had lived in South Africa for some twelve years or more, after marrying the daughter of a once well-known South African sportsman.

Bob turned to his new-found companion and said, ''Ere's the bloke I was tellin' you about, Chopper.' I winced at the name. Chopper smiled across at me and held out his hand, giving me a quick look up and down at the same time. He told me that his real name was Frank but everyone called him Chopper. I never did find out why.

'Glad to know you, Johnny,' he said in a very up-county

accent, and I winced again as I hate being called Johnny. He was friendly enough but there was something about him that didn't ring exactly true.

He chatted away about his position as general manager of a very big manufacturing company in Elsies River, an industrial suburb of Cape Town. He told me about his large American car and his speedboat and his attractive wife who was over twenty years younger than he was. I wondered what he was doing hanging around in the Regency bar when he had all those wonderful things to go home to. It suddenly dawned on me that behind his façade of bonhomie and his RAFVR tie hid a sad and lonely man, another of the world's walking-wounded.

From what he was telling me he also missed England and he seemed to be almost pathetically grateful for having met us. He said that Bob had been telling him all about me, which made me realise how sensible I had been in not letting on to Bob about Cynthia. Bob was already half-cut and I shuddered at the thought of what he might have told Chopper if he had known about Cynthia and me.

Bob had mentioned to Chopper that I had served in the RAF and Chopper had revealed to Bob that he had also been flying during the war. When I mentioned a couple of squadrons I had flown with in Bomber Command during 1943 and 1944 Chopper did a quick about-turn and said that his flying career had consisted of doing 'a spot of flying in gliders', and at a later date let drop that he had been mainly connected with airfield control in the Med. He was an amusing person and the evening passed quickly and pleasantly. Finally he glanced at his watch and said he would have to go home but would meet us there again soon, and with a wave he left.

Chopper was as good as his word and a few nights later he came into the Regency bar carrying a battered old leather briefcase. He had already enjoyed a few drinks before his arrival. Later I discovered that the briefcase, which he carried everywhere, contained nothing apart from a Scotch whisky bottle, usually almost empty. Poor old Chopper was a chronic alcoholic.

When South Africans are not discussing politics they are usually telling jokes, many of which are derogatory to black people. Chopper took a lengthy swig from his double Scotch and asked us if we knew what Kaffir roulette was. We didn't.

'Well, it's like this, you see. A white bloke takes a coloured bird into a telephone box. They start making love and he phones the police and they see who comes first!' Chopper wheezed with laughter: he really got a kick out of his own jokes.

Christmas was drawing nearer. On checking with my diary I found that it would be Christmas Day in less than three weeks.

Cynthia had already told me that she would be expected to spend Christmas Day and Boxing Day with her sisters and other relatives. Ramona, her eldest sister, shared a room with her husband and small son in her father- and mother-in-law's house in Kew Town, a bleak, uninviting Cape Coloured township in the Cape Flats. This sandy, windswept place was not so very far from the cottage at Rondebosch East. Space was at a premium in the small house but room would be found for Cynthia and her other sister Cathy to sleep during their short stay.

During our sojourns at the cottage Cynthia had told me a great deal about her sisters. I had asked her what they would have thought and said, had they known about her relationship with me. She told me that Ramona would have been very upset and angry because she didn't trust white people and would have assumed that her younger sister was merely being exploited; after all, how many white men ever kept their promises to a coloured girl? Apart from this she would also have been extremely worried in case Cynthia became involved with the police.

When I asked what Cathy's reaction would have been she said that she didn't think that Cathy would object to our relationship but she would have been worried about the risks we were taking and she also wouldn't want to see her younger sister in the hands of the South African police. Cathy was older than Cynthia by a few years but younger than Ramona.

Cynthia and I were sitting in the kitchen of the cottage one night enjoying a cup of coffee after our meal when I asked, 'Why don't you invite Cathy to have a special Christmas Eve supper with us here. What do you think she would say?'

Her eyes lit up in pleased surprise. 'Ooh! I think she'd love to do that but she'll have a shock when I tell her you're white.'

'Do you think we can trust her not to say anything to Ramona, at least not yet?'

Cynthia nodded her head. 'She wouldn't dare say anything to her, don't worry.'

Cynthia was excited about the proposal and she told me that she would have a quiet word with Cathy when they next met and it was left at that. When I dropped her off near the house in Camp's Bay she gave me a hug and a kiss before leaving the car. 'I'm ever so pleased about you letting Cathy have supper with us. You're nice.' And with this she was gone into the shadows.

As I drove back to Rondebosch I wondered what Cathy would think of the relationship when she heard about it, not to mention the risks involved in coming to the cottage. I took the line that as it would be Christmas Eve everyone would be enjoying themselves and would be too busy or too sloshed to notice what we were up to.

The following day was Saturday and I decided to invite Bob out for a meal; we hadn't seen anything of each other for a few days and I knew that he spent a lot of time on his own apart from when Beattie arrived to clean and tidy his flat. When I arrived there in the early afternoon he was sitting alone in the kitchen reading a World War II story. The kettle was on in no time and when I asked if he fancied a run in the car and a meal somewhere, his face lit up with pleasure, so shortly after finishing our tea we set off.

I drove through the city and made my way to the National Road which follows the foreshore for a few miles before turning inland. We drove slowly along enjoying the sunshine and the view of Table Bay over on our left with Table Mountain to our right. I continued around the bay, passing Paarden Eiland's power station and numerous factories, until we arrived at Blouberg Strand, a quiet little place offering the most stagger-ing view of Table Mountain with Cape Town glittering beneath its mass. On a clear day the view is outstanding and it is from Blouberg that most of the tourist photographs of the city of Cape Town and the mountain are taken. The beach is nothing to write home about, being a bit scruffy, and bathing was dangerous, but it was still a very popular spot for weekend drivers and their families.

During our drive Bob had mentioned that he and Beattie had become rather fond of each other, a possibility that I had already suspected, but I said nothing other than to warn him of the consequences should the police be tipped off. I omitted to mention my own situation and fears for the future.

We parked outside a small eating place, more a café than a restaurant. The name of the establishment escapes me but I distinctly remember that leaning against its rough white-washed outside walls stood the figurehead from an old sailing ship, possibly a naval one. It might even have come from one of Nelson's men-of-war during a trip to the Cape. Maybe the vessel foundered during a storm in the bay. Table Bay is noted for its spectacular storms and legend has it that the Flying Dutchman has been seen there many times over the centuries.

We spent a pleasant hour or so at the little café which served a delicious steak with salad followed by ice cream and coffee. And for some time afterwards we sat quietly enjoying the view and each other's company before setting off on our journey back to Sea Point.

We ended up in the bar at the Regency and after a few drinks we decided to call it a day as we both felt tired. It was getting late by the time I arrived back at the cottage and the road was deserted. I parked in my customary spot on the grass verge and closed the car door as quietly as possible so as not to disturb Marie and Dan. As I closed the front gate behind me I thought I noticed a slight movement of the curtain in the window of the house across the road. I didn't pause, and turning I walked up the path, mounted the stoep and entered the house. I made a mental note to oil the hinges of the gate. They had squeaked.

The following morning I was awoken by the sound of the wheezy harmonium from the chapel next-door. The sun was very bright through the drawn curtains of the bedroom and, stretching and yawning, I padded off to the bathroom for a quick shower before cooking some breakfast. I heard voices from the garden and after eating I opened the back door to say hello to my neighbours, not having seen them to speak to for some while.

Spot, the ungainly and friendly Dalmatian, was galloping around the garden and when he saw me he came to a sudden halt and stared at some imaginary object just over my left shoulder. His shiny, bulbous nose was sniffing in a businesslike way and when he recognised who the interesting scent belonged to he came bounding across to be made a fuss of. As I patted him Marie came over and greeted me.

'Hello, stranger,' she said in her strong South African accent. 'So you're still alive, are you?'

'Hello, Marie. How are you, love?' I countered. She told me that they were going out for the day for a *braaivlei* and would I like to join them. It would have been a very enjoyable experience if I had, from previous experience of Afrikaner *braaivleis*. I should have returned late at night absolutely stuffed with Boerewors sausage, chicken and steak, not to mention half a case of Cold Castle lager beer. However, I had already arranged to spend an hour or two swimming and sunbathing at the Pavilion swimming pool prior to meeting Cynthia at the Sea Point flat.

I thanked Marie for her kind invitation and asked her if she and Dan would care to join me for pre-Christmas drinks a day or so before the holiday started. She told me that they would be spending Christmas at her parents' home at Somerset West. I was delighted to learn this as it meant that there would be no unexpected visits from them during the time that Cathy and Cynthia would be at the cottage.

When I stepped back into my kitchen Spot stood on the doorstep with his nose poking inquisitively through the doorway. He was well-trained and would not enter the house. I decided that a modest investment in goodwill might be of value in the future, and when I asked him if he would like a piece of meat, he wagged his tail and cocked his spotted head to one side and sniffed hopefully. I opened the old fridge and took out a large slab of fresh, bloody topside and cut off a fairly hefty slice, watched closely now by the slavering animal. When I walked over with the meat and offered it to him, his reaction was almost comical to watch.

He could hardly believe his eyes or his nose. With a sort of 'Well I'd rather not but as you insist' look on his doggie face he removed the slab of meat from my fingers with the greatest delicacy. For a moment he remained on the step looking at me, almost stupefied with astonishment, before turning and trotting away to a far corner of the garden with his treasure. As I closed and locked the kitchen door I heard a raucous yell from Marie who had obviously noticed the juicy topside dangling from Spot's salivating jaws. 'Hey! Christ, man! You'll spoil the bugger.'

I dressed quickly and grabbed a clean towel, and a few minutes later I was turning on to the main road towards Sea Point. The flat was hot and airless when I stepped inside, and I opened all the windows and changed into my swimming trunks . . . Moments later I was flip-flopping towards the Pavilion. It was as hot as hell as it was now midsummer in South Africa. I wondered what the weather would be like in the UK and imagined all the shops lit up in Oxford Street and all the mums and dads and children muffled up against the cold, noses red and shining. For a moment I wished I could be there with them.

It was difficult for me as an Englishman to get into the spirit of Christmas in a climate where daily temperatures often soared into the nineties and where safari suits with shorts were standard wear. I remembered the previous year, walking around Stuttafords, one of Cape Town's prestigious department stores, shortly before Christmas and being quite surprised to hear 'Jingle Bells' and 'O, Come All Ye Faithful' being played on the store's intercom system. It took me a few moments to realise that it was because of the coming Christmas holiday. With everyone wearing summer clothing, and brilliant sunshine outside plus the store's air-conditioning, it was a bit difficult to appreciate that the festive season had arrived. Despite this, I later found myself walking along the road towards the cottage, with a Christmas tree over my shoulder and a carrier bag in my hand containing my turkey and a bottle of Scotch. It seemed a bit bizarre at the time. South Africans generally insist on a traditional Christmas Dinner, complete with plum pudding and brandy sauce and so on, but they do usually partake of this feast in the cool of the evening – not that it gets much cooler.

After a swim and an hour stretched out on a towel on the prickly lawn I decided that I'd had enough. It was just too hot and I felt hungry so I retired to a restaurant not far from the Pavilion and ordered a light meal. While eating it I reflected on the current state of affairs. I was giving much thought to Cynthia and the future. If we were caught there might well not be a future for us, at least not one that we would enjoy, and least of all together.

What would my friends say if they knew about my involvement with a non-white woman? They probably wouldn't believe it. I hadn't seen Basil or Brenda for ages and made a mental note to contact them before Christmas otherwise they would think that I had a reason for trying to avoid them.

There were the people I met through business too. Because of the nature of my work I had a wide circle of acquaintances. A favourite spot for advertising people in those days was the Tulbagh Hotel, known as the Toolbag. It was, and probably still is, situated in Tulbagh Square not far from the building where I worked. After a working day advertising folk would generally congregate there for drinks, political chit-chat, jokes, and gossip about various agency activities.

Looking around at the faces of some of the well-known figures of the Cape Town advertising scene I could not help but wonder what their reactions would have been if they had known that the quiet English chap, who joined them from time to time and laughed at their jokes, and nodded sympathetically at their political problems, was practically living with a black woman. I found it difficult not to laugh sometimes as I imagined the various expressions that would have appeared on their faces, along with the stunned silence that such an admission would have produced.

As I listened to their conversation, which often included comments on sex across the colour line along with rather selfish and derogatory remarks and comments on the less fortunate non-white citizens, I found myself drifting further and further away from their philosophies and attitudes. I was becoming an outsider; I would have been a social outcast in their eyes if they had known the truth. It was certainly a moment of truth for me. It was a hell of a thing really, when I thought about it seriously.

How much sympathy might I have expected from any of them if Cynthia and I were arrested and charged with an offence under the Immorality Act? I had one or two friends in Cape Town and Johannesburg who might have understood. I was breaking the law with my relationship, a harsh and unjust law and difficult to understand in free countries, but it was a judicially approved law nevertheless, and I was always free to leave South Africa if I didn't like it.

I had begun thinking about the possibility of Cynthia and I leaving together so that we could live our lives without having to wonder whether we were likely to be arrested at any time. I had already spoken to Cynthia about this possibility though not in detail. She told me that she knew that there was no future for her in South Africa, though if she left she would obviously miss her sisters whom she was very close to.

I looked at the clock and saw that I had the better part of three hours to kill before meeting Cynthia, so I decided to see if Bob was around. When I knocked at the door of his ground-floor flat there was no response and I found this curious as he seldom went out on a Sunday afternoon. I knocked again with our special coded knock, only louder this time, and after a few moments the door opened an inch or two and Bob peered out.

'It's me,' I said unnecessarily.

'I can see that,' he replied and he opened the door to allow me in. From the moment I stepped inside I knew he was up to no good. Nodding towards the kitchen he gave me a conspiratorial wink and his special ultra-crafty grin. It was a dreadful combination.

As I followed him into the kitchen I heard him say, 'It's all right, it's me mate!' Beattie and another young Cape Coloured woman were sitting at the table with glasses of brandy in front of them, a half-empty bottle of Oude Meester on the table and the remains of a meal. Bob introduced me to Beattie's friend. Her name was Chris and she had frizzy hair in an Afro style, a light complexion and grey eyes, an unusual combination but not all that rare in the Western Cape. Cape Coloureds varied from coal-black with genuine negroid hair to pale-skinned people with vivid blue eyes. The only thing that gave the latter away as being coloured citizens was their distinctive Cape Coloured accents.

Both girls were smartly dressed and seemed to be quite at

home in Bob's kitchen so I assumed that this was certainly not their first visit. I metaphorically took off my hat to Bob who had been more discreet than I would have given him credit for. The girls were amusing conversationalists and Beattie's vocabulary was interlaced with some rather choice expletives which I suspected she had picked up from Bob.

'I hope that no one saw the girls entering your flat, Bob. There are a lot of people around outside, you know.'

He gave me an excruciating leer and said, 'They 'aven't just arrived, you know. They crept in last night.'

I blinked. 'Since last night?' I said with wonder in my voice. I was hardly in a position to adopt an attitude of moral indignation so I left it at that and grinned at him.

'Do you live near by, John?' Beattie asked and as Bob's mouth opened to speak I trod on his foot and he yelped.

'Sorry, Bob,' I said sympathetically, smiling amiably, and with that I looked down at my watch and said I had to leave. After shaking hands with the girls I walked to the front door with Bob. I gave him a meaningful look. 'For Christ's sake, never tell either of them where I am living, do you understand? If I want a coloured girl to visit me, I'll make my own arrangements, if you don't mind. Anyhow, Bob, good luck to you but take care, all right?' and with this I strode off towards my own flat.

I arrived there shortly before three, knowing that as a rule Cynthia appeared around three-fifteen. On this particular occasion she didn't turn up until almost three forty-five. I was beginning to get a bit edgy when she suddenly entered the flat and closed the door quietly behind her. I took her in my arms and kissed her. 'Hey! What are you trying to do? Give me a heart attack? I've been worried stupid waiting for you.'

She nuzzled against my cheek and said she knew I would be worried but unfortunately the bus that she normally caught had arrived and left earlier than usual and she had had to wait for another one.

When we settled down with our now traditional tray of 'English tea' complete with cake, I asked her if she had spoken to Cathy about Christmas Eve. She giggled and put her cup down.

'She thought I was joking, John. Honestly, she couldn't take it in, but when she realised that I was not pulling her leg, she nearly had a fit.' I waited for her to continue. 'Anyhow, she calmed down after I told her the whole story about how we met and how kind and decent you are to me, but her main concern seemed to be that Ramona mustn't find out.'

I nodded. 'Of course,' I muttered.

'Cathy said that Ramona would kill me if she found out that I was "messing about" with a white man.'

After digesting this item of news I asked if Cathy had agreed to spend Christmas Eve with us and Cynthia said that she would as she wanted to see 'this white man' for herself.

After tea Cynthia washed up the cups and saucers and later we lay on the bed relaxing and planning the Christmas Eve meal. It would have to be something special as I wanted to make a good impression on Cynthia's sister. We made love, and later when the streets were quiet I drove her back to Camp's Bay.

A few days before Christmas Eve I invited Basil and Brenda out for dinner, but they told me that they were about to leave Cape Town as they had accepted an invitation to spend Christmas with Basil's parents in the Orange Free State. There was time for us to have a pre-Christmas drink together at their place before they set off. They had moved into an old but comfortable house high above Green Point and after exchanging presents and cards we sat companionably for an hour enjoying a few drinks and the pleasure of each other's company. When I rose to leave I shook Basil's hand and kissed Brenda and hoped they would have a safe journey and a super Christmas, and we promised to see each other again soon after their return. As I drove away from the house they waved goodbye to me from their balcony. I waved back and put my foot down for home.

Christmas Eve arrived. It was a hot, sunny day and Bob and I set off to do our Christmas shopping together. Although he knew nothing about Cynthia I had dropped a few mysterious hints about an attachment I had formed with a certain young woman and in due course he would know all about it. He tried to press me for details but I flatly refused to discuss the matter any further, so he had to be satisfied with my rather flimsy explanation.

I wanted something special for Cynthia and I decided to buy her some expensive clothes. We went into a shop in Sea Point which carried a range of exclusive fashions and an attractive model was showing off a very trendy combination. It consisted of a cyclamen-coloured silk blouse with long sleeves and long points to the collar, a pair of black trousers with extra wide bell-bottoms, and a dazzling black-and-white silk scarf wrapped casually around her waist. I didn't profess to being an expert on women's clothes but I knew that Cynthia would like this rig-out and that she would look terrific in it.

The model noticed us admiring her ensemble and she glided across. 'Do you think your wife would like something like this for Christmas?' she smiled.

'I'm sure she would,' I replied and asked her to wrap up a duplicate of each item after giving her the sizes.

She looked surprised. 'Shouldn't she try the garments on first?'

I smiled and said, 'Ah! but then it wouldn't be a surprise, would it? That's the object of the exercise, you see, to surprise her.'

The model seemed to be quite impressed and she spoke to a short, middle-aged lady who I assumed was the owner of the shop. She came over to us and gushed, 'How nice to find a husband so thoughtful. You must bring your lucky wife in so we can see how she looks in her new things.'

As I paid for my purchases I thought to myself, I could just imagine your face, love, if I did.

I took the clothes and other items I had bought back to the Sea Point flat and locked them inside the wardrobe, and after a quick drink Bob and I continued with our shopping. I bought a large duck having decided to prepare roast duck *à l'orange* for tonight's feast. Cooking has always been a hobby of mine and providing I was armed with a good cookery book I could just about cope with anything. Bob and I arranged to spend Christmas Day together and I told him that I had something special organised for him. He looked pleased and before we went our separate ways I treated him to a drink at the Regency.

I collected the stuff from the flat, drove quickly back to

Rondebosch and hurried into the cottage clutching my purchases. Although I had not yet had the pleasure of meeting Cynthia's sister, I had bought a small gift for her; some rather expensive toilet soap which I hoped she would like, along with a suitable Christmas card. It was stiflingly hot in the house and I opened the windows and started preparing the ingredients for the meal, sipping steadily away at the brandy at the same time. I was finding that I could hold my liquor better than most these days, no doubt due to my steadily increasing intake of the stuff.

When everything was ready for cooking I showered and changed into a new pair of white trousers and a white string vest; it was so hot it would have been unbearable to wear a shirt with a tie. After studying my image in the bedroom mirror I decided that I looked a bit like an attendant in a lunatic asylum so I exchanged the white vest for a dark blue one. I now looked rather like a croupier at a doubtful casino but it was a marked improvement.

Soon the house was filled with two things: the smell of roasting duck and the strains of 'Rock of Ages' from the next-door chapel where they were warming up in readiness for their Christmas Eve service. I was in a cheerful mood, and pouring out a liberal shot of Oude Meester I raised my glass in the general direction of the chapel and said aloud, 'Happy Christmas to you, you poor buggers!'

To make sure that my visitors would not be observed I had altered the normal schedule. On this occasion I was to pick up Cynthia and Cathy at the bus-stop not far from the cottage, where they were due to arrive shortly after 10 p.m.

Everything had gone according to plan in the kitchen and the meal was now ready so I turned off the gas burners. It could all be re-heated in a few minutes and as I was ahead of my cooking schedule I turned my attention to other things. I decided that we would eat in style so I manhandled the heavy table from the kitchen into the lounge. It soon stood resplendent with a new dark-red table cloth with matching napkins, wine glasses, gleaming silver, Christmas crackers for three, and in the centre of the table stood my *pièce de résistance*, a triple-candle holder made from white porcelain, complete with elegant, tapering white candles. I lit the candles and switched off the overhead pendant light and the change was dramatic. The atmosphere of the room had been transformed almost magically.

The presents were gift-wrapped and waiting beneath a white plastic Christmas tree on a small table in a corner of the room. I had decorated it with tinsel and the traditional coloured balls made from that unbelievably thin glass. The tree shimmered and coruscated in the flickering candlelight. I was pleased with the general effect and had to admit that the room looked impressive and quite romantic.

It was now twenty minutes past nine and I had time to enjoy a cigarette and another drink before setting off to pick up my guests. The house next-door was empty, so was the one across the road; I had remembered Marie mentioning that the people who lived there were going to spend Christmas at their daughter's home near Paarl, a famous wine-producing area in the Western Cape. This information was the perfect Christmas gift for me. It meant that providing reasonable care was taken, Cathy and Cynthia would be able to enter the cottage in a dignified way and could leave in the same manner.

At precisely five minutes to ten I left the house and drove off to welcome my Christmas visitors. I parked the Beetle a little way from the bus-stop and on the opposite side of the road, where I lit a cigarette and sat back to wait. On Christmas Eve everyone, including the police, would surely have other things on their minds and would not pay much attention to a white man waiting in his car near a bus-stop. It was one of the precious few occasions when meeting Cynthia that I felt totally relaxed and safe, and the brief feeling of euphoria was wonderful.

The lumbering double-decker arrived and two slim figures descended from it. The bus pulled away and whined off into the night towards the city and Cynthia and Cathy looked in the direction of my car. Then they hurried across the darkened road and climbed in. I had already started the motor and we drove off at once. 'Hello, darling,' I greeted Cynthia, and 'Nice to have you aboard, Cathy. I'll say hello properly when we get home.' Cathy said nothing and I guessed that she was a bit shy.

I told them that there would be no danger involved in

entering the cottage but to be on the safe side I dropped them about two hundred yards away and told them just to approach the house in a normal manner and to go inside. The door was unlatched and I would continue on around the block and join them shortly afterwards. They were still going strong in the chapel and I reasoned that no one would take any notice of two coloured women in the neighbourhood that night.

There were no problems and I was soon being introduced to Cynthia's sister. She was a charming young woman, a bit lighter in complexion than Cynthia and whereas Cynthia's hair was softly curly but not negroid, Cathy's hair was smooth and glossy black. She still seemed a bit shy but it was obvious that she was pleased to be with us and seemed to like me. I guessed that it must be proving a bit of an ordeal for her but I wondered if she was aware that it was an ordeal for me as well. I wanted her to approve of me; after all, I could end up being her brother-in-law. It occurred to me that this was probably the first time in Cathy's life that she had ever set foot in a white person's home.

Cynthia couldn't get over the changed appearance of the lounge and was quite excited by what I had done to make it more Christmassy. Eagerly she took her sister on a tour of the cottage and I could hear them laughing and talking animatedly in Afrikaans. It was a truly happy occasion, one of the few that we were able to share during our time together in the Republic.

I put a Christmas record on the turntable and the carols added to our Christmas atmosphere. The women would not allow me into the kitchen and I was deposited on the settee with a glass of brandy while Cynthia and her sister served the dinner. We sat around the table like happy kids and pulled the crackers and put on the paper hats from them. It was a great time and it was wonderful to see how carefree Cynthia was. Cathy, too, had come out of her shell and was obviously having a super time. I was glad that we had invited her along. Cathy told me more about how she, Cynthia and Ramona had spent their childhood in the orphanage, and they laughed as they recalled happy moments from when they were children.

After dinner we exchanged presents and there were many 'Ooohs!' and 'Aaaahs!' when Cynthia opened her packages and discovered what I had bought for her. She took her presents into the bedroom and returned a little while later wearing them. They fitted perfectly and she looked terrific. She made the lady who had modelled the garments look positively dowdy.

Cathy was very happy with the soap I had bought her and she gave me a large casket of cigarettes, and Cynthia had gift-wrapped a bottle of Oude Meester and a tie for me. It was the sort of tie that would not match any of my clothes but I kissed her and thanked her, and made a mental note to buy a suit to go with it.

That happy night passed all too quickly and at 1 a.m. I drove them home. There was little danger involved providing I drove carefully and didn't give the impression that I had been drinking excessively. The police were very alert in such instances. It was a twenty-minute drive to Kew Town and the roads were deserted when we stopped at the end of the street where they would be staying.

They thanked me for a nice night and we wished each other Christmas greetings before they got out and hurried away into the dark. I had given Cathy a brotherly kiss on the cheek and she tittered with embarrassment. I didn't waste any time hanging around Kew Town because white faces were not welcome and it was illegal for me to be there unless I had a good reason – such as being a member of the CID or a doctor.

Bob and I spent the better part of Christmas in an alcoholic haze when we were not sleeping. I stayed at the Sea Point flat and we cooked Christmas dinner at Bob's. It was an uneventful time but we enjoyed ourselves in our own way and we certainly had plenty to eat and drink. The special surprise I had promised Bob was his Christmas present – a well-illustrated book covering the history of the Parachute Brigade. He was touchingly grateful and was speechless for the better part of fifteen minutes. I also gave him a box of cigarettes. His gifts to me were a pocket diary and a bottle of Oude Meester, most of which he drank.

The Christmas holiday and New Year's Eve passed and it was back to the old routine once again. Basil and Brenda returned from their trek to the Free State and I took them to my favourite seafood restaurant for a good meal. Marie and Dan were also back and we were so pleased to see each other again that we all ended up in their kitchen having a bit of an impromptu party, the outcome of which was a classic hangover for me.

Cynthia enjoyed her Christmas reunion with her sisters and Cathy was as good as her word and said nothing to Ramona about meeting me, so there were no problems there. However, the first month of the new year was not without its traumas.

THE WATCHER

Early one morning after taking Cynthia back to Camp's Bay I decided to drive into the city through Sea Point as I wanted to make an early start at the office where a fairly heavy work-load awaited me. It was six forty-five on a Monday morning. I had time to spare and thought I would call on Bob and have a cup of tea with him before continuing into Cape Town.

It was a lovely morning and the buses were already rumbling along picking up small groups of early-morning workers. The sea looked flat and grey, and about a mile and a half off-shore I could see a massive tanker making its ponderous way towards the oil terminal at Cape Town docks. A few gulls were already swooping down along the shoreline, scavenging. I was in good spirits having spent a happy evening and night with Cynthia and also having made a safe and uneventful journey with her from Rondebosch East to Camp's Bay.

As I drove into the kerb opposite the forecourt of the garage in front of Bob's flat, I noticed that the light was on in his kitchen. At least the old sod's up, I thought. When I gave our special coded ring on the doorbell there was no response. I rang again: still no response. That's funny, I thought. He must have heard the bell, it's in the kitchen. I tried once more and the door opened a few inches and Beattie's frightened eyes looked out at me. When she saw who it was the scared look changed to one of relief and she opened the door to let me in.

'Oh! John, man. Thank God it's you,' she said as I followed her into the flat.

'What's the matter, love?' I asked.

She led me through to the recess where Bob slept and said,

'I'm so glad you came. I'm very worried about him. He can't breathe properly and he's hardly slept all night.'

The bedside lamp was on and in its glow Bob's deeply lined face was the colour of pewter. He opened his eyes and tried to sit up but the effort was too much for him and he grimaced with pain. I told him to lie still and to take it easy. I sat on the edge of the bed and Beattie said she would make some tea. I didn't like the look of him and I suspected what was wrong as I questioned, 'What's the matter, Bob? Have you got any bad pains anywhere?'

'Well, it's this pain in me chest,' he told me. 'It's not so bad now but it was 'orrible earlier on and I could 'ardly get me breath. Me shoulder and arm are hurting like buggery as well. Bloody 'orrible tingling feeling all down it and terrible pain. What do you think's wrong, John?'

I didn't need to be a doctor to know that he had suffered a bad heart attack but I didn't want to frighten him so I said, 'You'll be OK, Bob, there's a nasty bug around at the moment. A sort of tropical rheumatism or something combined with cold symptoms. Just take it easy and I'll get Howard to call in to give you an injection. You'll soon be fit again.'

Howard Levine was a local doctor and a very good one. We had known each other for quite a long time and we had become good friends. I had mentioned him to Bob on a few occasions. I needed to act quickly and I apologised to Beattie and told her that I hadn't got time to drink the tea as I wanted to catch Howard before he went out on early calls. I suggested that she made Bob comfortable and it would be wise of her to leave the flat before the doctor arrived. She could return later. She nodded agreement and began tidying the bed up. I gave Bob a reassuring smile and told him that I would call in to see him again at lunchtime and that he was to stay where he was and not worry.

I stopped at the first telephone kiosk I could find and luckily managed to get Howard on the line. I told him what had happened and gave him the symptoms and he listened without interrupting. When I had finished he asked me for Bob's address and exactly how to find his flat: he would go over right away as it didn't sound too good to him. He told me not to worry and that he would give me a ring at the office later in the morning to let me know the outcome of his examination of Bob. I explained that Bob was not in a very good financial position and that he should charge his fees to my account. He told me that we could discuss this some other time and promised to phone me as soon as he could.

About an hour after I had started work my telephone rang. It was Howard confirming that Bob had suffered a bad heart attack and was now in the Intensive Care unit at Groote Schuur Hospital. He couldn't have been in a better place as this is the famous hospital where Dr Christiaan Barnard pioneered heart transplant operations and it was at about this time that he was making a name for himself there.

Howard said that Bob's condition was stable at the moment and providing he didn't have a secondary major attack during the next twenty-four hours, his chances of survival were reasonably good. I was a bit shaken by what had taken place and found it difficult to concentrate. My sympathetic boss who heard about it told me to go home and take it easy, but I decided to stay and try to work otherwise I would have spent the day walking in circles at the cottage and taking in too much brandy.

At lunchtime I telephoned the hospital to enquire about Bob's condition and the Afrikaner nursing sister I spoke to told me that Bob was holding on but there would be little point in my going to see him as he was only partly conscious. As I drove home later that afternoon I felt quite depressed. For all Bob's shortcomings, I found him very amusing and valued his friendship.

The following day, during the lunch break, I drove over to Groote Schuur – which means Great Barn – to find out how he was. I was allowed to see him for a few minutes and he had tubes up his nose and wires attached to his body and looked weak and pale. I told him everything was going to be fine and that Beattie was OK and I would be giving her a report. He seemed pleased to hear this and after telling him that I would see him again the following day I left the ward. The sister in charge told me that Bob was in a stable condition and he stood a good chance of making a complete recovery. This was good news indeed and I felt more cheerful as I drove through the traffic back to the office.

In fact Bob made a remarkable recovery and within a few days he was sitting up in bed in a general ward, his old jaunty self, and looking better than I had seen him looking for some time. Despite this, his attitude hadn't changed, and for all the good work that the doctors had done and after all the trouble other members of the hospital staff had gone to to save his life, he couldn't find a good word to say about the services he had received or South Africa in general. He was moaning as usual and I lost my temper with him.

'Why, you ungrateful old bastard! Don't you realise that if it hadn't been for people like Howard Levine, who isn't charging you anything by the way, and the doctors and nurses here who had rushed around like crazy, you'd be bloody dead by now!'

He glowered down at the bedcovers for a while and had the decency to look ashamed of himself. 'Yer, I s'ppose you're right really, John,' he muttered. 'It's just that I wish I was back in England sometimes.'

'Well, thanks to these people here, you stand a decent chance of going back now which is a bloody sight more than you did yesterday.'

When I entered the ward the following afternoon I could hardly believe my eyes. Sitting next to Bob was Beattie. Non-whites were not normally allowed to visit whites in hospital unless there was some very good reason for them doing so. It seems that Bob had managed to obtain permission for her to visit him on the pretext that she was the book-keeper of his non-existent company and had to bring the books in for his inspection every day.

It was quite clear from the expressions on the faces of some of the patients and nurses exactly what they thought about it. It was very embarrassing and after what I considered to be a decent time, I said my farewells and got up, promising to call in the following day. Before I left I leaned close to Bob and whispered in his ear, 'You're pushing your bloody luck, my friend. Cheers!'

The next afternoon I was surprised to find Bob's bed in the ward empty when I went through to see him. Assuming that he was either outside taking a bit of fresh air or receiving treatment I asked the ward sister where I might find him. She looked a bit flustered and told me that he had been discharged earlier in the day and no doubt the senior sister would tell me more. I thanked her and made my way to the sister's office in the corridor outside. The sister was a pleasant-looking woman of about thirty-five and her name told me that she was an Afrikaner. She smiled and invited me to sit down. She listened to my enquiry and nodded politely as I continued, 'I know he can be a bit contrary at times. What has he done? Signed himself out or something?'

She gazed down at the clean white blotter on her desk and scratched a cheek thoughtfully for a moment before answering. Looking up at me, she said, 'I gather that you are a close friend?'

When I nodded confirmation of this she frowned and looked embarrassed and I wondered what was coming next although I already had a nasty suspicion.

'Well – to be perfectly honest with you, Mr Carr, we had some complaints.'

I tried to treat the matter lightly though I knew what she was going to say. 'Don't tell me the old sod made a pass at one of your nurses,' I laughed.

She looked directly at me with her cool, grey eyes. 'It would have been far better if he had,' she said crushingly. I said nothing and tried to look suitably surprised. She leaned towards me and in a conspiratorial whisper went on, 'Did you know that he was being visited by a coloured woman?'

The way she said it made me go cold all over. She made it sound as though Bob had been caught performing some highly indecent act in a public lift. 'Er . . . I understand that one of his employees visited him yesterday. A matter of book-keeping or something, wasn't it?' I said rather weakly.

She looked around as if we were being watched. 'I was told by one of the junior nurses that he and the woman had been holding hands underneath his meal tray.'

My God, how indecent can you get, I thought, and the incongruity of the situation nearly had me bursting into laughter but I had the sense not to. Joking apart, I was extremely annoyed by Bob's stupidity.

The sister told me that it had been decided that it would be 'in the patient's best interests that he should be discharged', but he would be reporting to the outpatients' clinic regularly and there was nothing for me to be worried about. 'All he needs is rest and no manual work any more,' she concluded and I thanked her for giving me her time.

I could hardly wait to get over to see Bob that night and when I did I really tore into him. 'If you are so anxious to see the inside of a South African prison, Bob, why be so subtle? Why don't you just step outside and kick the first policeman you see in the crotch. It will save you so much time and stress!'

Beattie discreetly left the flat and I continued, 'Look! I don't give a shit about your relationship with Beattie. That's perfectly OK by me. It's the way you're going about it that worries me. Did you think you were being clever? You're bloody dangerous, man. If you don't watch it you'll end up by putting Beattie and yourself inside, maybe even me. I'll see you some time.' With this I left – seething.

Cynthia and I had arranged to meet that evening. I was to pick her up from the corner of her road in Camp's Bay and we would then drive to the cottage. We deliberately hadn't seen each other for a few days, to help break up our pattern of movement a bit. I was looking forward to her company. I was depressed by this business with Bob and the resultant row I had with him.

I hated driving through the city of Cape Town with Cynthia hiding in the back of the car. I never knew what was likely to happen. Sometimes my imagination overdid itself which added considerably to the already unbearable stress. For example, what would I do if I found myself approaching a police road-block? They were not uncommon, after all. How would I explain Cynthia's presence in the car? How could there be any explanation that would be acceptable?

I had to be constantly alert all the time when she was with me. I had to drive ultra-carefully as even a minor scrape or accident could have led to a more complicated and potentially dangerous situation. It was getting me down, and I was now obsessed with security to the point where I almost found it difficult to trust anyone any more, even my closest friends. I suppose I must have been undergoing a character change. Would it be noticeable to anyone? My colleagues at work, perhaps? Was I beginning to look decidedly shifty? I certainly felt it.

When we arrived at the road in which the cottage stood I opted to drive past it fairly quickly and cast a glance across at the house opposite ours. The front windows were in darkness and the curtains were drawn and I assumed that whoever might be at home would be in the kitchen at the back of the house. It turned out later that I was wrong.

Instead of using our normal undignified but safe method where Cynthia had to go through the dreadful business of crawling into the house on her hands and knees, which I hated to see her subjected to, I decided that as the road appeared to be deserted and most of the neighbours seemed to have gone to bed, we would be safe in using the same tactics as we had used on Christmas Eve.

It went smoothly enough and soon Cynthia and I were embracing each other affectionately in the lounge before she went into the kitchen to make some tea. I went through my now-standard routine of peering from behind the closed curtains of my darkened front bedroom. All was still and there were no movements from the house opposite. But I could have sworn that the curtains of their front room had been closed when we drove by; now they were open and a door leading from the room into the hall was ajar and there was a soft light on in the hall.

Probably someone got up to go to the toilet and decided to see if it was raining, I thought optimistically. I was about to turn away to return to Cynthia to discuss this phenomenon when I saw a movement across the road. Someone was standing in the dark room looking out of the window. Whoever it was had assumed that because the room was in darkness they would not be visible. However, they had forgotten the light behind them which had given the Watcher away.

So I was right after all. My suspicions had been confirmed. I was being watched, and very closely it would seem, by the people living in the house opposite. A cold chill ran through me and I knew that Cynthia would have to leave as soon as I considered it safe enough. I didn't like this new development at all. Had Cynthia been seen entering our cottage? If so, had the Watcher been able to identify her as a non-white? I was not prepared to speculate on such questions and I certainly had no intention of ignoring the dangerous possibilities by allowing Cynthia to stay that night.

When I joined Cynthia in the kitchen I told her what I had seen. 'We must leave the cottage as soon as I think it's safe, darling, but don't worry. The fact that I was lucky enough to notice that shifty bugger, whoever it is, means that there is no way that we are going to be caught tonight, but we are going to have to be ultra-extra careful from now on.'

She looked a bit apprehensive and I felt sorry that she was having to go through all this, but when I suggested that perhaps we should break off our relationship for her peace of mind, she cried and wouldn't hear of it. We were in this together and we would see it through together.

We agreed that we would use the flat at Sea Point for a few weeks to let the heat die down a bit before attempting to use the cottage again. I went back to my look-out position in the front bedroom and this time the curtains of the room opposite were completely drawn and there was no sign of any light. I felt it would be safe to leave the house and after tidying around in the kitchen for a few moments, we went through our reversed procedure and left. As I sat behind the wheel of the Beetle I glanced across at the Watcher's domain, and although there were no active signs of life or anyone watching us, I had an eerie feeling that our every move was being closely observed and probably recorded.

We reached Camp's Bay without any problems and after kissing Cynthia goodnight I arranged to see her the coming Sunday at the usual time at the Sea Point flat. I could have stayed at the flat that night but I decided against it as it might have been the cause of further speculation by the Watcher. Before getting into bed, although it was now well past midnight, I decided to have one last look across the road, with the bedroom lights off, of course.

The house across the way had a dead look about it as if its spirit had departed. I knew instinctively that the front room was now empty and I got into bed and tried to read for a while as my mind was overactive. It was hopeless; my mind was on the Watcher and not the contents of my book. I got out of bed and padded off into the lounge. A stiff brandy and a Mogodon did the trick and ten minutes later I was back in bed and sound asleep.

One evening while sitting morosely in the kitchen with a half-empty bottle of brandy in front of me and an almost empty glass, I received an unexpected visit from Marie. When I opened the door to her knock she was standing on the step holding a skinny black kitten. Its bright yellow eyes stared at me with a look of fear in them.

'Can I bring it in?' she asked.

'Of course,' I replied, standing aside. She placed the kitten down on the top of the table and it remained in the same position it had been in when held in her hand. Terror-stricken-hunchbacked would have been a fair description of its posture. I wasn't exactly crazy about moggies at that time and I wondered what was behind the visit.

Remembering my manners I asked Marie to sit down. 'Would you like a drop of brandy, love?' I asked and she nodded. I sat down after giving her a glass of brandy and water and said, 'What's with the moggie, Marie?' She told me that she had visited her sister that afternoon and apparently her tabby had had a litter of kittens. The sister had managed to find homes for all the kittens with the exception of the specimen now cringing on my table, which happened to be the runt of the litter which nobody wanted. On looking at it carefully I could see why but I still failed to understand why Marie felt that this knowledge was of such importance to me.

Then the penny dropped and rather lamely I said, 'What the bloody hell would I want with that, Marie?' but I knew I had been lumbered. She had known me long enough to know that I was a soft touch with animals, kids and underdogs. 'All right! You win – this time,' I said, taking a gulp from my glass. Then, pointing meaningfully at the still panicky-looking kitten, I said, 'It's only got to shit on the carpet once and it won't have to worry about feeling unwanted any more.'

Marie laughed and said, 'I knew you'd want him as soon as you saw him. Cute, isn't he?'

I named the kitten Fred.

He was a ludicrous little animal and an equally silly name

seemed appropriate. He was extremely timid and spent the first few hours in his new home sniffing inquisitively around the house, leaking little puddles occasionally. I kept a beady eye on him in case he deposited something even more sinister. During the first night of his arrival, neither of us got a lot of sleep. He was too busy meouwling and in the end I had to open the bedroom door to let him in. I parked him at the foot of the bed and silence reigned from then on. Already, in only hours, he had established where he was going to sleep in future.

He was not only a nervous wreck but he appeared to be very underfed too, so I put him on a diet of beef topside and fresh milk. In a fairly short space of time he became a different animal. He had grown considerably and was now quite sturdy, with a glossy black coat. I bought him a rather posh cat basket complete with mattress and fitted blanket. He would have nothing to do with this whatsoever and on waking every morning I would usually find his whiskery head resting on my shoulder or against my face.

We became quite fond of each other, that was for sure. It was good to have him around because, when alone in the cottage in the evenings, I could work my way through a bottle of brandy most nights with no trouble at all, and as there was no one else to talk to I would usually end up talking to myself, or rather to my reflection in the mirror that hung on the wall. Fred changed all that, and he would sit on a chair nearby watching me inscrutably while I chatted happily away.

I trained Fred to travel in the car with me. The first few attempts were rather nerve-wracking but with perseverance, on his part as well as mine, it worked out in the end. He often accompanied me on visits to Bob's flat, much to the amusement of other road users either when they saw Fred leering at them from the window shelf at the rear of the Beetle, or when he perched himself on one of my shoulders. I suppose both of us were slightly eccentric.

Eventually I had to go to Johannesburg on a combination of business and pleasure and I decided to take Fred with me. A journey of almost a thousand miles from sea level to 6,000 feet was not the same as a short trip to Sea Point on a quiet Sunday afternoon, so certain training routines had to be adopted. I bought a large, blue plastic bowl to fit on the floor of the car behind the front seats: this was to be filled with cat-litter and would be Fred's travelling loo. Next I bought a Thermos flask for his milk and a wide-necked Thermos jar for his stockfish meals. Fred was already sporting a smart, pale-blue collar with a bell attached, so for good measure I bought him a matching lead. He would have to stretch his legs while motoring up to the old Transvaal and it stood to reason that I couldn't just open the car door and expect him to go for a stroll and return again. Clever though he might be for a mere mogulator, he was still a cat and not a dog.

We began training sessions late at night in the road outside the Rondebosch cottage. We held them late for fairly obvious reasons; I wanted to avoid embarrassing Fred and myself. I could just imagine what the neighbours would have said if they could have seen what was going on in the street: 'Thet bleddy med Englishman's et it again.'

The training sessions consisted mainly of me dragging Fred around on the end of the lead. Every night for some time I would take the poor cat for 'draggies'. He would place his bottom firmly on the road or the grass and that's where it would stay. Operating on the maxim that it is necessary sometimes to be cruel to be kind, I carried on walking, taking the view that sooner or later it would enter his feline mind that there would be no future in him wearing out his bum. It worked and eventually he began trotting obediently behind me while doing his best to make it appear that he wasn't actually with me.

Our first Great Trek was an enormous success and Fred appeared to have accepted my eccentricities with an understanding and nonchalance that filled me with pride. He developed one idiosyncrasy that I could never cure him of. While cruising along the National Highway at top speed, Fred's favourite spot was on my lap where he would sleep for hours on end. The snag was that on waking up he would yawn and stretch and then, looking up at me affectionately, he would proceed to sharpen his claws – on my chest. It took real self-control to slow down and ease off the road while he was scoring tramlines in my flesh with his needle-sharp claws.

Not long after our triumphant return to Cape Town Fred came home one evening swearing and spitting, with his tail at a peculiar angle. I telephoned the vet who came over at once and his visit resulted in the poor cat having to spend a few days in the animal clinic where his once-beautiful tail was amputated. I was never certain whether a dog had caused the injury or whether he had had his rudder slammed in somebody's gate. I suspected the latter.

It was a Wednesday night and I had arranged to meet Cynthia near the house in Camp's Bay. For some reason or other I felt apprehensive as I was driving over there. I didn't like the idea of waiting around in the road at Camp's Bay for too long and I hoped that she would be prompt, although it was at the discretion of her madam as to exactly when she would be allowed to go off duty.

We had not used the cottage for our meetings for some weeks and I felt that it would be safe to go there again, besides which Cynthia wanted to meet Fred. Before I set off from the cottage I had peered out from my usual observation point in the unlit bedroom, and the house opposite was in darkness. It looked safe enough to me and no doubt they would be fast asleep by the time Cynthia and I returned.

As I was well ahead of time I decided to call in at the Regency to see if Bob was there. He was and had a glass of lager standing in front of him. Howard Levine had warned him off the hard stuff and I was pleased to see that he had heeded Howard's advice in this respect. He told me that he was feeling quite well and was not doing heavy manual work any more. He had managed to find himself a job as workshop manager at a large multi-storey car park in the city, but how long he would last was anybody's guess.

'Seen anything of Beattie lately, Bob?' I asked mildly.

He gave me his customary crafty grin and leaning towards me said huskily, 'She's up at the flat now gettin' me dinner ready. Come an' 'ave some with us if you like.'

'You think it's safe enough, do you?'

'Course it's fuckin' safe!' was his cultured reply. I should have known better than to ask.

We finished our drinks and walked along to his flat. He gave the coded knock and a few moments later Beattie's friendly face appeared and lit up when she saw us. In no time we were tucking in to a pair of imported kippers each, with bread-and-butter and tea, and very nice it was too. I noticed that the kitchen was looking very clean and tidy. Beattie seemed to be good for Bob.

Clearly Beattie was now 'living in' but I made no comments about it; after all it was none of my business. They were genuinely fond of each other, that was quite obvious, and although Bob, who was in his early fifties, was quite a bit older than Beattie, the difference in their ages didn't seem to bother either of them. Good luck to them, I thought. I thanked Beattie for a smashing meal and asked Bob if he had given any thought to long-term plans regarding Beattie and himself.

'Well, first of all I've got to sort out me marriage problems, then Beattie and me are plannin' to slip across to good old England and that's where we're gonna stay. Right, luv?' He beamed up at Beattie who smiled shyly and went about her work at the sink.

Bob's estranged wife lived in Sea Point and was in charge of a successful play-school. He had taken me there one day to meet her. She proved to be a pleasant lady with a much stronger character than her husband and I could understand how their marriage had broken down.

At eleven fifteen I drove on to Camp's Bay and I timed it so that I should arrive a matter of a couple of minutes prior to Cynthia leaving the house, to obviate the necessity for hanging around late at night which might have been dangerous. I was on time but after five minutes there was no sign of Cynthia and I felt a bit uneasy. There was a street light opposite the house where she worked but I had parked beneath some overhanging trees and so I was in comparative darkness. I could see if anyone left or entered the house easily enough. It was getting on for midnight and I was growing increasingly agitated although I knew that I was safe enough where I was. Nevertheless my instincts told me that it would be more prudent to call it a day and drive quietly home. Cynthia would have understood. I was trying to think of a credible excuse for my being there in the event of a police truck stopping for the officer to question me. 'It's like this, Officer. I suspect my wife of having an affair with a bloke who lives in that house and I believe she is in the house now. I'm waiting to see if I can catch her leaving.'

It seemed reasonable enough to me but I suddenly realised that adultery is a criminal offence in South Africa, or at least it was at that particular time, and the good officer would probably have galloped into the house with gun in hand seeking promotion, leaving me to melt discreetly into the night. OK, so that wouldn't work.

Just then the headlights of a car swept up behind me and I sat as still as a statue on the illogical basis that if you don't move, you can't be seen. I waited for the car to pass me but to my horror it stopped immediately behind mine with the headlights on full beam, burning into the back of my neck. The driver switched off the engine of his car but not the lights. What the hell's he up to? I thought, thinking for a moment that he might be a police officer. Sweat began to trickle down my forehead and into my eyes but I dared not move my hands to wipe it away. I was petrified. At last the lights went out but the driver remained in the car.

As I began to relax slightly another nasty thought entered my mind: what if Cynthia came out now and walked across to my car and got in. She would be unaware that there was someone in the car behind mine but whoever it was would see that she was a non-white and where did we go from there? Sea Point police station, I supposed. I wished that some natural disaster would take place, like an earthquake or something – I was to remember this wish later on – anything that would distract the person behind me. Suddenly the door of the car behind slammed shut and I heard footsteps walking firmly away. I sagged down into my seat like a deflating balloon and was just about to turn the ignition key with a view to going home when a slim, familiar shape flitted across the road ahead. I opened the door and she was soon safely down on the seat behind me. I turned the key and drove away quickly.

'Where the hell have you been, darling?' I growled. 'I nearly had a bloody heart attack waiting there for you!' She had to work late as the madam had received unexpected guests. I unwound a bit and concentrated on getting us safely to Rondebosch. It was well past 1 a.m. by the time we arrived near the cottage and I told her that I felt that it would be safe for us to use the Christmas Eve technique. Although the front door was closed, the latch was up and it needed only a push to open. I had switched all the lights off, of course.

I drove past the cottage this time and dropped Cynthia about three hundred yards beyond the house. I then continued on and drove around the block fairly slowly to give her time to get into the house safely. Instead of parking on the verge outside the cottage I parked in a side-street a little distance away to eliminate the sound of my engine outside the house. This extra precaution made me feel a bit less tense. As I entered the dark cottage something furry rubbed against my ankle and a throaty *mrrreeowww* shattered the silence. It was Fred reminding me that I had forgotten to put out his supper earlier. Cynthia liked Fred and after sniffing her outstretched fingers he allowed her to stroke him. They were going to get along fine, I could see that. Although we were now into the wee small hours of the morning we were hungry so I fried some stockfish; this is a white fish similar to cod only smaller. We had this with peas and instant mash, and tea – not bad for a short-notice meal. I ran a bath which we shared. Running two baths would have been highly suspicious; Dan and Marie would have wondered why I was bathing twice. In any case the water-tank in the roof made an awful racket when re-filling.

Fred had some odd little ways. While we were bathing he sprang up onto the narrow edge of the bath and sat sphinx-like watching us through unblinking eyes. Quite disconcerting really, and I don't know how the hell he managed not to end up in the bath with us. We didn't get a lot of sleep that night but we were happy to be together and spent most of the night sitting close together on the settee listening to the record player with the volume well down. We managed to have a couple of hours' sleep and the alarm woke me at four-thirty. Oddly enough, despite these almost sleepless nights I always awoke alert and fresh, probably due to an increased flow of adrenalin because of the fear factor more than anything else.

The tricky part was leaving the cottage again without being observed. We had to get away before dawn and dawn came early in the Cape at that time of the year. While Cynthia dressed I gave Fred his morning milk and put him out of the front door. One morning, without thinking, I had put him out of the back door, almost into the waiting jaws of Spot. Once again the dog couldn't believe his good fortune, and the brief pause while he collected his wits was sufficient for Fred to reach safety.

Like most cats, Fred had very agile reflexes and the sight of a huge mawful of glistening white fangs, topped by a pair of disbelieving, red-rimmed, glaring eyes did wonders for his reflexes that morning. As I winced behind the kitchen door I heard a frenzied scrabbling sound as Fred navigated the lofty corrugated iron fence next to the chapel, followed milliseconds later by a frightening thud as fifty pounds of furious and frustrated Dalmatian hit it in its attempt to catch its arch-enemy.

This morning I went through my usual sneaky procedure in the front bedroom to make sure that all was silent across the road. There was no sign of life and I tiptoed back into the kitchen to tell Cynthia that she should leave the house and wait for me at the end of the road. We kissed affectionately before she slipped quietly out with her bag in one hand and her shoes in the other. Soon we were bowling along merrily towards Camp's Bay. Instead of driving all the way around Sea Point, I decided to go via Kloof Nek as it was quicker and quieter.

Dawn was beginning to break and I was glad when we dropped over the Kloof into darkness once more. There were signs of roadwork as we passed large earth-moving equipment parked silently at the roadside. We were almost there now and Cynthia was dozing on the rear seat. As we drove around a bend I saw the lights of a car ahead; it was pulled in to the opposite side of the road. Another vehicle was standing next to it and I wondered what was going on. As we drew nearer I recognised the outside vehicle as a police truck.

'Christ!' I shouted, 'it's the bloody police. We've had it now.'

In the rear-view mirror Cynthia's anxious face rose as she peered ahead over my shoulder.

'Lie down, for God's sake!' I yelped in panic.

She was much calmer than I was. 'If they see me lying down

they will be very suspicious and will know that we are up to something.'

As we drew nearer my mind was racing. What excuse could I give if we were stopped and questioned? The best that I could think of was that I was on my way to Camp's Bay and had stopped to offer her a lift and hadn't realised that she was non-white until she had got into the car. It seemed a bit feeble but it was all I could come up with at such short notice and the notice was getting shorter every moment.

Praying, I drove on at a normal speed and forced myself not to panic. I actually slowed down as we approached the police and leaned out of the window like a typical nosey driver, eager to see what was going on. How the hell I managed such nonchalance I shall never know when all that I wanted to do was to behave in a normal way – like having a fit or going into hysterics or something.

When we reached the point of no return I saw three police-men standing around an old Chevrolet which appeared to be crammed with Africans. Another policeman was standing on the other side of the road holding a revolver. He gave us a cursory glance and waved me past impatiently. I put my foot down and left the scene as quickly as decency would permit. If there is one thing that interests a South African policeman more than the sight of a white man – and was I white! – with a non-white woman in a car in the early hours of the morning, it is a car filled with Africans in a predominantly white laager.

As we drove on with me in my customary jelly-like state I wondered how much more of this my nervous system and general physical condition would be able to accept. I was already glugging down a bottle of brandy every night and smoking at least eighty cigarettes a day. Cynthia had a dis-concerting habit of giggling when nervous or under stress. From the sound of it she seemed to be thoroughly enjoying herself at the back of the car. I failed to see the humour of the moment.

I dropped her safely not far from the house in Camp's Bay and we agreed not to see each other until the coming weekend when we would spend the best part of the time in the cottage.

*   *   *

At that time there was, and I hope there still is, a bar called the Fireman's Arms. It was considered the nearest thing to an English pub that one could find in the city. I never suffered from homesickness but the idea of supping a pint of beer in such an establishment appealed to me, and so one evening I set off alone to find the place.

The Fireman's Arms was hidden away in a back street close to Cape Town's dockland and when I walked inside I was pleasantly surprised. The brightly lit bar certainly had an authentic English atmosphere and was a veritable museum of interesting artefacts, including a range of firemen's helmets from all parts of the world.

The walls were decorated with photographs of amusing and interesting characters who had been visitors at some time or another over the years, and there was also an impressive collection of ships' coats of arms, badges and neckties. The pub offered meals at the bar, many of which came out of tins, and the unusually large menu card displayed labels from tins indicating what was available.

The bar was also famous for the beer it sold – Hansa beer brewed by South Africans of German origin in South-West Africa, which at one time was German West Africa. The beer was brewed to traditionally high standards. It looked innocent enough with its pale amber body topped by a firm, creamy head but its looks were deceptive and it had quite a kick. I liked it so much that I drank five pints of the stuff and I left the bar slightly the worse for wear and had to sleep in the car for a couple of hours before attempting to drive. Anyone who has slept in a Volkswagen Beetle will understand how I felt during that journey home.

The following night the call of Hansa was stronger than my will and once again I found myself walking into the bar of the Fireman's Arms. The pub was empty as it was still early in the evening, and I spent a pleasant half-hour in conversation with the landlord who told me that his father used to run the pub until recently. I was enjoying my second pint of Hansa when another patron walked in and sat on the stool next to mine.

The red face, sunburnt aquiline nose, thinning fair hair and pale blue eyes indicated an English-speaking South African. I noticed the dark blazer and regimental tie and braced myself for another Chopper-type session. We nodded politely to each other and eventually got chatting and buying each other drinks. To my surprise he turned out to be an Afrikaner and from what he told me, he was a regular visitor to the Fireman's Arms.

After twenty minutes or so of harmless bar-room chat he began probing me on my opinions of the Republic, and although I was well into my third pint of the devastating brew a warning bell chimed at the back of my mind and I let him do most of the talking. I listened carefully to what he had to say, nodding from time to time to help him along. Like every South African that I had met, he wanted to know what I thought about the Republic, and I told him straight that much of it I liked but I felt that the oppressive political system might be its undoing one day.

At the same time, I softened the harshness of my words by admitting that I felt that South Africa had some unique problems which were not found in many other societies nor readily understood by the outside world, especially the UK. His eyes lit up when he heard this and I had a notion that his interest in my opinions was a bit more than casual, so I tried to find out what his game was.

I laid it on a bit thick, praising the early Voortrekkers for whom I have a high regard in any case, and saying how proud I was to be associated with such a progressive country. This was perfectly true but I omitted to mention my feelings of repugnance at a society that could treat other human beings with such contempt and cruelty.

He appeared to be fascinated by my rhetoric as I droned on, and when I paused for a mouthful of beer he clapped me on the shoulder and said, in a fervent voice, 'My God, man, how I wish we had a few more like you over here. You're exactly the type of English settler that we need in this country. You'll go far here, my boy!' I couldn't help thinking that Chopper would have applauded if he had been present.

By now I was enjoying a fourth pint of the dreaded Hansa and felt that I had had enough for one night – and not just the beer. My new-found friend, whom I will call Frikkie, had caught up with me with the aid of a couple of large brandies and both of us were feeling slightly tired. When I mentioned that I ought to be on my way home Frikkie insisted on my joining him in one for the road. I knew I couldn't manage another pint of Hansa so I accepted a brandy with plenty of water, which is the way most South Africans like to drink the stuff. In South Africa brandy isn't swirled in balloon glasses and sniffed at over coffee in posh restaurants. It is poured into tumblers containing what might appear to be one or two miniature icebergs, a liberal quantity of water is then added and the resultant mixture is swilled down with gusto; at least that's how they drank it in most of the bars and hotels I went into. After all, brandy is South Africa's national drink and it is available in qualities ranging from something resembling paint-stripper to exquisite KWV brandy, not to mention good old Oude Meester, God bless it.

Frikkie was sagging slightly on his stool and when he leaned close to me in a confidential manner and breathed fumes into my face I sensed that a spectacular announcement was going to be made. Looking me straight in the eye he said, 'You seem a decent enough type.'

I said nothing.

'How would you like to do the Republic a very special service?'

'Er . . . What sort of service do you have in mind, Frikkie?' I asked reasonably enough.

He looked around to make sure that no one else was showing unusual interest in our conversation. No one was. Turning back to me he stunned me with his next question.

'Fancy doing a bit of police work in your spare time?'

I nearly fell off the bar stool. He was, in effect, asking me if I would be interested in becoming a police informer. I stifled a desire to tell him to get stuffed, and decided that discretion was a better tactic. The man was obviously a policeman himself and no doubt a member of the dreaded Special Branch.

'What sort of police work do you have in mind, Frikkie?' I asked. 'I'd like to know what I would be letting myself in for, after all.'

He assumed that he had hooked me and with a knowing smile said, 'This isn't the time or place to go into details on this matter but I would like you to telephone me on this number and I'll arrange for a get-together with a few of my colleagues.'

He opened a wallet and removed a small business card on which was printed a telephone number and nothing else. Before handing it to me, he pulled a pen out of his pocket and wrote 'Frikkie' on it. 'Just in case you forget,' he smiled. I slipped the piece of card into the pocket of my shirt and rose to leave. As I was about to go he placed a hand on my arm and leaning towards me said, 'We can be very grateful for services rendered, man. Just think about it.'

That was my last visit to the Fireman's Arms and the piece of card with the name and number fluttered away into the night as I tossed it out of the car window.

The weekend was super in every respect. I had collected Cynthia from Camp's Bay on the Friday night at eleven o'clock and we had entered the cottage unobserved, or so it had seemed. The following morning, armed with a shopping list which we had prepared together over breakfast, I drove off to the stores in Claremont, a busy suburb not all that far away from Rondebosch. I was going to buy the groceries for the week. Poor Cynthia could not even enjoy this simple pleasure with me. She had to remain incarcerated in the cottage, scared even to flush the toilet for fear of the neighbours noticing that I had gone out. Who could be flushing the toilet? they would want to know – or having a bath – or opening a window – or playing a record?

Cynthia and I could not live like other people. We could not walk along a street or a beach hand-in-hand. We couldn't stroll around the neighbourhood in the cool of the evening watching the stars like huge diamonds against the black velvet of a southern hemisphere sky. We couldn't even go out into the garden. All we had was the cottage or the flat, the radio and record-player and each other. There was no television in South Africa at that time.

We played games to compensate for the everyday things that we were not able to do like other people. Silly as it might seem, my shopping trips became one of them. I would always buy a number of things that we hadn't listed. Things I knew would please Cynthia, little treats. On my return to the cottage, Cynthia would be agog with excitement, wondering what surprises I had brought this week.

I would adopt the most pompous and ridiculous stance. 'You have exactly fifteen seconds to get that kettle on for tea otherwise you won't know what's in this lot!'

Cynthia would scurry around like a mad thing to get the kettle on and we would laugh like kids – quietly of course.

Then, like a magician, I would produce the various items from the large Kraft paper shopping bags, accompanied by Ooohs! and Aaaahs! from an ecstatic Cynthia. It had occurred to me, of course, that the Watcher might have wondered why a single person needed so many bags of groceries every week. I was sure that this point had not been overlooked by the diligent observer across the road.

We often had some splendid meals during Cynthia's weekend visits. Although she was not much of a cook at that time, simply because no one had ever bothered to teach her, she was very interested and watched everything that I did in the kitchen and helped out enthusiastically. Plain English food had always been one of my specialities and one weekend I prepared roast leg of lamb with new potatoes, fresh garden peas, gravy and mint sauce. She was extremely impressed by this typical English Sunday lunch and was particularly taken with the mint sauce.

The following weekend Cynthia tried her hand at preparing curried lamb and I was left in the lounge with firm instructions not to appear in the kitchen as she was going to surprise me. She certainly did. The curried lamb was exquisite but it clashed a bit with the mint sauce. When I explained gently that mint sauce was eaten only with lamb, she countered by saying that we *were* eating lamb, and it became a bit complicated, but it sorted itself out in the end.

Another big hit with Cynthia was Yorkshire pudding. She enjoyed it so much the first time I made one to accompany the roast-beef dinner, that she insisted on having it with everything else for some weeks after. Eventually she became an excellent cook which relieved me of some of the household chores.

We were by this time very much in love with each other and

we lived for the moments we were able to spend together. The happiest times were when I was completely convinced that our entry to the cottage had gone un-noticed by anyone, especially the Watcher. I could seldom be really sure and when I had doubts it was impossible for me to relax; often I would abort the weekend and take Cynthia home, sometimes only an hour or so after she had arrived. She never argued with me but always trusted my judgement and went along with me.

As the months went by I became more obsessed than ever with safety precautions and security in general. I hated being on my own in the cottage or the flat and during these lonely moments I could spend the time worrying and drinking with my imagination running wild. I began to have sleeping problems although curiously enough I always had a good appetite. I must have been fairly fit in those days.

I did go through one period which was surely verging on sheer madness. Although I never touched a drop of alcohol during the working day and still managed to produce acceptable material at the office, I was more than making up for it in private, and on the occasions that Cynthia came to visit me she would search around the cottage looking for the places where I had started hiding booze.

I was drinking in excess of a bottle a day, which meant a bottle a night, in effect, during working days, and quite a bit more at the weekends. For hours, I would sit alone in the kitchen talking to myself and drinking while Fred would sit like a sphinx watching me. Cynthia became very concerned about my deteriorating condition and state of mind, but whenever she warned me that I might become an alcoholic I would fly into dreadful rages and rant and rave about the house. I told her of my fears and she reasoned with me and helped me to regain control of my senses, but I could not reduce the daily amounts of alcohol. When alone in bed at night, the darkness would crowd in all around me and I began to think that I was going insane. For some weeks I had to sleep with the lights on. What the Watcher must have thought of this I don't know.

From time to time I would get a 'feeling' about the Watcher and for several weeks we would stop using the cottage as a retreat. Of course I was just as nervous when we were using the flat. There was only one way in or out; no emergency exits that Cynthia could escape by should we be raided by the police. Consequently we had to be absolutely certain that no one at all could observe our clandestine comings and goings.

On one occasion Cynthia was given an unexpected day off by her employer and, rather foolishly, I agreed she could remain in the cottage during the day while I was at work in Cape Town. I had left her with plenty of magazines and told her that I would hurry home as soon as I finished work. I warned her not to do anything that might attract Marie's attention. 'Don't use the phone, don't run the taps, don't slam doors, walk barefoot, don't flush the loo, don't drop anything, don't have the radio too high – apart from all this, have a nice day.'

When I drove up onto the grass verge that evening I found Fred waiting patiently for me at the gate. I bent down to pick him up and fondle his ears and carried him to the house. As I slipped my key into the lock I sensed that all was not well and when I opened the front door and stepped inside, the hall was filled with acrid smoke. 'Oh! My God!' I gasped, 'the bloody house is on fire.' I made my way into the lounge, coughing, and there was no sign of Cynthia. I drew the curtains apart and opened the window as wide as possible. When I went through to the kitchen, Cynthia was there, coughing and wheezing and in quite a state. I led her into the lounge and sat her beside the window and waited for her to tell me what had gone wrong.

She had wanted to have a treat waiting for me when I came home and had decided to make a Swiss roll. Unhappily she had turned the oven thermostat too high and this, combined with an oven that needed cleaning, had resulted in all the smoke. Luckily Marie had been out and still was, otherwise it could have led to serious trouble. All would have been revealed – Swiss roll and all.

Some weeks later on a Saturday morning, Bob invited me to join him on a visit to a mate of his who had a service garage on the outskirts of District Six, then a Cape Coloured area of the city.

I followed his directions and we arrived at a rather scruffy street in which most of the buildings appeared to be derelict. Some of the so-called houses were inhabited by Cape Coloured families as I noticed small, ill-dressed coloured children sitting on dirty doorsteps staring sullenly at us as we got out of the car. They said nothing and looked apathetic.

After locking the car I followed Bob to a rickety old building that would have been condemned had it been in a whites-only area. We walked through a gaping opening which at one time had been protected by double doors. What was left of one hung crazily from the wall and the other had long since disappeared, probably having been used as firewood by the neighbours.

We found ourselves in what must have been the main workshop, for want of a better description. It contained a number of what seemed to be car wrecks. I glanced up and saw that the roof was sagging and looked as though it might fall in on us at any moment. At one time the roof lights must have contained sheets of glass.

'Eric!!' Bob bawled in a raucous voice.

This friendly salutation was followed by a heavy silence.

'Wonder where the old twat is?' Bob said amiably. I gave him a cigarette and took one myself and when we had lit up he yelled again. It was an excruciating sound and finished on a high note. 'Er . . . ic!!' A curious scrabbling noise from behind a mass of twisted metal heralded the approach of Eric and I watched, fascinated, as a slight, stooping figure picked its way delicately through the morass of wrecks, pools of green oil, masses of twisted wire and old batteries with splendid mushrooms growing from the terminals.

He was wearing a filthy boiler suit glossy with oil and grease. It was at least a couple of sizes too big for him. I mentally handed it to Bob: he certainly knew some characters. What was left of Eric's hair was sandy in colour and was now coated with a fine layer of white dust, and it lay flat on his thin, bony head. He had a red, hooked nose with a slit of a mouth beneath it. The mouth had a deep, vertical furrow on either side. He looked a bit apprehensive and furtive but his face cracked into a welcoming grin when he recognised Bob. Bob told me later that when Eric had spotted my cream-coloured Volkswagen through a crack in the wall of the building he had assumed that I was a CID officer. It seemed that Eric received fairly frequent visits from members of the CID anxious to locate missing parts from stolen vehicles.

Eric eyed me up and down suspiciously until Bob introduced us. 'This is the bloke I was tellin' you about, Eric – John, y'know, from England.' This seemed to satisfy him, as a thin hand on a stick-like wrist shot out of one of his sleeves. He had a surprisingly strong grip.

Eric, a panel beater by trade, had come out to the Republic to make his fortune. In view of the way in which South Africans drive he should have been a millionaire long since but unfortunately he wasn't a very smart businessman. From what Bob told me Eric spent much of his time dodging creditors and trying to avoid summonses for non-payment of bills. He also told me that he and Eric had been business partners at one time – a mind-boggling thought.

They soon got down to the main reason for my having been invited there. It sat in the yard at the back of the building, a trim, elderly Ford Prefect with a two-tone finish, white at the top and yellow at the bottom. Eric was asking R250 for it, the equivalent of £125 at that time. A reasonable enough figure. I had mentioned to Bob that I had been toying with the idea of buying a cheap second car. I intended keeping one at Sea Point and the other at Rondebosch. My Beetle had become a little too familiar at Rondebosch and I felt that a second car would help to sow some confusion in the Watcher and anyone else too interested in my activities.

I sat in the little car and turned the ignition key. It fired first time and I was quite impressed with the throaty chuckle that came from the exhaust. I took it for a run and it seemed perfectly OK. The brakes worked and the steering appeared to be reasonable. As I wasn't taking a very big risk financially I decided to buy it.

Back in the yard where Eric and Bob were waiting for me, I told Eric I would give him a cheque there and then. Eric said, 'Let's go into my office.' His office was a tent erected in the workshop. He led the way in and pointing at a not-too-clean oil drum invited me to sit down. I placed a newspaper on the top of the drum and sat on it.

Bob perched himself on the edge of what seemed to have

been a desk at one time. It tilted slightly and a large stack of yellowing letters and other documents slithered to the floor. 'Fuck it,' said Eric, with feeling, and presumably being a tidy sort of chap at heart he kicked the papers under the desk. I liked Eric.

'Randolph,' he squawked in a falsetto voice and a moment or two later a short, fat, Cape Coloured man appeared. This was Eric's one and only employee and principal assistant. 'Nip down to the caff, Randy, and get some coffee for us, there's a good lad.' Randy went on his way and I wrote out the cheque on Eric's behalf. Eric explained that a little work was still needed on the electrical system but he would be dropping the car in at the car-park workshop where Bob worked and the latter would finish off the minor wiring that was required. This was OK by me and I was told that the Prefect would be ready for me to collect on the Monday evening.

Monday was wet and windy and at the end of the working day I took a taxi to the garage where Bob worked. To my mild surprise, he had finished the wiring and the car was ready to be driven away. We had a cup of tea together in his office and I drove off. About fifteen minutes later while I was driving through the rainy night one of the windscreen wipers suddenly twanged off somewhere. I stopped the car and got out to look for it, and was almost run over by another vehicle. I was unable to find the wiper and when I climbed back into the car and angrily slammed the door closed, I found myself sitting there with the door handle in my lap.

Bob was surprised to see me when I returned to the garage. 'Don't worry, mate,' he said, 'I'll fix the 'andle and wiper first thing in the mornin' for you.' I took a taxi to Sea Point where I got slightly drunk and had an early night for a change.

The next morning was bright and sunny. I was in a cheerful mood as I hammered away at my typewriter and after a productive day I once again made my way to the workshop, hoping the car would be OK by now. When I stepped out of the lift and saw Bob's face scowling down into the engine compartment of the Prefect, my heart sank. I knew the news would be bad the moment he looked up and stared bleakly at me.

'What's come off now, Bob?' I queried as I approached him.

'It's yer bleedin' cylinder 'ead,' he yelped. 'The fuckin' gaskits 'ave blown!'

'The fuckin' gaskits seemed to be all right last night,' I replied, getting into the spirit of things.

I looked at the cylinder head bolts and they had been almost stripped of their threads. I turned to Bob. 'Just what did you do to the car today, Bob?' I asked with controlled emotions.

'Well, I fixed the 'andle on the door, then the wiper, an' as she seemed to be blowin' a bit I tightened up the cylinder 'ead a bit.'

I glared at him. 'I've seen you tightening up nuts "a bit" before, you silly old sod! You must have put about ten tons of torsion onto these bloody nuts, you twat.' I was almost dancing with rage.

He organised a cup of tea and gradually I simmered down. We arranged to meet for a drink at the Regency later in the evening. He promised me that come what may, he would have the car in tip-top condition the next night and like an idiot I believed him. The next night, much to my astonishment, the car was ready and waiting for me and I drove home without anything falling off; a marked improvement. I went over to the Sea Point flat to collect some clothes I needed and when I got back into the car my foot caught on some loose wire dangling beneath the dashboard. The car refused to start. I got out wearily and slammed the door, half expecting to see the car fall to pieces. By this time I had had enough and I set off for Bob's flat in a filthy temper.

When I told him about the latest disaster, he scratched his head and began, 'Well, I don't reckin on bein' much of an electrical expert on cars but I'll . . .'

'Just keep your bloody hands off the car,' I growled. 'Just get that sod Eric over here as quickly as possible. It's his responsibility and he should never have sold me the car in that state. If he doesn't fix it properly, and bloody quick, I'll have him in court and you can tell him that.'

Bob could see that I meant what I had said and he managed to contact Eric on the telephone. Eric arrived in a clapped-out Land Rover that he must have saved from a car-crushing plant in the nick of time. Despite its appearance, it managed to haul away the Prefect. Eric promised that he would arrange for the car to be fixed by a proper motor-vehicle electrician and that I could expect it back within a couple of days.

The next evening when I walked into the bar at the Regency there was Bob looking decidedly nervous. He opened his mouth to speak but I raised a hand. 'No! Don't tell me yet, Bob. Let me order a drink first, I have an idea I'm going to need one.' Reg, who had seen me walk in, had reached out for a glass and the drink was on the bar in no time. I took a couple of swallows and turning to Bob said, 'Right! Go ahead.'

He adopted a forced air of jollity but it didn't come over too well. 'Er. You know that bleedin' car of yours?'

'Only too bloody well,' I replied and waited.

'Poor old Randolph nipped over to Salt River to collect it from the electrical expert an' on 'is way back 'e was waitin' for the robots to change and some twat rammed 'im up the arse.'

I must have been going a bit purple by this time because Bob stepped back and looked apprehensive. 'You are joking of course, aren't you?' I managed to croak.

'That's not all,' he went on.

'Christ! Do you mean there's more?'

He told me the whole sorry tale. While the unfortunate Randolph had been sitting in the Prefect waiting for the traffic lights to change to green, a small van with faulty brakes ran into the back of him. The battery of the Prefect was not properly mounted and it had jumped off its seating due to the impact. It must have arced because there was an explosion and Randolph had been lucky enough to scramble clear of the car before it burnt out. I saw the funny side of it until I remembered the R250. I visited Eric the following morning and asked for my money back. He told me that he couldn't lay his hands on it right away. I told him not to worry, a couple of hours would do and failing that I would feel it my duty to let the CID know that he was trading without a licence. They would have closed him down immediately. I got my money within the hour.

THE PREGNANCY

Over the months Cynthia and I had become experts in the art of avoiding detection, or so we thought. If anything, we were over-confident and it wasn't until later that I realised that we had entered a very dangerous period. I had actually reached a state of mind where I began to think that everyone knew about us but nobody minded. Cynthia was now coming to the cottage on her own and the procedure was that if I felt it was too dangerous for her to enter the house, I would leave the living-room light on and the door into the front hall open. Cynthia was thus able to see the light through the frosted-glass panels in the front door without being seen by the Watcher. If the light was off, it would be safe for her to enter. This was madness but I was unaware of my lunacy at the time.

In other respects we had improved our security arrangements. The worst possible thing that could have happened would have been the police raiding the cottage during the early hours of the morning, a favourite time for raids by the Immorality Squads. The police did not choose houses or flats to raid at random. They usually acted after being tipped off by some high-minded citizen and I always remembered this whenever I saw our neighbours across the road.

We decided that if a raid ever happened Cynthia would have to get out of the cottage as quickly as possible in case the front door was forced by the police. She would leave through the back door and I would have to help her over the seven-foot-high fence separating our communal garden from the garden of the next-door chapel. She would then have to hide in the shrubs at the end of the garden and remain there until she received the all-clear from me, that is unless I had been arrested and taken away by the police.

One way to forestall the latter would be to make absolutely certain that no traces of Cynthia or her previous presence should be found in the cottage. With this in mind I hit on the idea of our using a large black plastic bag for her to put all her clothing and personal belongings in before going to bed. This bag was kept by the side of the bed so that she could grab it in an emergency and take it with her over the fence. Before we went to bed I would carefully go all over the house to make sure she had not left any incriminating items lying around. The bathroom received very special scrutiny. I had to check the wash-hand basin, bath, toilet bowl and shower cubicle for any black hairs and also the litter container for evidence of female visitors.

I could not keep any photographs of Cynthia on the premises, or notes or letters or cards or anything else that would indicate any relationship with a non-white woman. All the supper dishes had to be washed and put away before going to bed. It would not do if the police crashed in and found two lots of plates and knives and forks. Not that this would have been proof of fraternisation with a member of another racial group, but it could have led to some questioning which might have proved dangerous or at least awkward.

Early summer arrived and I had cause to visit a vineyard in the Tulbagh Valley to interview a client whose family had been farming wine in the Cape for over two hundred years. At that time of the year the valley was outstandingly beautiful and I thoroughly enjoyed the drive. The wine farmer told me that some of the vines growing in the valley were the actual descendents of vines brought over from Germany by early settlers. Some South African wines are superior to their European counterparts. One famous vineyard in the Western Cape produced an annual output of really fabulous wines, one of which was a spätlese; it was impossible to buy it in South Africa. The bulk of it was snapped up by a major retailing organisation in the USA and what was left was exported to Germany, the birthplace of spätlese.

The farmer and his wife were extremely courteous and hospitable folk and I spent an interesting hour or two being conducted around the farm, and the enormous cellars, so cool and dark in the warmth of the early-summer sunshine.

On my way back to Cape Town I passed numerous Cape Coloured farmworkers and reflected on the unhappy method of payment meted out by wine farmers. The coloured workers were usually paid a part of their wages in cheap wine and most of them spent their working days in an alcoholic haze. I couldn't believe this when I first heard about the system from an Afrikaner friend of mine. I thought it was absolutely diabolical at the time and I still do. Apparently the luckless coloured farm labourers received between three and four bottles of excruciatingly awful wine every day and consequently many of them were hopeless alcoholics by the time that they reached their teens. According to my Afrikaner friend, wine farmers didn't like the system but apparently they would not be able to find cheap labour unless they handed out their shoddy wine. Perhaps the system has changed since I was there. I pray to God that it has.

Shortly after driving past Stellenbosch with its famous university, I noticed a number of ostriches stalking majestically along behind a tall, wire fence. Not having actually seen these remarkable birds close up I stopped the car and walked over to study them for a moment. One of them stood in front of me and was not the slightest bit afraid of my presence. Its powerful legs and large claw on its foot could easily have disembowelled me if I had been on the wrong side of the fence. Large, penetrating eyes stared coldly at me and the unblinking stare was a bit un-nerving. With a polite 'Good afternoon', I returned to the car and set off home.

It was Wednesday and we had just finished our meal in the kitchen. I was about to start doing the washing up which we took turns with when Cynthia, who seemed a bit on edge, said, 'John, there's something I must tell you.'

I paused with my hand on the hot water tap. 'What is it, darling?'

She fidgeted with the tea towel for a moment and said, 'Please don't be angry with me!'

I was now intrigued and I walked over and put my arms around her and said, 'Why on earth should I be angry with you, love? Come on! Tell me all about it.'

'I think I am going to have a baby,' she said quietly.

For a minute or so I couldn't say anything. I just didn't know what my feelings were. I suppose I was struck dumb temporarily. Cynthia was gazing at the floor and I realised that she might have taken my speechlessness for anger or dismay. I hugged her fiercely. 'Good!' I said gently. 'I'm very happy to hear it and I want you to take extra special care of yourself and above all, don't worry about it. I'll do the worrying for both of us.'

She began to cry and I comforted her. 'You won't leave me, will you, John man?' she asked. 'I don't know what I would do if you should leave me now.'

I walked her gently into the lounge and sat with her on the settee. 'I have no intention of leaving you, darling, and I'm a bit hurt that you should even think such a thing.' I kissed her and wiped away her tears and we sat quietly together for a long time.

The prospect of becoming a father for the first time while in my early forties pleased me enormously, but I felt a chill run through me when I thought of the extra problems Cynthia's pregnancy would produce. I said nothing to her about my fears. Tonight was a night for happiness and I had to make her feel as secure as I possibly could in the insufferable circumstances under which we were compelled to live.

We laughed a lot that night. To me it was an incredible feeling. I was actually going to be a father after all this time. Me, of all people. Would it be a boy or a girl? What would we call our baby? Decisions, decisions, decisions. I turned to her and grinned foolishly; I simply couldn't stop grinning. 'Cynthia darling, would you be angry with me if I got a little bit pissed tonight?'

She laughed happily. I knew that she felt more secure now knowing that I had accepted the news happily and had no intention of deserting her – or the baby. 'Of course you can, love,' she said softly, 'but not just yet.' She lay back and drew me down to her.

At the weekend we met again and spent Friday and Saturday night at the cottage. I had bought a book on pregnancy and child care and a load of vitamins for her, and we sat talking excitedly about this new development in our already eventful lives. 'We'll have to start giving some very serious thought to the future now, love,' I told her. 'We can't stay in South Africa for much longer, can we?' I lit a cigarette.

Watching me with anxious eyes, she said, 'Do you think your family will accept me, John?' She looked down. 'You know. Me being coloured and all that?'

Giving her a hug I said gently, 'There isn't a lot of family to impress, darling. My brother will love you, I'm sure, so you can put your mind at rest on that point.' I asked her how she would feel about leaving her sisters and South Africa. For all its shortcomings as far as she and her race were concerned, it was still the land of her birth.

'There's nothing here for me. What future would there be for our baby if I stayed here? I want to get away from this country and start a new life somewhere where we can go out together and have friends.'

'What about Cathy and Ramona? They are going to find out sooner or later about the baby?'

Cynthia giggled. 'I think the later we tell Ramona the better,' she said. 'If I tell her she'll immediately think you will do a bunk and leave me in the lurch. I'll tell her in my own way and in my own time. I'm sure she will be understanding when she realises that you are trustworthy.'

I said nothing but I, too, hoped that Ramona would understand.

On the Saturday morning I was still excited about the coming baby and during breakfast I told Cynthia that I wanted to tell someone. 'I'm sure Bob will keep it quiet if I tell him. If he doesn't I'll murder the bugger,' I said.

'If you think so, John,' Cynthia replied. She was smiling at my obvious happiness and I could see that she was happy too. I said that I would slip over to see Bob during the afternoon as it would be a good thing for me to be seen leaving the cottage for a few hours. After breakfast we went through our usual weekend shopping routine much to Cynthia's delight, and I am sure that we were the happiest couple in the street that morning.

I left the cottage at about two-thirty and saw the Watcher and his miserable-looking wife working in their garden. I made a point of slamming the door of the car firmly so that they would be aware of my departure. The woman spoke to her husband and his grey head swivelled round, only to turn away again quickly when he saw that I was looking in his direction.

Bob and Beattie were both in when I arrived at their flat and the kettle was soon on. While we were enjoying a cup of tea I mentioned that I had some special news which I wanted to talk to Bob about, and suggested that we went along to the Regency for a chat. Beattie warned him not to drink any spirits.

'Don't worry, love. I'll keep an eye on the old sod,' I said, and with this we set off along the main road.

Realising that Bob would not be able to resist telling Beattie the news on his return, I stood firm on my decision not to give him the full address of the cottage. He knew that I had a cottage in Rondebosch, not far from Rondebosch Common, but I had always been a bit vague about the actual location. He never pressed me on the subject. I ordered a lager for him and, for a change, a large Bell's whisky for myself. A single measure of spirits in a South African bar is not much smaller than a double in a British pub. The first time I asked for a 'double' in a bar in the Republic, and the puzzled bartender finally realised what it was I was after, he said, 'Are you quite sure that is what you want?'

I gave him a frosty look and said, 'When it comes to the hard stuff I always know what I am asking for.' When he placed the South African 'double' before me my expression must have been something to see because he laughed outright. Reg knew what I meant by now.

Bob couldn't stand the suspense any longer. 'Come on then, you miserable git,' he said in his customary friendly manner, nudging me in the ribs with a bony elbow for good measure. 'What's all the bleedin' mystery then?' He had a grin on his foxy face.

'Well, it's no big deal, Bob. It's just that I'm going to be a daddy.'

He must have thought he had heard me wrong for a moment because his grin became a weak smile and he said, 'You're gonna be a bleedin' wot?' He looked quite startled.

'You 'eard, you old bugger,' I said, mimicking him.

'Christ! I mean, 'oo is she?' he squeaked, with froth on

his moustache and a look of puzzlement on his face. The combination was almost comical.

As he was about to repeat the order to Reg I said, 'Do you think one Scotch will give you a heart attack, Bob?'

'Not on your bleedin' Nelly.' He ordered two large Scotches.

He sat with his jaw hanging as I told him the story. 'You mean to tell me that you've been knockin' around wiv this bird for over a bleedin' year wivout tellin' me abaht it?' He shook his head with disbelief and sat in silence for a while. Giving me the elbow once more, again accompanied by his almost diabolically crafty grin, he said, 'You lyin' sod. You're 'avin' me on, aren't yer?'

When I shook my head with a tight little smile he said quite simply, but with great feeling, 'Well! Fuck me!' and for almost five minutes silence reigned.

I interrupted his reverie: 'She's a real cracker.'

He glanced at me. 'I'm sure she is, mate!'

I leaned across and said quickly, 'And she's coloured, too.'

For a moment I thought he was going to choke on his whisky and I regretted suggesting he should have one. He looked directly at me in awe.

'You're fuckin' jokin'. Christ, man! What are you gonna do?'

I shrugged. 'There's only one thing I can do, Bob. When the time is right, I shall take her back home and marry her. This isn't a one-off affair, Bob. We really love each other and that's that.'

'Wot I don't understand is 'ow you've managed to last so long without bein' nobbled by the law.'

I finished my Scotch and placed the glass down on the bar. 'Mainly by keeping my bloody mouth shut, mate, and while we're on about it, I'm relying on you not to drop me in it, especially with a baby coming along. If my girl ended up in prison in her condition, I wouldn't want to live any more.'

Bob found it all difficult to understand. He couldn't get over my news and for the rest of our time in the bar he sat deep in his own thoughts, interspersed with numerous 'Fuck me's and 'Fancy you's.

I returned to the cottage in a slightly euphoric condition but I very quickly sobered up when I heard what Cynthia had to tell me. During my absence she had been sitting in the kitchen playing with Fred when she heard Marie and another woman talking in the garden. They were both speaking Afrikaans which was Cynthia's first language. The woman was the Watcher's wife and she was asking some rather leading questions about me. Why were my curtains always drawn? How well did Marie and Dan know me? Why didn't I have a girlfriend or a wife? What was I up to coming and going at all times of night?

To give Marie credit, she told the nosey woman that I paid my rent on time and kept the house clean and tidy and was no bother. 'What he does in his own time has bugger-all to do with me,' she ended.

'Good on you, Marie,' I thought, but what I'd heard chilled me. She was out to get us, that cold-eyed bitch across the road.

THE HATFUL OF CHRISTMAS CHEER

The days were getting warmer as we approached midsummer. It would soon be Christmas and I remembered Cathy's visit on the previous Christmas Eve. Perhaps she might like to do the same this year. I decided to ask Cynthia to invite her again.

During the year I had seen little of Cathy apart from one occasion when I had to meet Cynthia to give her some magazines I had promised her. Cathy had been with her and we chatted for a few minutes before parting again. From what Cynthia had told me, Cathy liked me and also trusted me. Ramona was going to be the tricky one.

Again I marvelled at the brilliant sunshine and hot days we were enjoying in early December, and reflected on the differences between the northern hemisphere and the southern. To me, everything here still seemed back to front. Even water is supposed to run down the plugholes in the opposite direction in the southern hemisphere, and the moon looks as though it is lying on its side.

Winter in South Africa is at its peak in July and in the Cape manifests itself in the form of cold, wet, windy days with lowering grey skies. The Hottentot Holland Mountains, which are clearly visible from Cape Town, are usually covered with a light winter mantle of snow. It can get extremely chilly in and around Cape Town at that time of the year and log fires are customary for those householders lucky enough to have open fireplaces. I made do with a two-bar electric fire.

Winters in the Transvaal are different. Up in Johannesburg, six thousand feet above sea level, they have crystal-clear blue skies with hard, brilliant sunshine, but it is as cold as charity in the streets and parks and the icy winds can lance through the warmest overcoats. It is strange to see the busy streets full of people wearing heavy outer coats, scarves, gloves, hats – and sunglasses.

Cynthia and I discussed plans for the coming Christmas and we decided to spend it together at the cottage. It would be our first Christmas together and we were excited at the prospect of doing all the things that people do at Christmas time. We were determined not to let anything spoil it.

I began dropping heavy hints that I wouldn't be around during the festive season, to ward off potential callers. Marie and Dan would be staying next door and the Watcher would be remaining at his 'observation point'; we would have to take special care during the holiday so that our Christmas wouldn't be spoilt by unnecessary tension.

'One thing's for sure, love,' I said to Cynthia, 'there will be no spirit of Christmas with good cheer to all mankind in that bitch's heart. Her idea of a Happy Christmas would be to see us being carted away in a police truck.'

She looked a bit apprehensive. I cuddled her close. 'We'll have a smashing Christmas, darling, just you wait and see.'

During Cynthia's brief visits before Christmas, we began reorganising the cottage to make it as welcoming and as cosy as possible. After all, we would be spending several days incarcerated in it, and although I could always go over to Sea Point for a swim or a drink, poor Cynthia would be completely housebound and would not dare stick her nose out of the front door. It upset me that she was forced to live in such a humiliating and silly way but she never complained and seemed to be happy enough when we were together.

During a shopping trip into Cape Town I visited Stuttafords department store in Adderley Street. It was fairly crammed with people doing their Christmas shopping, and carols were drifting around the big shop from the broadcasting system. My purchases included a new plastic Christmas tree as the other one was getting a bit tatty. I also bought a box full of decorations for it and some gold and silver tinsel. A copy of Bing Crosby's classic record of Christmas songs was added to my bounty.

Choice of presents was no problem. Like any young woman of her age Cynthia loved new clothes and I remembered her reaction when I gave her clothes the previous Christmas. How could I go wrong with a repeat performance? I bought a complete new outfit for her including the accessories. For Cathy I bought a cardigan and jumper and for Cathy's little baby girl a simple plastic toy.

Bob, who wasn't supposed to smoke or drink, got a bottle of whisky and a couple of hundred cigarettes. If I hadn't bought them for him, he would have done so himself. I had already explained to Bob that I would be spending the holiday period with my 'girlfriend'. I had not as yet told him Cynthia's name as a minor precaution. He understood the situation but insisted that he and I should have a few drinks together on Christmas Eve, to which I agreed. He was dying to find out where the cottage was in Rondebosch but I refused to tell him, though I did mention that I would arrange for him to meet Cynthia some time in the New Year.

Not many months previously I had struck up a friendship with a young Englishman and his wife. Terry was a representative and we had met at the Tulbagh Hotel. Although he had been born in Britain he had spent most of his life living in what was then known as Rhodesia. We met from time to time and eventually he invited me to have supper with himself and his wife Di, a charming young Englishwoman who had met Terry during a visit to relatives in Salisbury, Rhodesia. They hadn't been living in Cape Town very long and consequently they had not, as yet, made many friends. I liked them and impulsively asked them to have a meal with me at the cottage. As they left we agreed that we would meet again after the Christmas holidays and probably organise a day's fishing at Gordon's Bay or possibly a *braaivlei* at Saldhana Bay. I was pleased I had met them.

Cynthia visited the cottage a few days before the holiday period as I was eager to show her the changes I had made in the house. She was excited at the prospect of our spending our first 'family' Christmas together and was overjoyed when I told her that I had bought all the ingredients for her to bake her first Christmas cake and to make our Christmas pud. We were going to have a capon instead of a turkey and we intended to enjoy it with all the trimmings: baby sprouts, creamed potatoes, game chips, chippolata sausages, sage-and-onion stuffing, bread sauce and gravy. We also agreed to have our Christmas dinner in the evening as it would be far too hot to even think about Christmas pudding in the middle of the day.

At nine o'clock on Christmas Eve, Cynthia and Cathy made a safe entrance to the cottage. The table was already laid in the lounge and the candles lit, and with the glitter of tinsel and the Christmas tree, supported by the mellifluous tones of Bing singing 'White Christmas', we knew that the festive season had started. This was the one time of the year that I felt a little homesick and I wondered how my brother was and what he was doing.

Cathy mentioned that Ramona suspected that Cynthia had found herself a boyfriend. I asked why Ramona assumed this and Cathy said that as Cynthia hadn't visited her eldest sister as regularly as she used to, Ramona had, quite rightly, put two and two together. It would be only a matter of time before Cynthia's condition would become noticeable. Then Ramona would have to be told about the situation as Cynthia would need all the help and support she could obtain from her few relatives and especially her sisters.

After spending several minutes studying the street and the Watcher's window I felt it was safe enough for Cathy to leave and we managed to get away unobserved. I drove her to the little house in the coloured suburb of Athlone which she shared with an aunt. After wishing her a very happy Christmas I went on to Sea Point to have the promised drinks with Bob. Cynthia was quite happy in the cottage and would be perfectly all right in my absence. I had told her that I might be a bit late coming home but I would not have too much to drink.

When I walked into the cheerful bar of the Regency a large, brightly decorated Christmas tree stood at one end of the bar and Reg was doing his stuff wearing a paper hat. Bob and Chopper were locked in animated conversation and didn't notice my arrival until I tapped Bob on the shoulder. He turned and said, ' 'Ang on a minute.' The two of them were vociferating about the differences in working conditions in South Africa as compared to those of the United Kingdom, especially with regard to non-white labour. This was a depressing subject and one that should not be discussed on the eve of Christmas.

'Ah! Johnny!' boomed Chopper, placing a welcoming hand on my shoulder. 'What would you like? Brandy?' He turned to catch Reg's eye but Reg was already reaching out for a glass and nodding a greeting in my direction. 'This mate of yours, Johnny, is going to get himself into a lot of trouble one of these days, sounding off in public about South Africa's short-comings.'

I wished him good health and took a drink from my glass. 'He's entitled to his opinion, Chopper, and if he hurts anyone's feelings, well . . . what can they expect? I agree with much of what he has to say in any case, but you're right.' I turned to Bob and wagged a finger under his nose. 'Don't push your luck too hard, mate. You never know who's listening in these places.' Taking another drink I signalled to Reg that we needed a refill and told him to have one as well. 'Come on,' I laughed, 'it's Christmas. Let's change the subject and have a few laughs for a change.'

I lit a cigarette and said to Chopper, 'One thing that I have learned is that everyone is right and no one is wrong. The *verkrampters* [the hardline ultra-right wing of the National Party of South Africa] will offer you a convincing argument in favour of apartheid; after all, in their opinion, *they* are right. On the other hand, I will counter with my own argument which, if logically delivered, will prove conclusively that *I* am right. OK? But not to them. In their opinion I'm wrong. So you see, we're both right really, aren't we? It's only a matter of opinion, after all.'

Chopper stared thoughtfully at me for a few moments and shook his head. 'I've never heard it put like that before but there is a certain insane logic in what you say, lad.'

I finished my drink. 'The only snag is that man spends most of his time trying to bend the will of others to accept his point of view. This leads to bloody wars.' We seemed to be choosing some strange subjects to discuss on a Christmas Eve.

Bob nudged me. 'Can you come back up the flat wiv me when we leave? I've got something I want to give you.'

'Fine, Bob,' I replied.

Chopper looked at his watch and picked up his briefcase. 'I'm glad you popped in, Johnny, I wanted to ask your opinion on something but I'm a bit late now and I'll have to dash.

Could you come and have dinner with us after the holiday?' When I nodded he said, 'Super!'

I promised to telephone him at his office early in the New Year to fix a date and off he went. Bob and I had one for the road after which we walked back to his flat. I had already collected his presents from the car along with a small bottle of good perfume for Beattie.

Beattie and Chris were waiting for us in the kitchen when we arrived. They had both been drinking and were slightly the worse for wear. Bob vanished into the interior of his vast but unfurnished lounge which was now in darkness. He returned carrying two gift-wrapped parcels which he handed to me self-consciously. ' 'Ere,' he said, 'these are yer Christmas presents.' One of the parcels was heavy and made a swilling noise and I guessed correctly what it was. The other one was soft and pliable and on it written in large black letters was the following cryptic message: TO MISS X – John's girlfriend. I thanked him and gave him the presents I had brought for him and Beattie. 'Don't open them until the morning. OK?' I said and after exchanging repeated Christmas greetings I managed to get away. They were obviously disappointed that I was leaving so soon but I explained that someone was waiting for me and would be worried unless I arrived home.

Although it was now past midnight the roads were very busy and one or two cars were weaving unsteadily along the National Road. I kept well away from them. A couple of big passenger liners were moored in the harbour, brightly lit and decorated with pennants which fluttered from their masts and rigging. I wished all aboard a very happy Christmas and began singing Christmas carols to myself.

It was almost half an hour after midnight when I reached the cottage and Cynthia greeted me with a warm smile and a kiss. 'Happy Christmas, darling,' she whispered and I held her close and said, 'A very happy and safe Christmas to the three of us, love, and with Fred that's four.' She laughed happily. Fred rubbed himself against my ankles and it was good to be home. I placed Bob's presents under the Christmas tree along with other packages and as we sat on the settee listening to Jim Reeves warbling happily away she said, 'Can we open the presents now, darling?'

I gave her a stern look. 'Certainly not! I've never heard of such a thing. They're supposed to be opened in the morning after breakfast. Didn't you know?'

She glared at me in mock anger.

'Of course, I might be persuaded to change the rules if someone would make me a cup of . . .'

She was off to the kitchen like a shot and a few minutes later I sat back sipping my tea watching her happily tearing the wrappers off her presents like an excited child. Her beautiful young face was flushed with pleasure and anticipation as she opened the packages, and I smiled with delight at her reaction on seeing what I had given her. The biggest parcel was a sort of Chinese-looking dress with a high collar decorated with gold embellishments. It had long sleeves with matching gold twiddly bits on the cuffs. The other packages held shoes, stockings, handbag, underwear – all the accessories. She gave me a big kiss and seizing her loot disappeared into the spare bedroom. Ten minutes later she came back into the lounge wearing her new things. She looked absolutely wonderful, yet somehow I suddenly became depressed. Any man in his right mind would have been so proud to be seen in the company of such a stunningly lovely young woman, yet here we were living like this. I couldn't take her anywhere and it all seemed a mockery.

She sensed that I was unhappy and came over and sat down beside me. 'What's wrong, John, man? Are you annoyed with me?'

I took her in my arms and held her. 'Of course I'm not annoyed with you, love. I'm sick that we have to live such a stupid bloody life. It's wrong that you should be stuck here, hiding like a criminal.'

She snuggled close to me. 'Come on,' she said, giving me a little shake. 'Don't be so silly. Let's enjoy our Christmas. We won't live like this for ever, will we?' I hugged her and held her close and wondered what the future held for us.

We opened Bob's presents. Mine was, predictably, a bottle of Oude Meester brandy and Cynthia had received a very pretty scarf and a baby-suit. Typical of Bob, I thought. There was a little note pinned to the small suit:

Dear Miss X, Please accept this little present for your baby. We hope it turns out to be what you are hoping for and I hope that your miserable 'old man' will soon let us meet you. Happy Christmas from B and B XXX.

We were delighted by Bob's thoughtfulness and Cynthia was touched. 'He seems to be a very kind man,' she said, 'and wasn't it nice of him to send the baby-suit?' Cynthia's presents for me were a whacking great bottle of Richelieu brandy and a carton of my favourite cigarettes. I was well geared for Christmas. It was early morning before we got to bed and it was one of those occasions when my vibrations told me that we were safe. Someone had told me that they had never heard of anyone being arrested for immorality during a Christmas holiday. I considered this to be a doubtful concession on the part of the South African police but as it was Christmas and as I didn't want anything to spoil it, I believed it.

Christmas morning was bright, sunny and hot and when we awoke at about nine o'clock we could hear the people arriving at the chapel for their annual Christmas Day service to be followed by a grand party. Fred *meerouwed* from outside and I padded into the hall and opened the door to let him in. He scampered through to the kitchen looking for his breakfast. I hadn't yet put it out for him and as it was a special occasion I opened a tin of salmon and left him chomping happily before returning to bed.

'What are we going to call the baby?' I asked Cynthia. She said it depended on whether it was going to be a boy or a girl so we laughed and decided that we would have a girl. 'Rosemary?' I suggested.

'She'd be called Rosie for short. Sounds like a barmaid.'

'What about Margaret?'

'Don't like Maggie very much either.'

We lay thinking about different possibilities for some time. I said, 'What we must try to do is find a name that will be difficult to turn into a nickname. One that can't be shortened . . . Wait a moment, I think I've got it. What about Hanna – H-a-n-n-a.' I spelt the letters out.

She looked at me and repeated it slowly: 'Hanna.' Then she smiled. 'Yes. I like that. It's a nice easy name to remember and it is different, isn't it, darling?' So Hanna it was going to be.

I put a hand on her stomach. 'You're beginning to swell a little, my girl. We won't be able to hide Mother Nature's handiwork for much longer.'

She bit her lower lip and looked at me with a troubled expression on her pretty face. 'I'm so worried about Ramona. I wonder what she'll say when she finds out?' She paused for a moment. 'I'm sure she won't want any more to do with me.'

I cuddled her. 'Come on, love, I don't think that your elder sister is going to reject you. She will be angry at first, I'm sure, but that will be her immediate reaction. I think you'll find that she will accept the situation, especially after I've met her and assured her that I have no intention of deserting you. I shall take good care of you and it won't cost your sisters a cent. Everything is going to be all right, you have my word on that.'

Cynthia looked up at me through anxious eyes. 'She'll have a fit when she finds out that you're a white man.'

I shrugged. 'Well! She'll just have to get over it, that's all. There's nothing I can do about my colour.'

I lay beside her thinking about it all. I came to the conclusion that the sooner Ramona knew about Cynthia's condition the better it would be for everyone. After the initial explosion, Cynthia's mind would be at rest. I didn't want her fretting any more than was absolutely necessary in view of her condition. We had enough to worry about as it was.

Blood is thicker than water, I thought. Ramona might well be bitterly opposed to our relationship but I couldn't see her turning against her young sister. I knew that things were going to get a lot worse before they got better and we would be glad of whatever help we might get from any sympathetic quarter – including Ramona.

I turned to Cynthia and kissed her. 'I think that you should let Ramona know after Christmas. If you're frightened about it I'll come with you.'

She let out a long sigh and shook her head. She agreed that she should tell her sister the truth but she wasn't very happy at the prospect of facing Ramona's sisterly wrath. She also felt that it might not be such a good idea for me to be present during her confession. 'I think it would be as well to give her one shock at a time,' she said, twisting the bedcover in her fingers, no doubt at the daunting prospects that lay ahead. 'It will be enough to tell her about the baby. After that I can gradually lead up to who the father is.' I told her not to think about it too much today as we didn't want to spoil our first Christmas together.

'Yes, you lazy old so-and-so,' she giggled, ruffling my hair. 'After all I am pregnant, and expectant dads are supposed to make a fuss of expectant mums. What about a cup of tea in bed for me for a change?'

I grabbed her feet and began to tickle them until her shrieks of laughter brought me down to earth and I remembered the neighbours. I hoped that they would think it was part of the high jinks taking place in the chapel which was almost visibly shaking by this time.

I put on the kettle and told Cynthia that I had better visit Marie and Dan to wish them the compliments of the season or they might take it upon themselves to pop in to see me, with possible embarrassing results. I had a quick shower and then donned my personal Christmas present to myself. A rather flamboyant safari suit complete with Boy Scout-type stockings and desert boots. I admired myself in the mirror looking a bit like Sanders of the River.

I had bought cigarettes and booze for Marie and Dan and a small present for their son. As I walked out of the house, Spot greeted me in a friendly way and I gave him a pat and wished him a happy Christmas. The little boy was playing on his swing and his eyes shone when I gave him his gift-wrapped present, and after offering me a shy 'Danke' he rushed off to his mother yelling excitedly in Afrikaans.

Marie appeared with her hands and arms covered in flour, and her face lit up when she saw me. 'Happy Christmas, you old bugger,' she called. 'Come in and have a drink with us.' An appetising smell filled her kitchen and their Christmas dinner was obviously well on the way. The table was laden with home-made pies and cakes and a large, crispy loaf of fresh-baked bread stood on top of the refrigerator. She saw me eyeing it hungrily and said, 'I've made one for you too.' She took another loaf from her cupboard and handed it to me along with a meat pie sitting proudly on a white plate.

From a corner of the cupboard she removed a gift-wrapped package and thrust it into my hand. 'Here, man! It's not much but we hope you enjoy them.' I knew that Marie and Dan found it a bit hard sometimes to make ends meet on Dan's not very high earnings and I was touched by their kindness. I hadn't expected anything from them other than a friendly drink.

In the lounge Dan was sitting comfortably in his underpants and sandals in front of a small table. He was puffing contentedly on a Dutch cigar and enjoying his first drink of the day. He half stood. 'Kom, man.' He pulled another chair forward. 'Sit down and have a tot with me.' He held his hand out and with great dignity and obvious sincerity, wished me a happy Christmas. After an exchange of compliments he apologised for his informal dress.

'I'll be doing the same later on, Dan, don't worry.' We enjoyed a couple of shots of brandy together and chatted about nothing in particular. Marie came through and asked me what I would be doing for Christmas dinner and I assured her that I had received plenty of invitations but I had decided to spend Christmas in my own house and was expecting someone to share it with me later.

'Oh! Yes?' she said, cocking an enquiring eye at me. 'Male or female?'

I shrugged. 'You never know!'

She laughed and said meaningfully, 'I often wonder what bloody larks you get up to, my lad.' I felt it was time I finished my drink and left before there was any more speculation.

Cynthia had been busy; the bird was already stuffed and in the oven and she was preparing the vegetables when I walked in. 'Have they started cooking their Christmas dinner yet?' she asked.

'Yes. Marie's almost finished it. They must be having their meal at lunch time.'

That Christmas Day passed quickly enough but it was wonderful in every respect and we were so happy just being together at that special time of the year. We spent a good deal of our time talking about the future and wondering what it would hold for us, and we also agreed that it would be better for us to remain in the Republic until the baby had been born, despite the difficulties that we were bound to experience. I didn't think that the Immigration officials at our point of entry into the UK would be very enthusiastic about welcoming a foreign girl arriving 'for a holiday' in an advanced state of pregnancy.

Cape Coloured women were allowed to have their babies in the maternity unit of Groote Schuur Hospital providing that they registered well in advance of delivery. I told Cynthia that she had better register at the hospital early in the New Year because she wouldn't be able to have the baby at home. In any case we were not even sure where 'home' was going to be by then. She wouldn't be able to keep her job for much longer so another set of problems were presenting themselves to me. However, I would cross that bridge when I came to it. I tucked her into bed after a very happy day and made a cup of Irish coffee as a special treat. After checking through the house carefully and making sure that the black plastic escape bag was nearby, I put Fred out for the night and went to bed.

Early the next morning I left a note by the bed to let Cynthia know that I was going for a swim and would be back later in the morning. Fred slipped into the house as I left. After a quick dip at the Pavilion I called in to see Bob and Beattie. He was still in bed when I arrived and Beattie was wearing a rather sensual looking nightie which turned out to be one of Bob's presents to her.

'Have a heavy night, love?' I queried, eyeing the bags under her eyes.

'You should have seen your English gentleman friend last night,' she said over her shoulder as I followed her into the kitchen. 'He was pissed out of his mind and he fell over twice. In the end I had to drag him to bed.'

I sighed. If Bob carried on like this he would end up in the intensive care unit again – or the public mortuary.

Beattie made me a cup of tea and after a while shuffling feet heralded the approach of Bob. What a dreadful sight he looked, but despite his dissipated appearance he was cheerful enough.

'Wotcher think of the presents then?' he greeted me with a grin.

'Terrific, Bob. The baby-suit was very well received and won top prize, I can tell you.'

He seemed genuinely pleased to hear this. 'Why don't you bring the girl over here for a drink tonight?'

I thanked him for the invitation but I would no more have thought of risking Cynthia's freedom by taking her to Bob's than I would have thought of stamping on a South African policeman's foot. There was nothing wrong with his flat but it was on a rather exposed site with a brightly lit forecourt in front of it, and cars pulling in and out of the garage every few minutes. The only reason that Beattie and Chris escaped undue notice was because the flat was part of a large block and it was obviously assumed that the girls were employed as servants. I wondered how long it would be before Nemesis in the form of a police raid spoilt things. I had warned Bob about this possibility but he had always given me his customary crafty grin of wisdom and tapped the side of his nose. I never found it very reassuring.

While in the district I paid a quick call on Basil and Brenda. They were pleased to see me and Brenda wanted to know why I hadn't been round recently. As I made my excuses Brenda busied herself in the kitchen with the preparation of coffee. Basil was still lounging in bed and I heard him call out, 'Hey, man, where the hell have you been? Let's have a look at you.' He was lying back on the low bed wearing a pair of pyjamas that were so flamboyant and dazzling that they would have sent Fred into a fit if he had been there.

'Where the hell have you been hiding yourself, man?' he asked me, leaning up on one elbow.

'I've been busy with a new project and it has taken up a great deal of my personal time.'

At that moment Brenda walked in with a tray containing mugs of coffee and a plate of biscuits. 'Well, whatever it is you have been doing, you look remarkably well on it,' she laughed, handing round the mugs.

Out on the sunny balcony looking over to Greenpoint Stadium with the sea beyond, we flopped down into comfortable cane chairs and Basil asked me what I was up to. I explained that I had been working on a design project for what I hoped would be a revolutionary new range of furniture. 'Can't say too much about it at the moment but I'll let you have a look at it all when I have made the prototypes. I'd like your opinion, Basil.'

After a few pleasant banalities and good wishes for the coming New Year, I told them that I would have to leave as I was expecting a visitor. They walked with me to the front door and we promised to have a meal together early in the New Year. It was getting on for ten o'clock before I drove off towards Rondebosch and I didn't want Cynthia to start panicking, thinking that I might have had a change of heart and left the country.

When I walked into the cottage, Cynthia was dressed in her new clothes and she had put on a little make-up. She looked lovely and I told her so. She blushed beneath her delightful coffee colour and said that she wanted to look extra specially nice for me on my return. She got a kiss and a cuddle for that. I told her that I had seen Bob and thanked him for the present for the coming baby, and that pleased her.

For lunch we had cold chicken salad, avocado pear with shrimps, and ice cream and home-made fruit salad. After washing up and tidying around generally, we settled down for a quiet and lazy afternoon, me with a good book while Cynthia listened to some records and played with Fred. We were content and very happy in each other's company – all was well in our world.

There was a loud double knock at the front door. I sat up with a start and Cynthia froze where she was kneeling by the record player. I raised a finger to my lips. 'Shhh!' I was glad that the record player was turned down low otherwise whoever it was at the door might have heard it. Another heavy double knock came from the door and I suddenly realised that my car was parked on the verge, which was a dead give-away.

'Oh! Hell! I wonder who the dickens it can be?' I said to myself, rising to my feet. I peeped down the hall and could see the distorted images of two people through the frosted-glass panels of the front door. Cynthia was standing beside me.

'It's all right, love. No need to worry. Just do as I say and everything will be fine. Grab everything that is yours from the lounge and the kitchen and I'll lock you in the spare bedroom until they've gone. You'll have to lie down and be very quiet. I'll soon get rid of them. OK?'

She nodded and did as I suggested and disappeared into the spare bedroom. I locked the door after her and slipped the key into my trouser pocket.

Glancing around quickly to make sure that there was no evidence of her presence in the cottage, I walked along the hallway and opened the door. It was my English friend Terry and his wife Di. 'Happy Christmas!' they chorused and I gave a forced smile and made a valiant effort to try to look as if I were glad to see them.

'Hello there!' I said. 'Please come in. Nice of you to call.' I led them through to the lounge and invited them to sit down and asked them what they would like to drink.

Di looked around with interest and said, 'Oooh! doesn't it look nice in daylight?' She meant the cottage lounge, of course. I could have kicked myself for having invited them for that meal. Delightful people that they were, they had certainly chosen an unfortunate time to visit me.

Terry had a large brandy and Di chose a gin and tonic, and several drinks later I realised that an hour had slid past effortlessly. I suddenly had a sick feeling in my stomach as it dawned on me that they had settled in for the rest of the afternoon and possibly the evening as well. I hadn't the heart to make an excuse to get rid of them. They seemed genuinely pleased to be with me and Di even mentioned that it didn't seem right for me to be spending Boxing Day on my own.

I was concerned about poor Cynthia. What on earth would she be thinking, stuck there in the bedroom? She must have been bored to tears. There was a banging at the back door next and I thought, Oh, shit! The whole bloody street is calling in now. I hoped that my visitors would put the fact that I was sweating profusely down to an exceptionally warm afternoon, but it wasn't only because of that.

When I opened the back door Marie and Dan were standing there. Dan was holding a partly empty bottle of brandy and looked as though he already had a skinful. 'Have a drink, man!' he chortled. I shrugged inwardly and stepped aside from the doorway to let them in. There was nothing I could do about the situation; it was getting a bit out of hand. All I could think of was Cynthia incarcerated in the bedroom. What a bloody Christmas, I thought as I followed my latest visitors into the lounge.

After the introductions, Di took over as acting barman allowing me to sit down and chat a while. I was barely six feet away from poor Cynthia on the other side of the bedroom door. Here we were, just a few friends enjoying each other's company for a while at the time of year when peace and goodwill were supposed to abound, yet, because nature had given her a different skin pigmentation to us, she had to remain hidden as though she had leprosy. How bloody unfair, I thought. How fucking ridiculous!

Terry and Di were now fairly well loaded and Marie and Dan were not far behind them. Despite the amount of brandy I had consumed, I remained stone-cold sober and under the circumstances I doubted whether I would be able to become tiddly. All it needed now was for the Watcher and his wife to roll in to join the festivities and I would have been a candidate for a strait-jacket.

It became a torment and I could hardly believe the situation I was in. Much to my chagrin, Terry and Dan hit it off and I envisaged a long, agonising session. By now I could not look at the spare-bedroom door any more and I began to have nightmarish thoughts. I half expected Cynthia to emerge at any moment, furious, telling everyone to go to hell. I learned later that she was even more scared than I was.

The brandy and gin were now flowing like water and I made tremendous efforts to appear cheerful and glad to be with them. It was one hell of an effort but I seemed to succeed.

After another almost unbearable hour, Marie and Dan rose unsteadily and thanked us for a very nice time and with apologies for having to leave so early they made their way out of the back door. As I sat down I asked Di if she and Terry planned on having a family. 'Yes, we're both very keen on children and we intend trying for a child as soon as we have settled a bit better down here.'

I felt like saying, 'Well, there's no time like the present. Why don't you both bugger off and do something about one today?'

Terry pushed his shoes off – a bad sign – and Di excused herself and went to the bathroom. Cynthia had been locked away in that damned bedroom for five hours now and I was praying for them to leave. There hadn't been a sound of any sort from the bedroom and for a moment I wondered if Cynthia had taken an overdose or something. The fact that she might have wanted to go to the toilet had never entered my head.

Di returned from the bathroom with what I thought was a mysterious expression on her good-natured face. She made another round of drinks and asked me if I had a steady girlfriend.

'Not really, Di. No one would fancy a miserable old sod like me.'

At that moment I noticed that Fred had hopped through the lounge window and was now sniffing around at the bottom of the spare-bedroom door. I rose as if to go into the kitchen and gave the cat a surreptitious kick as I went by, sending him scuttling to the other end of the lounge where he sat glowering at me. It was the first time I had treated him badly and he was very hurt. I felt rotten about it at the time.

I made some coffee and carried it through to the lounge on a tray with some slices of fruit cake. After handing the coffee and cake around I sat down and began sipping my coffee. Suddenly Terry said, 'John, don't be upset or take what I am going to say the wrong way, but we're both broad-minded.'

I wondered what was coming next and tried to appear casual and slightly surprised by his remark. Terry looked a bit embarrassed and Di chimed in. 'John, when I went into the bathroom a while ago I saw some make-up on the shelf and a pair of black false eyelashes.'

I cursed the make-up and eyelashes. Cynthia had wanted to try them out and I had bought them for her for a laugh. It hadn't turned out to be as amusing as I had hoped. I knew the game was up and in a way I was glad.

'As the eyelashes are black, we were wondering if your girl-friend is a brunette,' Di continued.

'Er . . . all over, that is,' said Terry.

I felt the tension draining out of me as I sighed and lay back in the chair. 'There's no point in me lying. The poor little bugger has been locked in that room for almost six hours,' I said, completely resigned to the consequences.

This remark had an electrifying effect on Di. 'Why, you rotten cad!' she exclaimed. 'Why didn't you say so ages ago?'

I rose to my feet and headed for the bedroom door. 'How the hell could you expect me to?' I protested, my voice rising with irritation. 'Anyhow, she isn't staying there a moment longer,' and I unlocked the door and went inside.

Cynthia had dived beneath the bedcovers, terrified by this latest development, and wouldn't show herself despite Di's soothing and reassuring words. Eventually Cynthia peeped out at her and Di smiled and said, 'Well, whoever you are, you're certainly very pretty.' A muffled giggle came from under the bedcovers. 'Come into the lounge, there's a darling, and join the party,' Di said but Cynthia wasn't having any.

'It's all right love,' I joined in. 'They're not going to tell anyone. Come on, there's a good girl. I've been so worried about you.' Even my words of reassurance had no effect. She was plain scared and that was all there was to it.

'Right!' said Terry. 'Take her legs, Di. She's going to join us whether she likes it or not,' and with this, they carried the highly embarrassed Cynthia into the lounge, complete with bedcovers. It was at least an hour before she could calm down and join us in the conversation. Eventually she unwound, and the day ended on a happy note after all. During the evening Di and Terry realised that this was no casual romance and they promised faithfully that they would never mention a word to anyone. I knew that I could trust them.

After they left Cynthia giggled nervously and tracing an invisible pattern on the carpet with her toe she said, 'I did something naughty while I was alone in that room.'

I smiled encouragingly at her. 'What do you mean, love?'

She stared down at the carpet. 'Well, I was in there for a long time and there was nowhere else.' She looked up at me and for a brief moment she was like a child caught with its hand in the biscuit jar. I waited patiently. 'You know your hat, John?'

I knew my hat very well indeed. I had bought it in Johannesburg and it had cost me a lot of money. It was made of suede and had been hand-made in St Louis, USA. I was very taken with it and it never failed to arouse favourable comment whenever I wore it. I wouldn't have parted with that hat for anything.

A slight chill of unease ran through me. 'Yes, darling, go on, what about my hat? You didn't stand on it accidentally, did you?' I asked anxiously. I laughed at the thought.

'Oh! No! Nothing like that,' she said and relief flooded me. I smiled.

'As a matter of fact I peed in it!'

The smile froze and my eyebrows rose fractionally. 'Peed in it?' I said in astonishment. Then, 'Don't worry, love,' I went on bravely, seeing her expression. 'If it's weatherproof outside it must be pee-proof inside.' And with this seemingly logical statement, I went to the bedroom and looked around for the hat.

There was no sign of it and I bent down and looked under the bed and found it in the appropriate place. Reaching out, I took hold of the brim and attempted to draw the hat towards me and it remained firmly in place. For a moment I thought she must have nailed it to the bedroom floor, but as I gripped it more securely I felt my thumb slide beneath the surface. It was literally full to the brim. I drew out my once magnificent hat and carried it pathetically off to the bathroom to empty it.

Cynthia followed me in. 'I'm ever so sorry, John. I'll buy you another one, please don't be angry.'

I wasn't angry, just a bit preoccupied. I turned and kissed her on the tip of her nose. 'I'm not angry with you, darling. I'm angry with me for not having thought about an eventuality like this before. It's not your fault, love.' I had emptied the hat and I gazed down at the soggy object.

'Throw it away,' she said.

I could hardly believe my ears. 'Throw it away?' I yelped with mortification. 'Throw away a perfectly good hat with years of wear left in it?' I put the plug into the bath and after half filling it with water, I dunked the hat and left it there for the rest of the night.

The following morning, I rose early and hung the hat on the washing line in the garden with a couple of clothes pegs. I forgot the effect that the summer sun might have and when I went out into the garden to collect it later in the day it was bone-dry and hard looking. After a good brushing it looked as good as new again, but when I tried it on I discovered it had shrunk by almost one size and it perched ridiculously on top of my head. It was never the same hat after that.

During the remaining days of the holiday we spent much time evaluating our present security procedures; we had been shaken by Terry and Di's visit, even though the outcome had been a happy one. One of the problems we gave thought to was that of Spot, the Dalmatian. He and I were firm friends but he had never encountered Cynthia directly.

Sometimes when the afternoons were uncomfortably warm we would sit near the open lounge window. This window looked out on a thick hedge between our cottage and the chapel next door. On one occasion while we were enjoying a breath of fresh air, Spot sniffed his way to the window and on seeing Cynthia he began to bark and growl. I closed the window but it generated the germ of an idea in my mind. I encouraged Cynthia to slip the occasional tit-bit through the window to Spot and gradually he took a liking to her and eventually they became good friends. He never barked at her any more and gave a friendly wag of his tail whenever he saw her at the window. This augured well should we ever have to do a bunk into the garden and have to put 'operation fence climb' into practice. As it turned out, our foresight paid handsome dividends later on.

THE TWO WORLDS

From time to time Cynthia visited her aunt and uncle who lived in the small town of Malmesbury. On these occasions I used my free time to catch up with outstanding social visits. On one Friday evening while Cynthia was away, Bob told me that it would be Beattie's birthday the next day. They were going to a family party at Beattie's family home which was in a non-white area near Elsies River. Beattie had asked Bob to invite me along as well but I didn't like the sound of it.

'Christ, Bob! That would be asking for trouble, you know. I'm sure we would be as welcome as the flowers in May by Beattie's family, but other coloureds might not be so hospitable. In any case, if we're seen there by the patrolling police, we shall have a bit of explaining to do, won't we?'

There were some very pleasant non-white suburbs around Cape Town at that time with charming and friendly non-white residents. Unfortunately Elsies River was one of the less salubrious coloured areas and if the residents were suspicious, to say the least, of white people, one could hardly have blamed them for lobbing the odd brick at us. It was in places like Elsies River that the Choppers of South Africa found a ready supply of cheap labour. In return for their work many of these people received sub-standard wages on which they quite often had to support large families.

My immediate response to Bob's suggestion was a flat 'No!' He assured me that it would be perfectly all right because several of Beattie's relatives had promised to guarantee our safety if we visited them. I wasn't particularly reassured by his confident manner but I felt that it would be interesting to see with my own eyes how some of the poorer coloured families lived.

I was to rendezvous with Bob at his place the next afternoon at three o'clock. When I arrived I found him spruced up to the nines. His thin face was cleanly shaven, his moustache neatly trimmed and his hair was plastered down with a parting as straight as a ploughman's furrow. He was wearing a navy-blue suit which I had not seen before, and was sporting a small yellow buttonhole. He still wore his Parachute Regiment tie. I felt positively shabby next to him, wearing my Sanders of the River outfit. We strolled along the road to the Regency and over a couple of drinks Bob announced that we would be on our way as soon as we finished them.

I was astonished. 'If you think that I'm going to be seen driving around the rough end of Elsies River in broad daylight on a Saturday afternoon, you've got another think coming, my lad,' I said, glaring at him.

'What the bleedin' 'ell's the matter with you?' he rasped with a look of contempt on his face. 'Ain't you got any guts?'

I scowled angrily. 'I'm not short of guts but I intend hanging on to them a while longer if you don't mind.'

Bob turned abruptly away and sulked. For some minutes the atmosphere was decidedly unpleasant. I ordered another round and seeing this as a sign of weakening on my part he turned back to me and whined, 'Wot you don't understand is that I promised the old lady a 'and in gettin' everythin' organised for tonight and as I ain't got a bleedin' car I'm gonna drop her right in the shit, ain't I?'

I shuffled my feet in embarrassment and muttered, 'Why didn't you tell me this last night? I could have refused there and then.'

He leaned sideways in a peculiar attempt to add emphasis to his words. 'I didn't fuckin' well know last night, did I? Beattie asked me this mornin' before she went orf over there an' I gave her me word.'

He whined on and on until I relented and said, 'OK, but let's have a couple more drinks first. I'll have to get a bit pissed or I won't have the nerve to go there. If I get nicked the worst that will happen is that I'll be charged with drunk driving. It will be better than being charged for driving around a non-white area without good reason.'

We had a couple more drinks and went on our way. As we drove along steadily, I wondered what I had let myself in for again. Every time I helped Bob out with something I always ended up in the cart and I cursed myself for allowing myself to become involved in the affair.

When we reached the robots at the Elsies River turn-off we headed towards the scruffier area of this uninviting district. The landscape and its dreadful-looking shacks became more and more depressing. Finally Bob directed me into a long straight sandy track which turned out to be the 'road' in which Beattie's mother and family lived. I was shocked by the miserable conditions under which these unfortunate people were expected to live. Compared to it, the near-slum in which I had lived as a small child in the dockland of Hull was a pleasant, middle-class area.

The houses, if they could have been described as such, were in various stages of mouldering decay and through occasional gaps between them I could see piles of rusted corrugated iron in which other families were living. The track was littered with broken bottles, bricks, stones and other debris and it got worse as we proceeded along it. We were now almost at the end of this track and the decrepit group of shacks built from rusting corrugated iron sheets which we were approaching was our destination.

A number of thin, ragged children were kicking a ball around in the sand. As we drew nearer they moved aside for our car to pass and watched us with sullen expressions. They might have thought that we were a pair of CID officers looking for someone. A fierce-looking man dashed out from a gap in a corrugated iron fence and stood glaring defiantly at us. I didn't like the atmosphere at all and despite Bob's squawk of dismay I pressed my foot down on the accelerator and sped past the heaps of rusty iron. I didn't stop until we had turned into another so-called road, which was empty and quiet.

'Look, Bob,' I said, turning to my agitated passenger, 'it's just too bloody dodgy for my liking; if you want to risk your neck I'll drop you near the place but I'm going back to Cape Town.'

Bob glowered at me. 'Wot the bleedin' 'ell's the matter with you, man?' He gave me a cigarette and we lit up.

'I didn't like the look of the welcoming committee, that's all.'

'Do you mean Jaapie? The bloke 'oo shot out of the 'ouse?' He laughed aloud. 'That's Beattie's brother-in-law.'

I turned and stared at him.

'Why, 'e's a lovely bloke. 'E only wanted to welcome us.'

I shifted uncomfortably in my seat. 'Well, someone must have upset him,' I replied. 'If that's what he looks like when he's being hospitable, Christ knows what he would be like if he was annoyed about something.'

Bob leaned back, laughing his head off. He dug me in the ribs and said, 'Don't be so bloody daft. They're as good as gold. Come on, let's get over there or 'e'll think we've buggered off.'

I gave a sigh of resignation and started the motor. I had abandoned all hope of leaving the neighbourhood alive and a fatalistic calm descended over me. When we stopped in a sandy hollow beside a crude compound surrounded by a rickety fence, a shambling figure appeared through a gap in it, and with its nut-brown face wrinkled into a broad, toothless grin, clamped a large hand on Bob's shoulder and gave him a friendly shake.

Bob returned his greeting. ' 'Ello, Dick, 'ow's the old lady?' The old lady was Beattie's mother and Dick was Beattie's uncle.

I was introduced to Dick, a short, thick-set man, stooped with the hard labour of his younger days. He had grizzled white hair and wore an indescribable pair of baggy trousers complemented by a shrunken grey pullover. There was no shirt beneath it. His left knee protruded through a long slit in the trousers and he was barefooted. Despite this he was a cheerful and friendly soul and he told us to go into the compound. As we left him, Dick squatted down next to the car. His job was to see that no harm should come to our vehicle. I noticed that he was holding a stout stick and I didn't doubt his ability to use it should the occasion arise.

There were stagnant pools of water inside the sandy compound and a few rather sickly chickens lurched around in search of non-existent scraps of food or plants. We turned right and as we walked between two of the rusty hovels a nasty-looking mongrel dog appeared from beneath one of them and bared rabid fangs at us. As it snarled in a menacing way Bob said, 'That's Dinky, 'is bark's worse than 'is bite.'

'I'll take your word for it,' I replied, moving to the other side of Bob.

We walked out into an open area of sand on which a small fire was burning, a silent group of coloured men sitting around it. As we walked past them and nodded politely, they just stared at us without a word of greeting. Small children, excited by our arrival, scurried about shrieking in shrill voices. All were thin, ill-clad and barefooted.

'Poor little sods. What future have they got to look forward to?' I said quietly to Bob as we trudged on. 'Thank God they're happy at the moment. When they grow older they'll discover that life isn't so amusing, 'specially when they realise that they're Cape Coloureds living in South Africa.' What a pity they couldn't remain children for always.

We came to a door that at one time had boasted at least one coat of green paint. Now it was scabrous, and to open it one tugged on a length of dirty manilla twine which dangled from a roughly drilled hole in a rotting lintel. Bob banged on the door with his coded knock and yanking on the string entered the house, beckoning me to follow.

The inside was dark and cool and appeared to consist of a maze of small, low-ceilinged rooms, clean but badly in need of decoration. The floors were stamped earth. We entered a dimly-lit tunnel which led to a closed wooden door. Bob tapped on this door and bawled, 'Anyone at 'ome?'

There was a creaking noise from inside the room and a harsh, voice answered, 'Kom, lad!'

Bob opened the door and a flood of light entered the dark tunnel from a window in the room beyond. Standing against a wall was a sorry-looking wardrobe with one door missing. There were two single beds in the room and on one lay the owner of the voice, an elderly Cape Coloured lady. She was wearing a long dark-brown skirt and a maroon, long-sleeved cardigan. On her head was the customary Cape Coloured head-scarf popular with the older women. She had the flat features and raised cheekbones of a typical Cape Coloured matriarch and I remembered that the group originated from the original Hottentot tribes who lived in the Cape at the time the early Dutch settlers arrived.

She held her thin arms out to Bob and greeted him as if he were her son, and he hugged her and planted a loud smacker on her sunken cheek. Her black, penetrating eyes sparkled with pleasure.

"Ello, Ma!" he said with a grin, "Owyer keepin' then, eh?"

She held his arms and said, 'It's good to see you, son.' She turned her searching gaze in my direction and I knew that she had the measure of me in one long, appraising look. From the friendly gleam that appeared in her eyes I gathered that I had passed muster.

I extended my hand and walked over to her with a smile. 'Hello there,' I said. 'Bob has told me a lot about you. Are you well?'

She took my hand in a warm, firm grip and told me that she was feeling great and was happy that I had accepted her invitation. I sat down on the bed opposite while she and Bob chatted quietly to each other.

Two small, thin children came shyly into the room with the obvious intention of inspecting the strange white man who was visiting them. How very odd, they must have been thinking. They were two of Beattie's nieces, neat little things with their black, shiny hair in twin plaits. Both were barefooted and wore their best dresses, brightly coloured garments made from cheap cotton material. They were ready for the party and looked cute. At first when I spoke to them they were quiet and rather shy, but later when they realised that I was friendly and harmless they lost much of their shyness, and began to ask me many questions about where I came from. Had I been to London? What was it like there? Did black people live there? and so on.

They wanted to know if I had met the Queen. I explained that the Queen was a very busy lady and had over fifty-five million subjects to think about. 'She would dearly love to meet us all, I'm sure, but there are just too many of us.' They thought deeply about this for some time. I noticed their matchstick legs and arms and asked the old lady how old they were. I was astonished when she said that they were twelve and fifteen years old. I thought they were both about ten years old. I put it down to lack of proper diet and vitamin deficiency. Whoso shall offend one of these little ones . . ., I thought.

As the evening progressed, people began to arrive until we were all called into the main parlour. I was quite surprised when I entered the fairly large room. It was neatly papered in pink wallpaper with a floral pattern, with a number of framed religious texts on the walls. The sloping ceiling was recently whitewashed from the look of it and red satin curtains hung from the windows. There were a number of low wooden chairs, and an old-fashioned settee sat proudly against one wall. The main attraction was a huge table in the middle of the room. It was decorated with different coloured crepe papers and laden with an assortment of foodstuffs – cakes, jellies, salads, fruit, cold meats, avocado pears, bread-and-butter and bowls of jam, and plates of biscuits. There were cups and saucers and tumblers, and in the centre of the table stood a big birthday cake covered with white icing with the following legend in wobbly pink lettering: Love to our darling Beattie XXX.

The room quickly filled with coloured people dressed in their best clothes who smiled shyly at me when I looked towards them. One of Beattie's aunts automatically became the Master of Ceremonies and she handled the big family affair with authority and skill. She was obviously a kindly woman and she put herself out to make Bob and me feel at home. I was glad that I had plucked up the courage to stay.

We were all made to stand around the massive table to sing hymns and to offer prayers before being allowed to sit down to eat. I looked around at the people gathered there and I was touched by their kindness and simple faith and my heart went out to them. I wondered what Chopper would have thought had he seen it all. The Choppers of this world miss out on an awful lot.

Beattie and Chris had arrived earlier in the day and had been busily engaged in helping to prepare the gargantuan meal. Bob's principle contribution to the festivities had been chatting up the old lady during the afternoon, a not unworthy contribution considering the pleasure it seemed to have given her.

After we and the other guests had demolished the enormous feast, Beattie was made to stand up to make a speech, then we all retired to another room which was also big and spacious. This turned out to be the kitchen and was where the dancing was going to take place. Within moments of our entering the room a Kwela music record was thumping out its catchy rhythm and soon we were all dancing happily. Wine and brandy flowed like water and the four bottles of hard stuff that Bob and I had brought with us ensured that everyone was able to enjoy themselves.

I had long forgotten my doubts and fears and was really enjoying myself when Bob tapped me on the shoulder and said, 'Time to be going, mate.' I was surprised to discover that it was almost one o'clock. The night and the party had passed too quickly.

The following week I kept my promise and telephoned Chopper, who invited me to supper a few days later. He gave me careful instructions and I had no difficulty in finding the house in a very exclusive white suburb called Bishops-court; it was large and stood on a big corner plot. The house was double-storeyed and resembled a typical middle-class suburban English house. It looked as if he had had it designed and built to his own specifications. He had. I parked my Beetle, feeling a bit conspicuous in a neighbourhood noted for bigger and more affluent cars. When I pressed the bell-push next to the imposing front door it opened almost immediately, but instead of the usual coloured servant whom I expected to see I was greeted by a woman who appeared to be in her early thirties. She was Chopper's long-suffering wife.

She smiled and said they had been expecting me at any moment, and led me into a large hall where an impressive staircase swept up in a broad curve to a wide landing above. On the walls were one or two excellent reproductions of paintings of wartime RAF planes. I half expected to see a bust of Chopper standing somewhere on a plinth.

We found the master of the house doing his country-squire bit in the large, ornately furnished lounge. He was leaning against an imitation Adam fireplace that must have cost him a shilling or two. An expensive-looking French ormolu clock was gracing the mantelpiece, while suspended above it in a magnificent gilt frame was a very good reproduction of a painting by Gainsborough. The floor was covered from wall to wall with dark green, silky carpet and the walls with a Regency-style design of embossed vertical stripes. Furniture consisted of two comfortable wing-back chairs and a matching three-seater settee covered with posh-looking green velvet. A number of small, round, occasional tables were placed around the room and a Regency-style bookcase and cupboard stood against one of the walls. French windows looked out on a large stoep containing tubbed plants and shrubs. It was exactly the sort of set-up I would have expected to find Chopper inhabiting.

His wife was a quite attractive woman but she was quiet and colourless and seemed to blend into the background in her husband's forceful presence. She went off somewhere leaving Chopper and me alone. 'Ah! Dear boy!' came his characteristic greeting as he walked across the room with hand outstretched. His red, shining face was beaming with pleasure. 'Welcome to our little place.'

He was wearing a green corduroy jacket, a pink shirt and a matching tie, which was a nice change from the RAFVR tie he usually flaunted. Perhaps the latter was for public viewing only. He made me welcome and in a matter of moments I found myself grasping a large balloon glass holding a massive shot of brandy – neat. 'That's the real stuff; French, y'know.' If he had made that remark in the bar of the Regency he would have been instantly deported. To any patriotic South African the 'real stuff' is produced in and around Stellenbosch. 'You don't drink that with water, my boy,' he boomed.

As soon as we had finished our pre-dinner brandies, he led me through to the dining-room. It was furnished in a different style to the lounge but was equally elegant and a lot of money had been spent on it. It was panelled in knotty pine. There were several racing prints around the walls and the large table and six matching chairs were beautifully made from pine. Three places were laid and Chopper nodded to one and we sat down. They did not employ a servant – 'Can't trust the buggers,' said Chopper when I made a mild enquiry on this matter. His wife, Daphne, did everything and she looked a bit tired and careworn. She quietly served up the meal but made little contribution towards the conversation.

Our meal was simple but well-prepared and we drank a

bottle of Nederberg Cabernet. It was not until we were on the cheese and biscuits that Chopper brought up the reason he had invited me over. A brick-built servants' quarter standing beside the house was empty. He wanted to turn it into a replica of an English pub, for private use only, of course. We strolled outside and he took me into the building and switched on the lights.

I saw at once that the building could easily be converted into a most attractive bar and I became quite enthusiastic about the possibilities. When I suggested a design for a repro- duction of an English inn-sign to incorporate his family name he was as pleased as Punch with the idea. I told him how to go about obtaining odds and ends such as beer mats, dummy bottles and advertising material from brewers in the UK, and he was almost beside himself with delight.

While we had one for the road I said I would rough out a few sketches and jot down an idea or two that might help to get the 'pub' off to a good start. He gave me a plan of the building and I told him that my ideas would be ready for his approval a week later. It was agreed that I would join them for supper again one evening next week.

When the evening arrived I found Chopper waiting eagerly for me in his front garden. His eyes lit up when he saw the roll of plans and sketches under my arm as I pushed his gate open. They were quite ordinary suggestions with nothing outstanding about them but he was almost drooling over them and treated me as though I were some sort of genius. Later at the dinner-table he waxed enthusiastic about his pub idea until I began to get a bit fed up with hearing about it. I changed the subject and asked him to tell me more about the factory he was running in Elsies River.

The products his company manufactured were useful to the wine trade and he took a great pride in explaining to me the economics involved in the running of his organisation. His red face was glowing with smug satisfaction as he continued, 'We have a twenty-four-hour operation, y'know, and as we turn out X pieces an hour which we sell at Y cents each we are making a bloody fortune.'

I listened with great interest to all this. 'So you run a three-shift system, do you, Chopper?' I asked.

He looked at me with a wily leer, and shook his head. 'Two, dear boy.'

I digested that. 'So your workers do a twelve-hour shift, do they?' I queried. 'I suppose they're glad of the extra cash, poor buggers.'

He beamed happily. 'That's right, and they work like buggery, too. They know bloody well that there are plenty of others waiting to jump into their jobs if they get stroppy.'

I looked thoughtfully at my drink for a moment before eyeing him. 'I suppose they are compensated for the long hours they work?'

He nodded affably. 'Oh yes! Our top operator picks up twenty-four rand a week clear and the others don't do too badly either.'

I could hardly believe what I was hearing.

He made the mistake of continuing, 'The buggers can't go on strike either, so how can we fail to prosper?'

His wife was staring down into her lap. I took a long pull on my drink and after putting my glass down carefully I looked pointedly at his RAFVR tie which he was sporting on this occasion. 'You know something, Chopper, me old mate?'

He cocked an eyebrow and smiled patronisingly at me.

'A long time ago, some very good mates who flew with me during the war were killed fighting to stop some shit called Hitler from doing to Jewish people what you are doing to these poor bastards in the Cape!' His face had frozen in disbelief as I went on, 'When you have your inn-sign hanging outside, I suggest you take your RAFVR tie, which you disgrace, and hang yourself from your sign with it!' and on this note I walked out of his house. I never spoke to him again.

THE FIRST MOVE

One evening towards the end of January we were having supper when Cynthia said to me nervously, 'John, I must leave my job.'

My heart sank momentarily for I knew her employer must have detected her condition by now. I reached out for her hand. 'Can you stay there for a few more days while I see what can be done about finding somewhere for you to stay?'

She nodded but looked very worried.

'Hey!' I leaned forward and smiled at her. 'Now what did I tell you? I'll do the worrying and you concentrate on having the loveliest little girl ever. OK, Mum?' I squeezed her fingers gently and she smiled back at me.

It was as well that Cynthia was unaware of my true feelings. Where the hell was I going to find a safe place for her to stay during her pregnancy? She would not be able to stay with Ramona; there simply wasn't enough room and if she did, it was possible that Ramona would prevent Cynthia from seeing me. That was no good. I had discussed this coming problem casually with Bob who suggested that Cynthia should stay with Ma at Elsies River. This was totally unacceptable for a wide range of reasons. To start with, I feared that we would be quickly exposed to the authorities should we take that course. But I realised that Bob meant well and had Cynthia's best interests at heart. I thanked him and said I would discuss it with Cynthia and let him know.

The situation was becoming a bit of a nightmare. It had been perfectly all right in the early days when our problems had been bridges to cross in the future. One very big bridge now lay ahead and needed to be crossed soon. Scanning the small-ads pages of the *Cape Argus* one evening while alone in the cottage, I spotted what appeared to be just what we were looking for. Someone was offering to let a small, unfurnished room for a single Cape Coloured girl, must be respectable etc., etc. The advertisement mentioned that the room was in Wynberg which would be ideal for us.

I wrote a carefully worded letter of application there and then and gave it to Cynthia later in the week. She copied it carefully in her own handwriting and signed it and I mailed it off for her. There must have been scores of applications for the room as accommodation for coloured people was at a premium in Cape Town at that time. Something about our letter must have captured the attention of the advertiser, because after a few days Cynthia received a reply inviting her to call at an address in Wynberg to meet the landlady.

Cynthia was very nervous at this prospect but I told her that we had no choice. I gave her plenty of money to take with her so that she could offer three months' rent in advance. My experience of human nature told me that not many of the coloured applicants would make such an offer and the landlady would not be able to resist. I was correct, thank God, and a very excited Cynthia visited me at the cottage a few nights later.

She told me what the landlady was like, and all about the room which was part of a small annexe of a large house. The annexe was rented to Cynthia's future landlady, Rosanna. The annexe's front door was shielded by a white-painted brick wall which stood immediately in front of it. The front door opened directly into a small kitchen with a bathroom beyond. To the right of the kitchen was a reasonably large room which was being used as a bedsitting-room by Rosanna and her twelve-year-old daughter Anne. To the left of the kitchen was a smaller room; this was to be Cynthia's.

Rosanna was, according to Cynthia's description, a coloured woman of medium height with long chestnut hair and yellowish skin. She seemed friendly enough and thanks to the new duffel coat I had bought Cynthia, she hadn't noticed the 'bump' under it. Apparently she had taken a liking to Cynthia and the feeling was mutual. When Cynthia mentioned that she would be very happy to pay three months' rent in advance, the deal was clinched on the spot and it was agreed that she would move into the room the coming Saturday. The next problem would be furnishing it.

When I told Cynthia that she could have my furniture from the Sea Point flat she was delighted, and I received a big kiss and a hug for that announcement. 'It will be lovely having your things around me, darling,' she said, smiling happily. 'It will make me feel as though I am with you all the time.' I told her to make her way to her new abode on the Saturday and I would arrange for the furniture to be delivered to her during the afternoon.

Bob had previously introduced me to a couple of Cape Coloured blokes whom I had got to know over the months and quite liked. One of them, whose name was Johnny, had the misfortune to be hunchbacked, but despite his handicap he was a good-natured little chap and quite strong. He had a weakness for the bottle but promised me faithfully that he would supervise the furniture move without imbibing.

He had a friend who owned a lorry which would be used to transport the furniture from Sea Point to Wynberg. We agreed on a transportation and removal fee which was quite generous, and I promised them a bonus if they carried out the operation efficiently. There would be three men involved: Johnny, his friend who owned the lorry, and another bloke who would help with the carrying. I gave Johnny a sketch to show him how to find the Sea Point flat and it was agreed that Bob would act as my agent by being at the flat to supervise the collection. The lorry with its crew and load would then make its way to the cottage at Rondebosch for further instructions from me, and Cynthia had money to pay them when they delivered the furniture to her.

Before Johnny left me, I slipped five rand into his hand and told him that this was extra and was a goodwill payment. He grinned broadly and said, 'You can rely on me, Mr John.'

Saturday afternoon found me pacing irritably around the cottage. They were already a good half-hour behind schedule and I hoped that nothing had gone wrong. I strode through to the lounge where an open bottle of brandy stood on the table. I had already consumed one or two and as I poured out another generous measure I couldn't help reflecting on the complications that had developed in my life. It hadn't been so long ago that I hadn't had a care in the world, and look at me now.

Just then I heard a strange rattling noise approaching along the road; this curious noise was supported by some rather heavy backfiring from a motor vehicle. I raised my glass to take a drink when it suddenly occurred to me that the noise was now stationary, right outside my front door. I hastily put the glass down and hurried through to the front bedroom and looked out of the window.

The most dreadful open-topped lorry of unknown origin stood vibrating out in the road. I saw my furniture stacked immediately behind the derelict driving cab which still had a few patches of blue paint where the rust hadn't eaten through. Lying down on his back next to my furniture was a coloured man wearing voluminous green overalls. He appeared to be dead. The passenger door of the lorry opened and through a haze of smoke Johnny fell out of the cab. He rolled to the grass verge and lay there for a while, until at last, making what appeared to be a terrible effort, he managed to stagger to his feet where he stood swaying until he suddenly spotted me glaring at him through the window.

He gave a cheery wave and began tottering towards my front door. I opened it and hissed, 'Johnny! You're as drunk as a fiddler's bitch, you silly bugger. Come in!' He reeled after me into the lounge and eyed the brandy bottle. I ignored the appeal in his eyes and asked, 'Any snags, Johnny?'

He shook his head and tugged off his greasy cap. 'Everything OK, Bossie.' He told me that 'Mr Bob' had fixed everything. I was relieved that Bob had not let me down.

'Do you know where you're supposed to be going with the stuff, Johnny?' I asked. He assured me that he did; diving his hand into a pocket he tugged out a slip of paper with Cynthia's address on it. I nodded and told him that they had better get a move-on now as they were late and Cynthia would start worrying.

As he weaved his way unsteadily towards the gate I recollected the prone figure on the back of the lorry. 'What's up with him?' I called.

Johnny grinned broadly. 'He OK, Mr John. He just drunk but good lorry engineer.'

The driver had cut the engine and peace reigned over the street, much to my relief. The whole thing was a bit embarrassing and one or two neighbours had started taking an interest in the tableau outside. I shook my head in puzzlement and after waving Johnny goodbye I re-entered the house and closed the door behind me, hoping they would clear off as quickly as possible.

I went back into the lounge and started where I had left off with the brandy. It wasn't until at least five minutes had passed that I suddenly realised that I had not heard the old lorry departing. With a heavy feeling in my stomach I walked back to the front bedroom and took up my position behind the net curtain at the window. Johnny and the driver were staring pessimistically into the engine department of the lorry. Something was patently wrong and I sensed disaster unless a miracle took place soon. It did, before my very eyes. Johnny lurched around to the sleeping figure and began to shake him and shout something in Afrikaans. Life slowly returned to the man and with jerky movements he heaved himself up, and rolling to the edge of the deck descended to the ground the same way that Johnny had. Johnny helped him to his feet and they staggered towards the front of the lorry. After tinkering under the bonnet for several minutes, the engineer yelled something to the driver who had climbed back behind the controls.

A moment or two later there was an ear-splitting explosion and a great cloud of filthy black smoke belched from the shredded exhaust pipe of the vehicle, which started to shudder in a peculiar way. This procedure was repeated, much to the pleasure of a growing crowd of kids who had appeared from nowhere. With a choking roar the old engine fired and caught and the whole contraption vibrated wildly. The kids were now poking fun at the lorry's crew who completely ignored them and prepared for take-off. Johnny clambered into the cab and hauled the engineer in after him. The last I saw of them was the door being slammed on the engineer's leg as they lurched away.

I heard someone knocking on the back door and when I went through and opened it I found Marie standing there, grinning. 'Did you see that bloody lot outside your cottage?'

I winced. 'The buggers were trying to find their way to Diep River and chose my house to ask at. Some people have all the luck, don't they, Marie?'

The road where Rosanna lived was in a quiet, respectable area which was shared by white families. This made it easier for me to be seen in the neighbourhood when collecting Cynthia or dropping her off. The procedure was that I would stop my car in another road around the corner from the one in which she was staying.

After a week or two Rosanna began to ask Cynthia some leading questions. She had quickly discovered that a baby was on the way, but to her credit and my enormous relief she had not suggested that Cynthia should find somewhere else to live. No doubt she was grateful for the money we were paying her plus the fact that Cynthia was a quiet, undemanding tenant. Furthermore she got along well with Anne and was proving to be a welcome companion for the younger girl.

Nevertheless Rosanna kept pressing Cynthia to tell her who the father was: 'The fact that he has never shown his face here could make me believe that he might even be white.' Cynthia, who liked Rosanna, felt that she could be trusted so she admitted that the baby's father was white and told her what we had already gone through together and how I had stood by her.

'Well, he sounds a decent enough chap; you might as well ask him to come in the next time he's over this way.'

Cynthia and I were pleased about this because we felt that we were pushing our luck by using the cottage as a rendezvous all the time, and we both had a premonition that sooner or later the police were going to raid the place.

A few nights later I met Rosanna. When we arrived at our usual parking place near the annexe I felt a bit nervous at the prospect of entering the house but Cynthia assured me that it would be all right.

'OK,' I said, 'you go ahead and I'll follow in a few minutes. I want to be sure that there's no one skulking around who might see me.' I remained in the Beetle for about five minutes looking around and listening carefully in case some of the neighbours were enjoying a breath of fresh air on their stoeps before retiring for the night.

It seemed safe enough so I got out of the car as quietly

as possible and practically tiptoed along the road towards
Rosanna's little home. When I reached the gate, I again looked
around behind me and along the quiet road to make certain
that no one else was about. Finally, satisfied, I walked quietly
up the path and stepped thankfully behind the white brick
wall which hid the front door from the road.

Through the glass-panelled front door I could hear a strident
female voice and assumed correctly that this would be
Rosanna. She made me think of a corncrake. I tapped politely
on the glass and the voice stopped, then the door was flung
open and there was Rosanna. She was exactly as Cynthia
had described her and she smiled hospitably while obviously
weighing me up at the same time. At Cynthia's request I had
put on a collar and tie which I suppose added a degree of
respectability to my appearance.

'Come in, John,' Rosanna said cheerily, 'we don't stand on
ceremony here.'

I stepped inside, noticing the neat cleanliness of the place.
It was cosy and homely and I tacitly congratulated Cynthia
and myself on having been fortunate enough to have found
such a seemingly nice place for her to live.

'Come and meet my big daughter,' Rosanna said, leading
us into her own private room. A young girl sitting on a
double-bed, reading, looked up and smiled as we entered.
'This is Anne,' her mother said proudly.

I shook hands with her. 'Hello, Anne. Nice to meet you.'

The child blushed and lowered her head to continue reading.
She was obviously embarrassed by the sudden intrusion of this
strange white man. Her straight, black hair and ivory skin
were a sure indication that she had mixed blood and I was
convinced that her father was white, but I made no comment
on the subject.

In addition to the bed, the room contained a double-fronted
wardrobe, a kitchen cabinet acting as a sideboard and dresser,
a large wooden table covered with a crimson plush tablecloth,
three dining-chairs, a record player and a radio. There was
still plenty of room for moving around.

Rosanna invited me to sit down and she went out into the
kitchen. I heard her striking a match as she lit one of the gas
burners to make a pot of coffee. Cynthia sat demurely on the

edge of one of the dining-chairs, too shy to open her mouth.

Rosanna came back carrying a tray with cups and saucers and what looked to be the best coffee pot. She placed the tray on the table and reaching into the kitchen cabinet she took out a big cake-tin. She opened it and lifted out a honey cake. 'You'll have a slice of this, won't you, John?' she asked, turning to me. Unfortunately I had a tooth that needed filling but, rather than hurt her feelings as I could see that the cake had been home-baked, I nodded and tried to look enthusiastic about the prospect of an agonising toothache. Sure enough, the first mouthful found the cavity and I tried to look as happy as possible under the circumstances.

Rosanna got straight to the point without preamble. 'What do you intend doing about this girl, John?'

I had been expecting this and I told her quietly that I wanted to marry Cynthia and we would be leaving the Republic as soon as possible after the birth of the baby, and I hoped to make a future for the three of us in England.

She looked at me thoughtfully and nodded to herself. 'Not many white men stick by coloured girls, you know.'

I shrugged. 'I can only speak for myself,' I said, sipping my coffee in an attempt to wash the honey cake away from my throbbing molar.

She told me her own rather unhappy story. She had met Anne's father before the days of apartheid and the Immorality Act. At the time they met, Steve was a Royal Marine whose ship was visiting Cape Town. They had met and fallen in love and he had returned to Cape Town later where they married and subsequently had Anne. Unhappily, the marriage had failed and they were divorced. Not long after this the Immorality Act was made law in the Republic. Rosanna and Steve later became reconciled, but because of the new law they were not able to live with each other again nor re-marry. So now Steve was more or less in the same position that I was. He usually visited Rosanna and Anne at weekends which they spent quietly together. If they had been detected by the police they would have been treated with leniency in view of their marital history, but it still didn't alter the fact that they were breaking the law in sleeping together.

The following weekend I met Steve who was a red-faced,

cheerful Londoner of about fifty-five years of age. He was completely sympathetic towards Cynthia and me and advised me to 'Get her and yourself out of this bloody country as soon as you can or you'll end up inside! If that happens, you'll never be allowed to see each other again and the baby will be taken away from her and stuck in a home and she will never see the child again either.' With these chilling words ringing in my ears I made my lonely way back to the cottage where I spent the rest of the night sitting drinking in the kitchen and talking to myself.

On another occasion I asked Steve why he hadn't done something about taking Rosanna and Anne out of the Republic. 'Well, if I do,' he replied, 'I could only take them to England and what the hell would I do for a living there? What sort of a job would I get at my age?' he went on. Steve was a civil engineer and was then employed as a supervisor on bridge-building work. He was earning about R100 a week plus productivity bonuses and in addition he owned a small but profitable scrapyard somewhere out of Cape Town. 'If I go back to the UK I might be bloody lucky to earn twenty quid a week, that is if I could find a job. Besides, I'm getting too long in the tooth to start pulling up roots now. I've got a nice little house not so far from here and nobody bothers us. Why give it up?'

I nodded in agreement. His situation was quite different from my own and I had to admit that he would be better off to stay where he was. I asked him how he thought Cynthia and I would be received back home with her being coloured.

He shrugged. 'Depends to some extent on where you live, I suppose,' he said. 'No matter what you read about in the newspapers, there's a lot more colour prejudice around than you might think. Even so, you can go where you like there and do as you please as long as you don't go breaking any laws. At least you and Cynthia will be able to go out together and you'll be able to sleep in peace at night without wondering if the "gestapo" are on their way.'

I told him about an incident that I had experienced not so long before. I had pulled in to a petrol station on the foreshore where I had not been before. It was on a Sunday morning and it was very quiet. Mine was the only car standing at the pumps. A short, coloured man had come over to serve me and when he spoke he had a real gor-blimey accent. Naturally I was surprised to hear the sound of Bow Bells on Cape Town foreshore and my curiosity got the better of me. 'Where do you come from, my friend?' I asked, and he told me his interesting tale. He had left South Africa some eleven or twelve years previously and had lived and worked in one of the southern suburbs of London as a motor mechanic.

'Here for a holiday?' I enquired politely.

'No, my missus and the kid and I came home about six months ago and we live in District Six now.'

I could hardly believe what I was hearing. 'You mean to tell me that after living in a free country like England for all that time, you have come back to live here where you are looked upon as a second-class citizen?'

He looked at me quietly and said, 'At least we know where we stand here.'

This was an eye-opener for me and I have never forgotten the incident. Steve listened intently and nodded. 'Yes, I can understand his feelings. Tough, though, isn't it?' I decided that whatever happened in the future Cynthia and I would have to get away somehow. I was sure that we would find somewhere where we could live happily together.

Cynthia began attending the ante-natal clinic at Groote Schuur Hospital in readiness for baby's arrival, which was due some time during July. She had been rather apprehensive before making her first visit as she knew that she would be asked to give the father's name. I made up a story and told her not to deviate from it. We rehearsed it in the privacy of her room at Rosanna's.

'Tell them that you had been invited to a beach *braaivlei* late one night and when you arrived you found a number of white people there as well. Tell them you were dependent on someone else for a lift home otherwise you would have left. Instead you stayed and someone must have put something into your drink because you passed out and were taken advantage of while unconscious.' It sounded a bit feeble to me but it was better than nothing and the best that I could come up with on the spur of the moment. 'Just stick to your story and stare them straight in the eyes,' I told her. We looked at each other and burst out laughing.

Cynthia told me that the welfare officer listened to her tale of woe with a straight face and when she finished, the woman patted her sympathetically on the shoulder and said, 'Don't worry, dear. We'll find the bugger!' From then on, whenever Cynthia visited the clinic she made a special point of dodging the attentions of the welfare officer, who always said emphatically whenever she saw her, 'Don't worry, dear. We'll find the bugger!'

Not if I can help it, Cynthia thought, scuttling out of the clinic.

We were now facing the problem of finding and securing the services of a non-white midwife so that Cynthia would receive proper attention after the birth of the baby. Cathy, who knew about Cynthia's condition, knew of one but Cynthia would have to visit her personally to make the necessary arrangements. An appointment was made for an after-dark visit and I decided to take a chance by picking up Cynthia and her sister and driving them into the heart of Athlone, another non-white township. There I was, driving *two* attractive coloured women in my car, and one of them pregnant. By now I had become a complete fatalist and no longer bothered about trying to make up stories in case we were stopped by inquisitive policemen.

We found the street in which the midwife lived and Cynthia and Cathy walked from gate to gate looking at the house numbers until they found the correct house. I parked across the road as there was a street light nearby and I preferred to sit in a dark, safe area. Momentarily I saw the expression on Cynthia's pretty face and my heart went out to her. She looked so young and vulnerable and somehow reminded me of a beautiful and timid deer, trusting its handlers that no harm would come to it. It was a rotten position for the girl to be in. She was totally dependent on me now and obviously scared of the whole situation but it was too late for either of us to turn back. After all, there was a third party to consider. I sat smoking nervously in the car and thinking about what the future would hold for us. Supposing we survived all this and got away without too many mishaps. What about the years ahead? Would I be ostracised by society in the so-called free world? It was wonderful, this relationship between this lovely girl and myself, but would we still be happy when we were away from this country? What would my few remaining relatives think about my coloured wife? What would my brother truly feel inside? Would being married to a coloured girl affect my ability to get a decent job to provide for her and the baby?

I felt suddenly depressed. It would have been easy for me to walk away from all these doubts and fears. I could simply resign from my job and find a better-paid one in Johannesburg. There would be nothing to prevent me from supporting Cynthia and the child financially; I would be able to send her a monthly remittance that would enable her and the baby to live comfortably. It would take the dreadful strain of our present existence off her young shoulders immediately – mine, too, come to that. Yet despite my line of thought and my doubts and fears for the future, I knew that I could never desert this young woman. We had been through hell together and we loved each other very much.

Not so very long ago I had become very ill, through self-neglect and too much boozing, I suspected. I had picked up a particularly vicious flu virus that had been making its rounds in the Cape and on top of that I developed a form of jaundice. I have always kept myself fit but when I tottered out of bed one night to go to the bathroom I was shocked by my appearance in the bathroom mirror. My face had a yellowish tinge and my eyes had sunk out of sight. I looked ghastly and feared I was going to die. I saw my doctor who prescribed various antibiotics and other medication and told me to take it easy for a few days. The office was notified and I assured them that I would be OK.

For the next couple of weeks I was really ill and could hardly fend for myself. Cynthia had thrown all discretion to the winds and had come to the cottage every night at around eight-thirty. She was so worried about me that she hardly bothered with the simplest of safety precautions, and I was too ill to care. Every night she washed me and changed my pyjamas and forced me to have a meal of some sort. She half-carried me to the bathroom and bathed me and shaved me. Goodness knows how we survived those two weeks without receiving a visit from the police. I began to develop a lot of faith in God at that time. He must have covered us with some divine mantle of protection.

I thought now about that period when Cynthia had put my welfare before her own safety. I thought about the many other instances where she had shown her real affection for me. All that she seemed to care about was making me happy. I knew that I could never find another woman like her and in my heart I knew that I was doing the right thing, for everyone's sake – especially my own. I swore that I would stick with her to the bitter end, come what may. To hell with those who were against us and God bless those who were with us. There were not many of those.

The girls returned to the car and climbed into the back.

'How did you get on, love?' I asked, half-turning to Cynthia.

'Fine!' she exclaimed, 'but she's a real nosey bitch. She wanted to know how I was managing to live when I was not working or living at home. When I paid her quite a bit on account and told her not to worry about the balance she soon shut up.'

As we were already in Athlone I was soon able to drop Cathy close to where she lived. I then drove over to Wynberg and had a coffee with Cynthia and Rosanna before setting off to Rondebosch East. I changed my mind on the way as it was not very late and I turned on to De Waal Drive and headed for Sea Point.

As soon as I saw Bob hunched over his drink in the Regency bar, I sensed that doom had struck him once again. It didn't take long for the story to come out. It was due to Bob's usual problem: money – or lack of it. He had been dodging a horde of creditors for some time but one of them had caught up with him and a summons had been served on Bob that afternoon. He wouldn't tell me much about it but his reaction was quite characteristic.

'They can get stuffed!' he said. 'I'm moving me job anyway and I'll shift out of that flat. They'll get no bleedin' money out of me,' he went on.

'Christ, Bob, you're carrying on as if they are out to get you. They only want what's due to them, after all. That's not unreasonable, surely?'

He shrugged indifferently and continued with his beer.

'How's the ticker?' I asked. 'I'm pleased to see that you are keeping away from spirits.'

He nodded glumly. 'Yeah. They told me at the clinic that I'll 'ave to lay off the old brandy snaps and fags for some time.'

He had a 'fag' stuck between his fingers, I noticed. 'You should try to pack in the smoking, Bob. I think that would do you more harm than brandy, to be honest with you.'

He shrugged disconsolately. 'Christ! If I can't 'ave a bleedin' fag now and again what the 'ells's the point in goin' on?' He was quite miserable and I couldn't do very much to cheer him up.

'How's Beattie?' I asked, changing the subject.

'She's up at the flat, been there all week,' he said. He told me that she had now moved in permanently, and I again warned him that he was asking for trouble in view of the exposed entrance to his flat. As the atmosphere was rather depressing and there appeared to be no signs of it improving, I told him to cheer up and that I would drop in to see him later in the week. Then I went to the Sea Point flat and swept it out and tidied around a bit as it was getting rather scruffy and neglected. I would spend the coming Saturday there to give it a good clean-out and to enjoy a swim at the Pavilion.

The next night I had an invitation to supper at Rosanna's place. I cooked a bit of topside for Fred's meal and gave it to him, receiving a brief ankle-rub and a polite *meerouwl* before he turned his attention to it. I showered, changed, wrote a couple of letters and prepared to depart. Before doing so I went into the unlit front bedroom and had a peep through the curtains across no-man's-land to find out if there was any enemy activity. The light in the front room over the road was off but I could see that the Watcher was on duty because he had once again forgotten about the light in the hall behind him which presented his silhouette clearly to me.

'So that's your little game, is it, matey?' I said softly as I stepped back and walked out of the room. I thought about it as I drove over to Wynberg. What endless pleasure I must have been giving these people who lived opposite me, and what empty lives they must live. It was a great pity that South Africa refused to have television at that period. The Watcher and his wife seemed to spend a hell of a lot more time spying on me than I did watching them. In some ways I felt sorry for them. They were part of a sick system and if they were sick too, who was to blame?

Since Cynthia had been staying with Rosanna a good deal of strain had been lifted from our shoulders. We were able to stop using the cottage as frequently now for I felt that it was growing increasingly more dangerous to meet and spend nights and weekends together there, especially in view of Cynthia's ever-burgeoning condition.

I was on time for my supper date and as I approached the annexe I could hear Rosanna's shrill voice from the road. Something had upset her, that was for sure, and she obviously didn't realise, or care, how far her voice could be heard from the house. She quietened when she heard my knock, and a few moments later the door was opened by Anne who was looking a bit fed-up. When I greeted her she tried to smile a response but it failed in its effect. Rosanna's piercing tones broke the silence. 'Is that you, John? Come on in, man, we're waiting for you.'

I found Rosanna and Steve seated at the table with what was left of a gallon jar of white wine between them. From their appearance they must have been glugging away most of the day. My heart sank instantly, even more so when Rosanna leapt from her chair and seizing me began waltzing me around the room to the music from the radio. Steve raised an eyebrow at me over her shoulder as much as to say: Humour her for Christ's sake. I endured the insane romp while we narrowly avoided hitting the furniture and falling onto the bed several times, until at last she grew weary and flopped back on the chair, brushing aside her hair which had fallen untidily across her eyes. 'You're a lovely dancer, man,' she said, reaching out for the wine jar. 'Have a drinkie, man!' she giggled as she grabbed an empty glass. At that moment Cynthia came quietly into the room and as I smiled at her she made a little face in the direction of Rosanna who had her back turned to the door.

Steve, no doubt used to these performances, stolidly swigged away at the wine and kept his own counsel while Rosanna worked her way steadily through the rapidly emptying container. I accepted the glass she had filled for me and it wasn't a bad drop of wine considering that it was a cheap brand.

Anne left the room and Cynthia cleared the table ready for

supper. Anne returned carrying a large casserole containing one of South Africa's most popular dishes known as pickled fish, a combination of stockfish with tomatoes and vegetables cooked in a special blend of herbs, water and vinegar. It was well cooked and we thoroughly enjoyed it. After the meal Rosanna put on another record and insisted on my joining her in another wild prance around the room, to Cynthia's disgust. However, the alcohol plus a long, energetic day had their effects on her and she finally sagged down onto the bed and promptly fell asleep, much to my relief.

As it was getting late by this time I said my goodnights and Cynthia and I went into her room to talk for a while. She seemed tired and I suggested that I should not stay too long so that she could get some rest. Her room was neat and tidy and I saw that she had touched up a long scratch on the wardrobe – a legacy from its eventful journey from Sea Point – with some shoe-polish. It was a nice little room and she seemed to be happy and comfortable there. 'How have you settled in, darling?' I asked, placing an arm around her.

'Fine!' she replied. 'But I am worried about Rosanna and her drinking. When she's sober she is so nice and kind but when she gets drunk she starts shouting at Anne and banging things around and making a nuisance of herself.'

I asked if Rosanna troubled her at all and she assured me that there were no problems in that respect. Certainly Rosanna seemed to like Cynthia a lot.

Rosanna's tendency to drink too much worried me too, as it represented a weakness in our security. 'If Rosanna speaks out of turn to someone while she's pie-eyed, it could put us in a nasty situation,' I pointed out, and decided that I might have to try to find a safer place for Cynthia. It was becoming a wearing and worrying nightmare, twenty-four hours a day, seven days a week.

One afternoon at about four o'clock I was sitting in my office digesting a new job brief when the phone rang. It was Bob, in a dreadful state of panic. 'Is that you, John?'

I confirmed my identity with a sigh of resignation. 'Yes, Robert?' I queried gently.

'I'm inside!' he exclaimed with what could only be described as a vocal flourish. It reminded me of the epitaph on the hypochondriac's gravestone: There you are, I told you I was not well.

'Inside what?' I replied with deliberate thickness.

He was sitting in the Prisoner's Friend's office at the High Court. 'They're going to send me to Roeland Street prison if I don't find the money,' he yelped. The creditor had finally caught up with him and he was now well and truly up the creek without the proverbial paddle.

I stared bleakly out of the office window at Table Bay. At that precise moment I wished that Bob had been in the middle of it – without a boat. The judge had sentenced him to three months' imprisonment but he would be released if he could pay the debt of R85 to the plaintiff's attorney.

'Don't let them do this to me, John,' he squawked and I wondered why I felt that I needed a friend like Bob. 'You've got to get the money down 'ere straight away, mate. I'm due to leave on the next van to Roeland Street if you don't.'

I couldn't help enjoying the situation in a perverse sort of way. He needed a lesson, the silly bugger. 'Of course I'll get the money down straight away, Bob. Whereabouts did you leave it in your flat?'

There was a choked silence for a moment or two. 'Don't be bleedin' funny, you know I ain't got the money otherwise I wouldn't be 'ere now!'

Fearing that he might have a sudden heart attack I told him to sit tight and to tell the Prisoner's Friend that the money was on the way. 'Simmer down, Bob, and give me the name of the people you owe the money to and the name of their attorney.' He did so and after making a few telephone calls I learned that Bob would be released providing that the money was in the hands of the plaintiff's attorney no later than five p.m. The banks were closed and I hadn't got the full amount on me but I managed to borrow the difference from a friend at work. The office messenger went off to the court with it at about twelve minutes to five.

That evening I visited Bob at his flat and found him dejected and pale. He was grateful for the help I had given him. 'Christ, John! That was bloody close I can tell you. I thought I was a goner that time. If it hadn't been for you I would be inside now.'

I told him to forget it but on principle I expected him to repay the money to me even if he paid just a few rand every week. He promised me faithfully that he would repay every cent of the money but I knew better. I put it down to my own stupidity. Half an hour later in the Regency, with his moustache dripping froth, he was his old cocky self again. I told him that if he got caught at his flat by the police on an Immorality charge all I would be able to do for him would be to cry. I suggested that it might be a good idea if he took over my own little flat at Sea Point, as it would be a lot safer than the one he was living in at the moment.

He looked at me in amazement. 'Blimey! Do you mean it?' he asked in open disbelief. When I nodded he was so excited that he couldn't wait to get home to inform Beattie. I told him that he could move in whenever he wanted, which turned out to be the next day.

I called round one evening soon after to find out how he had settled in. The place was in darkness, and when I gave our usual coded knock there was no response. I looked for him at the Regency and the other places where he might have been but there wasn't a sign of him anywhere – nor of Beattie either. Perhaps he had gone to the cinema; he liked an occasional visit to the cinema. I decided to enjoy my own company at the Regency for a while, then try to contact Bob again.

At about twenty minutes to midnight I went back to the flat once more. He would be sure to be home by this time as the cinemas usually closed at about eleven p.m. and it wouldn't have taken him more than twenty minutes to reach home. The flat was still in darkness and I thought he might have returned earlier than I had calculated and gone to bed. However, after trying our private knock a couple of times I knew the place was empty. I was puzzled and a bit worried about his absence as I drove back towards Rondebosch.

The following morning at about ten-thirty, Bob phoned me with a cryptic message. He sounded nervous and I knew at once that whatever the news was going to be, it would be bad. He asked me to meet him at the Regency that evening as he had something interesting to tell me.

'When would you like me to be there?' I asked.

'As soon as you can get over.'

I tried pressing him for some indication as to what had happened and all that he said was, 'I can't say anything on the phone but I'm sure you will guess before we meet.'

The only thing I could think of was that, somehow, he must have ended up in the hands of the law. I hoped that he hadn't involved me in his meeting with the police – if that had been the case, that is.

When I parked not far from the front entrance of the hotel that evening, I found him waiting at the door with a glass of what looked like brandy in his hand. He could hardly wait to tell me what had happened. 'Let's go through to the lounge,' he said. 'It's a bit more private in there.' We walked through the thickly carpeted foyer past the hotel manager's cubicle. He acknowledged our nods with a friendly grin as we went on into the large, mirrored lounge where we sat at a low circular table in the corner. The lounge was hardly ever used except for special functions or wedding parties, so we could talk without fear of being overheard.

Bob told me his story while I sat, enthralled. Two evenings before, he and Beattie were in the little flat together. She had been drinking heavily and when she did so she usually became unreasonable and sometimes violent. On this occasion she and Bob had a flaming row which almost ended in a stand-up fight. At about eleven-thirty that night she slammed out of the flat, swearing never to return, much to Bob's relief. Bob remained behind and after sitting alone mulling over what had taken place earlier he went to bed.

At about one a.m., while he was still alone in the flat, there was a thunderous knocking at the front door. Thinking that it was Beattie, back for another session, he leapt out of bed intent on telling her to bugger off and stop making a noise. When he yanked the front door open he was faced by two burly CID men who strode straight into the flat. Without saying a word to him they inspected the kitchen and bathroom and the interior of the wardrobe, and seemed disappointed to find him on his own. He suspected that someone had tipped the police off and they had arrived expecting to find Bob and Beattie in the flat together with signs or evidence that they had been sharing the same bed. Unfortunately for the police this wasn't the case, but it was still bad enough as far as Bob was concerned.

First of all the wardrobe had many of Beattie's clothes hanging there and in addition to this find, the two officers were particularly interested in the selection of Beattie's family photographs which were neatly arrayed on top of the dressing-table. They searched every item of clothing, his suitcases and drawers, and read all his private letters from his few friends, his son in Johannesburg and his aged father who lived in Hastings, despite Bob's angry objections. One of the men looked bleakly at him: 'You're not in your own country now, my friend, so shut your trap. We do things our own way here – and we don't like people like you.' On this menacing note, Bob decided that discretion was the better part of valour and, for once, he had enough sense to keep his aggressiveness to himself.

While they continued searching and reading his private mail, Bob was rehearsing his story and was ready with a somewhat implausible tale when at last they turned to him.

'Who are these coloured people?' one said, flicking the stack of photographs which now lay on the bed. 'And who do these clothes belong to?' They pointed to the wardrobe containing Beattie's garments.

Bob launched himself into his explanation and I had to laugh as he told me the story. He had said that the clothes and pictures belonged to a coloured woman called Beattie who used to work for him when he was running a garage in the city. This was true and could easily be confirmed. She had been thrown out of her sister's home and had nowhere to put her things while she was trying to find somewhere else to live. She trusted him and had asked if she could leave her few possessions at his flat as she didn't know anyone else she felt she could rely on. So far, so good.

'Kindly tell us why you have these family portraits prominently displayed in your room?'

She had left the pictures in one of the drawers of the dressing-table, he told them, and he had been studying them himself, and had been leaning them against the wall, one after the other, as he finished perusing each of them.

Luckily, Bob and Beattie had agreed on this yarn between themselves in case of such an eventuality. At some time after three a.m., while the police officers were more or less winding up their inquiries and seemed to be preparing to depart, having given Bob the benefit of the doubt, who should walk through the partly open front door but Beattie, who was almost sober by this time. When they questioned her she came out with a story almost identical to the one that Bob had already delivered.

Although the policemen had no option but to accept their story they still took them down to headquarters in Cape Town for further interrogation. They were questioned more or less continuously for the rest of that night and for the better part of the next day but refused to deviate from the story they had already given. Finally the public prosecutor told the police that the case against Bob and Beattie for a charge of Immorality was not strong enough to stand up in court and they were released, but not before they had both been warned of the direct consequences if a similar situation ever arose between them. They were allowed to leave separately later that evening.

Later that night, Beattie removed all her belongings from the Sea Point flat and took them to her sister's home, and moved in with her for a week or two to let things cool down. After listening to Bob's frightening description of what had taken place, I told him that he would be very foolish to let Beattie move back into that flat with him. 'They'll have an eye on you from now on, my lad,' I told him, but my advice was completely ignored and within three weeks, Beattie was back again – complete with the family portraits.

Some months after all this happened, Beattie discovered that the police had been tipped off by a former friend of hers, who had been going around saying that Beattie was too high and mighty now because she had a wealthy white boyfriend whom she was living with. Foolishly, Beattie had allowed this woman to discover the location of Bob's new flat. I heard through the grapevine that the informer had been waiting for a bus late one night on Main Road, Sea Point. Unfortunately for her, Beattie appeared from a nearby alleyway and after a brief altercation dragged the woman into the alley and almost killed her. The informer was taken off to hospital suffering from multiple injuries and after recovering left the district permanently. Cape Coloured people can be extremely vindictive when wronged and Beattie, although she had a heart of gold, was an extremely tough bird; if given a choice, I would have preferred taking on Muhammad Ali for three rounds rather than Beattie for one. For one thing, Muhammad Ali would have fought fair.

Another horrific incident took place not long after this. I was sitting alone with Cynthia in her little room at Wynberg when the door opened and in reeled Rosanna in a drunken state. This would not have mattered if she hadn't brought with her a next-door neighbour, also a coloured lady.

'This is the little girl I was telling you about,' Rosanna slurred. 'And this is her nice English boyfriend. He's sticking by her, you know.'

I said nothing but I was absolutely stunned at this stupid performance on Rosanna's part and I knew at once that I would have to seek another refuge for Cynthia.

The whole thing was getting out of hand and I was bone-weary with worry and tension. No wonder I was drinking brandy – and now Smirnoff Blue Label vodka – as if there would be no tomorrow. I knew that if I carried on like this for much longer it would begin to affect my mental health seriously. As it was I had become almost paranoid in my moments alone. I actually began to think that even my few close friends such as Basil and Brenda had somehow discovered my secret and were laughing at me behind my back, just waiting for the right moment before having us arrested so that my own happiness and life would be totally destroyed. I even suspected Bob of being a clever member of the Special Branch who had been planted on me. I couldn't speak for Cynthia's state of mind. She took it all well enough but I could tell, by the way she would sit for long moments lost in her own thoughts, that she was dreadfully anxious about our situation. If I had been in her position, and carrying a baby, I honestly don't know what I would have done.

From then on, we decided, I would visit her at Rosanna's in the early hours of the morning. Rosanna would be asleep by then and there would be less chance of her bringing in more 'sympathetic' strangers to have a good look at Cynthia and me. The arrangement was that I would arrive around two or three a.m. I would alert Cynthia with a gentle, coded knock at the window which was just above her bed, and she would get up and let me in quietly through the front door. We kept this routine up for a couple of weeks but it began wearing us both down. I developed magnificent bags under my eyes which sparked off some dirty remarks at the office, and apart from my own discomfort, I was interrupting Cynthia's sleep. For an expectant mum, this was not a satisfactory arrangement.

During one of my visits Cynthia told me that some people had called in to see Rosanna and had warned her that they had heard a neighbour telling someone else that 'a white man calls there to see a pregnant coloured girl'. As soon as I heard this latest bit of heart-warming news, I realised that our little arrangement with Rosanna had come to a shuddering halt. I told Cynthia not to be alarmed about this as I would not allow her to be subjected to any unpleasantness. 'Just quietly get your things together, darling,' I told her. 'You're moving out of here tomorrow.' Rosanna had no idea where I lived in Rondebosch, and I decided there and then to take Cynthia and her precious 'bump' to my cottage where she would just have to stay quietly for a while until I managed to find another permanent place to move her into.

She was as worried about this as I was but we agreed that we had no alternative. The next night I told Rosanna that Cynthia's sister's husband had managed to obtain a bigger house for his family and they were prepared to take Cynthia in with them. I told her how grateful we both were for her kindness and when I slipped her two bottles of good quality brandy and twenty rand as a bonus, she was very happy about the arrangement. She agreed to let us leave Cynthia's furniture there for a few days and I said I would pay her rent while the stuff was in her room.

We packed a few things that Cynthia would need on an everyday basis and made our way safely to the cottage, where we received a warm and friendly welcome from Fred who appeared genuinely pleased to see Cynthia again.

THE POLICE RAID

Cynthia remained in hiding in the cottage for five weeks. It was murder, especially for her, and though she never complained it was not easy to keep her cheerful all the time. I was acutely aware of her condition as she was now seven months pregnant and I was anxious about her well-being. She couldn't go for regular walks or get proper exercise and she had no company apart from myself, Fred and an occasional stealthy visit from Cathy. Cathy usually had to go through the same silly entry procedure to the cottage that Cynthia had used so many times, although there were occasional nights when the Watcher and his wife were out and she could walk into the house in a normal, dignified way.

Marie was a bit puzzled as to why I always left the curtains drawn while I was at the office. She had also been used to popping in on the odd occasion to give the place a bit of a clean-out for me. This was simple kindness on her part; she would have been insulted if I had offered to pay her for this little service. Dreadful though I felt, I had to discourage this homely act. Poor Cynthia was tremendously limited in her movements during the times that I left her alone in the house. She constantly had to remind herself not to flush the toilet or make any suspicious noises while there on her own. Marie might have thought a burglar had broken in and she would have forced an entry which would have been disastrous.

Our little ploy to gain Spot's friendship began to pay off. I told Cynthia that she would have to have some gentle walks around the garden and get some fresh air otherwise lack of exercise might affect the baby and herself. We took to getting up at four-thirty every morning, just before dawn broke, and we would walk silently around the garden, with my arm around her. At first Spot didn't know what to make of this, but a bit of topside kept him quiet and happy and eventually he took no further notice of us. It was a good idea and Cynthia loved the little breaks outside. The cool, fresh air against our skin was wonderful after both being cooped up in the house, apart from when I went into Cape Town to the office and returned in the evening. Cynthia was also going short of sunshine so when I came home in the evenings, and at the weekends, I would open the windows in the lounge and she would sit there taking a bit of sunshine in as it filtered through the hedge.

One afternoon, while we were both sitting near the open window listening to the turned-down record player, I heard the snap of a twig outside in the little walkway that ran from the garden along the side of the house. As quick as a flash I hauled Cynthia up and almost thrust her into the spare bedroom just before Dan's cheerful face appeared at the open window.

'Sorry to disturb you, John. Just clearing away a few bits of dead wood from the path.' We chatted for a few minutes until he heard Marie calling for him. I closed the window and drew the curtains and called Cynthia to come back to the lounge. It was a narrow squeak. The squeaks seemed to be getting narrower and my recovery time from them, longer. To the brandy bottle once more.

Each night we would go through a tiresome but vital safety check before going to bed. I had bought a monocular at a camera shop in the city and used it every night to scrutinise the Watcher's domain through the curtains in our unlit front room. After this procedure, we would go into the kitchen to make a final cup of coffee and say,

'What do you think?'

'Do you *feel* safe?'

If we both *felt* safe we would go to bed reasonably early after my now normal bathroom-scanning routine, and making sure that the black plastic escape bag was in its place beside the bed ready to be seized in an emergency.

If for some reason neither of us felt safe we would sit quietly in the kitchen, drinking numerous cups of tea or coffee until possibly two or three in the morning, before going to bed. During this time the escape bag would be with us in the kitchen. On reflection I realised that we had now been living this surrealistic existence for almost two years. We read, with a mixture of sympathy and horror, the accounts which appeared in the newspapers describing immorality cases. Most of the unhappy couples involved didn't seem to have lasted very long with their illicit relationships, and it struck me that we had probably achieved some sort of record for keeping out of the clutches of the authorities.

Cynthia, because of her youth no doubt, was holding up a lot better than me under the strain imposed upon us by our own actions. She wasn't working her way through a bottle a day for a start, I thought wryly. I was becoming short-tempered and irritable and I must have been a bit difficult to live with at times. If Cynthia thought so she never reproached me and was a great comfort when my morale was at a low ebb. Despite my problems and my predilection for brandy and vodka – what a combination – I still got through a good day's work every day and there were no complaints. I was earning pretty good money at that time and we needed a good income with the baby due to appear in the not-too-distant future. I couldn't afford to find myself out of a job under these circumstances. What helped to keep my spine stiff was the knowledge that I was going to be a father. The child nestling in Cynthia's womb was totally dependent on me and that was a good enough reason for sticking it out and not cracking up.

Bob indicated one evening that he knew of a way that we could make eighteen thousand rand for an investment of only five hundred. I was suspicious at once as he passed this confidential information to me over a drink in our corner of the lounge at the Regency. He was in one of his particularly furtive moods and kept casting beady glances around, not that there was a soul in sight apart from our many reflections from the large, ornate mirrors surrounding us.

He asked if I could raise a couple of hundred rand. I nodded and sat waiting. It appeared that his car-dealer friend Eric had made a strong contact with a person from South-West Africa who wanted to dispose of a tobacco-tin full of illicit diamonds and was prepared to do so for the modest sum of five hundred rand. I asked Bob if he had seen this tin of diamonds himself, at which he shook his head.

'Wot do you think?' he asked as he stood up to fetch another drink.

I pointed towards the bar. 'Fetch the drinks and I'll let you know when you come back.' I then told him that I preferred to stick to good old-fashioned immorality. 'If I get caught red-handed, I might find myself getting seven years' hard labour but would probably do only two.' I tapped my fingers on the arm of the chair. 'On the other hand, if I get caught by the police for buggering around with Illicit Diamond Buying, you know as well as I do that I'd get ten years HL and would disappear from the court so fast that my feet wouldn't touch the floor.' I had heard of a number of people who had made themselves rich for the rest of their lives by dabbling in IDB. I had also heard of several others who were still languishing in some tough South African prison after many years. I wanted nothing to do with such a caper.

Bob reacted to my views with what could only be described as 'feeling': 'You can't turn down a chance like this, man. What about your future, and your baby who's on the way?'

I shook my head slowly as I told him, 'I want absolutely nothing to do with his venture, Bob; I'll make my money my own way if you don't mind. And one of my main reasons for turning the offer down *is* the baby and its future. Thanks all the same.' But I said I would be interested in knowing how it would all turn out. 'If ever a bloke needs a break it is Eric so I hope his dream becomes a reality, Bob. Wish him luck from me.'

Two nights later when I walked into the Regency bar, I found Eric talking to Bob; rather surprising as Eric seldom visited the Regency. When he saw me, he nodded a bit sheepishly, no doubt still smarting after our difference of opinion about the Ford Prefect. I greeted him with a friendly smile and a handshake to put his mind at rest as I don't bear grudges. I ordered a round and Bob winked craftily in the direction of the lounge. I took the hint and followed him and Eric, and we sat around our usual table in the corner, but before Bob or Eric could start I said,

'If it's anything to do with what you told me the other day, Bob, I can tell you now that you will be wasting your time if you're planning on including me in the deal. If we are just going to have a few drinks and a laugh together, then that's perfectly OK by me.'

Bob ignored my comments. 'Look, John, I don't want to see you lose out on this deal. You could regret it for the rest of your life.' He went on to tell me that the bloke with the diamonds would be on his way back to South-West Africa within the next few days and time was running out for us to take advantage of the offer.

I looked across at Eric. 'Have you actually set eyes on these stones, Eric?' I asked.

'Yes!' he said eagerly.

'And would you know what an uncut diamond looks like?' I went on.

'Well, actually,' he said, 'they look a bit like a lot of small pebbles.'

I took a drink from my glass. 'What makes you think that they are anything other than just pebbles?' I persisted.

Eric seemed to have been won over by the man from SWA and was convinced that what he had been shown in the old tobacco tin had been the real thing. 'Good industrial stones' was what the dealer had described them as.

They were looking at me expectantly and I repeated that I wanted absolutely nothing to do with any deal that would make my life any more complicated than it was already. 'Look, Eric, let me give you a word of advice. If you insist on getting involved in this business don't discuss it with anyone else and furthermore before buying insist on examining the stones under a black light.' Eric looked puzzled. 'Ultra-violet, Eric. You can buy UV bulbs if you ask around.'

Bob chipped in. 'What happens when you put the stones under UV light?'

'When the dealer opens the tin it will look as if it is full of blueish-white fire. If it doesn't, you had better hold on to your money.'

I heard from Bob a day or two later that Eric had taken my advice. When he had insisted on looking at the stones in ultra-violet light, the dealer had promised to arrange it but that was the last that Eric saw of him. He was probably an *agent provocateur* from the South African diamond squad deliberately trying to trap us.

Cynthia was in very low spirits from having been more or less locked away in the cottage for over five weeks. Something would have to be done to cheer her up. Against my better judgement I decided that I would arrange to take Bob to the cottage to meet her and we could have a nice little supper together. Although he had his faults I felt that I could rely on him to keep his mouth shut. I suggested that he might like to stay with us for the weekend in which case I would collect him on the Friday.

He was very flattered by the invitation and when I went to pick him up on Friday evening I found him sitting expectantly in the Regency bar wearing his navy-blue suit and looking very spruce and dapper. On the floor beside the bar stool was a small weekend bag.

When we parked outside the cottage just after eight o'clock I wondered what the Watcher might be thinking – if he was on duty. Probably that I had gone queer or something. Cynthia had cheered up considerably and had been busy tidying around in my absence. She was genuinely pleased to meet Bob and made a fuss of him and while she was making coffee in the kitchen, Bob looked across at me and said,

'Blimey! No wonder you've been keepin' 'er to yourself, you crafty old sod!'

Bob's naturally homely manner made Cynthia feel at ease with him and it was good to see her in the kitchen, happily humming while she cooked a meal for us.

The weekend was a great success and Bob stayed with us until Sunday evening when I drove him back to Sea Point where Beattie was waiting for him. Before I left to return to Rondebosch, we arranged to meet in the Regency one evening in the coming week.

During one of our quiet moments that week, when we were content to sit back on the settee just talking and planning our future, Cynthia nestled close to me and said softly,

'Do you think she'll be dark like me?'

We both seemed to know instinctively that the coming baby would be a girl.

'What do you mean, dark? You're not so dark; a nice coffee colour really. If I'm crackers about you, are you seriously suggesting that I might reject my own daughter if she is the same colour as you?'

I had noticed that the Cape Coloureds had their own colour

prejudices; the darker the person, the lower down the social scale they were placed. Once while I was walking through Cape Town two coloured women were hurling insults at each other from opposite sides of the road. The lighter-skinned woman had the last word when she yelled out at the darker lady, 'You bleddy Hottentot!' which was a reflection on the unfortunate victim's ancestors.

Cynthia was no exception to this prejudice and she desperately wanted her baby to be as light-skinned as possible. I continually assured her that it was of little importance as far as I was concerned but I could see that it was of great importance to her.

I went through to the kitchen to make coffee for us before going to bed and heard Spot sniffing at the gap under the back door. I opened the fridge and cut a slice of topside for him, which he received with wagging tail and slavering jaws; he trotted off into the darkness with his booty and I stood on the step for a few minutes waiting for the kettle to boil. It was a nice night, dark, cool, but not chilly.

The kettle was boiling and I closed the door and locked and bolted it. I made a practice of oiling the locks, hinges and bolts of all the doors in the cottage, just to be on the safe side. When I carried the two cups of coffee into the lounge, Cynthia was lying back against the settee with her eyes closed. I put her cup down on the table and tickled the end of her nose.

'Come on, Mum, don't go to sleep here. Drink your coffee, there's a good girl.'

We sat side by side enjoying our nightcaps. It was now getting on for one o'clock and I felt relaxed and safe. I always convinced myself, wrongly of course, that if we remained 'unvisited' until about this time in the morning, the chances of our being raided were extremely remote.

We finished our coffee and I helped Cynthia up; she was beginning to get a big girl by now and I would be a father in two months' time. I helped her into bed and made her comfortable before going on my rounds and tidying up in the kitchen. When I returned to the bedroom Cynthia was already asleep; she had had a long day and it was hardly surprising that she was tired out.

I lay beside her and put out the bedside light, and she

moved in her sleep and slid an arm over my tummy. I kissed the top of her head and whispered, 'Sleep well, my love.' I was still wakeful; perhaps my subconscious was over-alert or something. After a final cigarette I lay down and tried to sleep. I kept wondering about how we would fit in if we managed to get to England. I had read in South African newspapers about reluctance among some British people to accept the presence of coloured people in their society.

I had read, too, about the Race Relations Act. Society could introduce as many acts as it wished to punish people for being unkind or inconsiderate to people of other races, but they couldn't bring in a bill to make people like each other. It occurred to me that if we had all been the same colour there would have been plenty left for biased people to moan about: never trust anyone with red hair, for example, or, have you noticed how people with flat feet always smell. Then, of course, there were always the different religions to fall back on. I turned to Cynthia and putting an arm around her closed my eyes.

Something woke me with a start and I heard Cynthia's voice, hoarse with fear: 'John! Quick, wake up, it's the police!' I sat up in alarm. For a moment I thought it was just a bad dream but when I suddenly heard the guttural sound of Afrikaans being spoken from a mobile radio system outside the house, and the thrumming of the exhaust of a truck, I knew what we had been dreading for so long was actually happening.

I leapt out of bed. 'Do exactly as I tell you and we'll be all right,' I whispered, wishing that I felt as confident as my own words. Cynthia was already out of bed and in the subdued light of the window I saw that she had grabbed hold of the escape bag.

Silhouetted against the drawn curtains were two figures; one was wearing a peaked hat and the other one was bareheaded. I couldn't understand what they were saying, as they were speaking in Afrikaans to each other. I grabbed Cynthia by the arm and we scurried down to the kitchen. There was a thunderous knocking at the front door and for a moment I thought that my bowels were going to let me down.

I threw her duffel coat around her shoulders and with shaking hands fumbled with the bolts of the back door. I was in such a panic I could hardly breathe. When I tried to whisper words of reassurance to Cynthia, I found myself lisping with fear. It was a most terrifying moment. I thanked God that we had taken the precaution to win Spot's friendship. Apart from sniffing around Cynthia's ankles and growling in a subdued manner, he showed no vicious intent.

There was silence from the front of the house and at any moment I half-expected to hear the breaking of glass and the splintering of wood as the police forced an entry. They had been known to do so. Although it was not very cold, Cynthia was shaking and so was I. I told her to put her coat on properly while I fetched a chair from the kitchen for her to stand on, so that it would be easier for her to get over the fence.

As we both climbed up onto the swaying chair, Spot suddenly took off and headed towards Marie's back gate which led into the road at the front. The police were trying to get in through it. Spot started barking and snarling savagely and would have gone for them if they had got in. Meanwhile Cynthia and I were experiencing some difficulties. Our combined weight had caused the two back legs of the chair to sink into the soft earth.

'Grab the fence, love, and heave yourself up and I will lift you at the same time.'

She pushed herself up and with a superhuman effort on my part I managed to get her safely over the fence. There was a thud from the other side and I winced and prayed to God that she and the baby would be all right. I heard her making her way down the garden to the shrubbery at the end and I hid the chair at the side of the house and quickly filled the holes in the earth by scuffing my foot hurriedly across them. After this I shot back inside leaving Spot barking excitedly outside the back door.

There was no sound from the front of the house and I went into the bathroom and put on the lights and went through the motions of making normal use of it, including flushing the toilet. If they recommenced battering the front door I intended to open it with the excuse that I suffered from chronic constipation, hence the delay in answering their knock. At the present time, chronic constipation was the last thing I was suffering from – quite the contrary actually.

Fortunately there were no further knocks at my door and with forced cheerfulness I attempted to whistle but didn't seem to be able to control my lips. After a while I left the bathroom and hurried along the hallway towards the front door. There didn't appear to be anyone outside but they could have been standing to one side or perhaps out in the road. As I opened the door my legs felt boneless and my very appearance would have aroused any self-respecting policeman's suspicions immediately. To my relief there was no one there but I saw the back end of a police truck with the red rear-light blazing angrily in the dark road. That was enough for me and I quickly closed the door again. I'd done my duty as a good citizen: the police had knocked – for lack of a better description – I had duly answered their knock and if they had taken it upon themselves not to be there when I opened the door, then that was their bloody fault.

I scuttled back to the kitchen and went through a quite gutless procedure of hand-wringing, trembling and muttering mindlessly to myself. It must have been a very convincing performance at the time and although I can smile when I think about it now, it was far from funny to me then. I was worried about Cynthia and hoped that she was all right. By this time my shocked nervous system needed fortifying and a very large Smirnoff Blue Label soon stopped the hand-wringing. I suddenly realised that I was a bit chilly which was not surprising as I was only wearing underpants. The cool night air from the garden plus the after-effects of shock were catching up with me, and I made my way rather stealthily back to the bedroom where I slipped on a pair of casual pants and a sweater. The police truck was still parked in the road and I heard footsteps and the door of the truck slammed shut. A moment later someone started driving off and I kept my head cocked to one side as I heard the truck disappearing in the distance. I waited for a few minutes to see whether they might return but nothing untoward happened.

I peered through the front window, but the Watcher's house was in darkness and there was a suspicious stillness about the road and the shadowy garden across the way. I was surprised. After the noise the police had made I would have expected half the street to be awake wondering what was going on.

Something was bothering me. I couldn't put a finger on it but I knew something wasn't right out there and I continued my vigil for some little while before returning to the back of the house. This sixth sense of mine was fairly acute and I had ignored it twice previously, to my cost. The first time was when I was on a motor-cycling holiday in Cornwall. Shortly before getting up in the little inn I had stopped at for the night, I had a vivid dream which involved me in a motor-cycling accident. It was so realistic that it woke me and I could remember now the feeling of relief that I experienced when I realised that it had only been a dream. Less than an hour later, after I had breakfasted and ridden away from the hotel, I was involved in exactly the same incident that had taken place in the dream. If I had taken the route I had originally planned instead of suddenly changing it, would this accident still have happened? I have often wondered.

Another time, I had been staying at a hotel in Durban while visiting the city on business. I had just finished lunch and was waiting with a small group of people for a lift to take me up to my room. There were two lifts, one was manually operated and one was fully automatic. A few days before I had taken a sudden dislike to the manually operated lift and from then on used only the automatic lift. While waiting for the lift I prayed that the automatic lift would be the first to arrive.

Unfortunately the manually operated lift arrived first and when the doors opened I couldn't step back because of the crowd behind me. I was more or less impelled into the lift. Shrugging indifferently I put my feelings down to foolishness. A few moments later the lift, while on its way up to the top floor, suddenly paused between the fourth and fifth floors and then plummeted down to the basement. Fortunately no one was seriously injured and apart from a few bruises I was unhurt. However, it took engineers some time to get us out of the lift car because it had crashed down well below floor level and had to be manhandled with crowbars. Since then I have treated my sixth sense with more respect and this is why I felt extremely uneasy about the house across the way.

Back in the kitchen I put the kettle on as Cynthia would need a hot drink after shivering at the end of the chapel garden for the best part of an hour. It seemed safe enough now at the back of the house, and I unbolted the kitchen door and stepped outside into the garden. All was still and quiet and Spot came over wagging his tail with delight; he obviously thought that this was some kind of eccentric game that humans enjoyed and he was more than willing to participate.

Wedging the chair against the fence once more and this time finding a firmer surface for it to stand on, I climbed up gingerly and peered hopefully down towards the shrubs at the end of the garden. There was no movement and I attempted a subdued little whistle, but my lips were still not functioning properly so I called out quietly, 'Cynthia! It's me. Come on, it's OK now.' Silence, so I tried again, only a little louder this time.

There was a rustling noise and Cynthia emerged huddled up in her duffel coat and clutching the escape bag. She had dressed but she looked cold and frightened. I raised a finger to my lips to caution her to be quiet. Leaning over I whispered, 'I think they have gone now but I am not happy about those buggers over the road, so you had better hang on there for a while longer. I've made you a hot drink.' I passed the steaming mug over to her and she smiled bravely. 'Go back down the garden, love. I won't be very long. I told you we would be all right.' She slipped silently away and vanished into the shrubs and I got off the chair, stuck it in its hiding place and went back into the house.

I flopped down wearily at the kitchen table and poured myself another stiff drink. So this is what it's like, I thought as I sipped the strong liquor. I knew then how Jewish people must have felt in Germany during the evil days of Hitler in the thirties. Hounded down at all times of day and night because they were 'different'. Waiting for the dreaded knock of the Gestapo in the early hours of the morning.

Here I was living in a country that had actually helped to destroy Naziism during the war but now, in many ways, was adopting against its own citizens tactics of terrorism not so far removed from those used by the Nazis. Black people were compelled to carry passes, reminiscent of the period when the Jews in Germany were compelled to walk around with racial identification marks on their clothing; whole families were uprooted from areas that they had lived in and loved for generations and made to settle in areas they disliked; anyone who was not white was a second-class citizen and any who criticised the system or actively broke the laws of apartheid were considered to be active communists – or insane!

In falling in love with this beautiful coloured girl I had committed a most heinous crime according to South African law. If we could have been allowed to live openly and freely together in love and peace, South Africa would not have lost anything; on the contrary, she would have gained three – with Hanna – very proud and patriotic citizens. There was and still is much that I admire and love about South Africa.

As I mentally rambled on, reflecting on the curious laws of the Republic, I remembered another little anomaly which took a bit of understanding. At that time, the Japanese were buying large deposits of iron ore from South Africa. The twisted, two-faced logic of Pretoria granted all Japanese citizens Honorary White status in the Republic; for example, a visiting Japanese businessman could, if he so desired, take a white lady out for dinner somewhere, but was not allowed to marry her, at least not in the Republic. On the other hand, Chinese people were considered to be coloured.

During this period there was a well-known drinking and dancing haunt in Cape Town known as the Navigator's Den. Inside it was so dark that half the time it was difficult to know who the hell you were dancing with. To cut a long story short, a Japanese crew from a fishing boat bumped into a crew of Chinese sailors and, probably as a result of the crazy racial policies, it was put about that members of the Japanese crew were ribbing the Chinese sailors. The outcome was one of the biggest knife fights ever seen by the police in Cape Town.

With one more look out of the front-room window and after satisfying myself that it would be safe to bring Cynthia back over the fence again, I went out into the garden and went through the chair-climbing routine once more. Cynthia came out of hiding and after a good deal of heaving and hauling and a few muttered obscenities, I managed to drag her back over the fence unharmed. The chair heeled over ominously as we stepped down. Picking it up, I led her gently back into the house and locked the door behind me. She was chilled now, I could see, and I brought the electric fire into the kitchen and she sat by the glow as I made her another hot drink. She had been very brave and I was proud of her, but very upset at what she had been forced to go through.

She looked down at the mug of coffee in her hands and spoke. 'I don't have to tell you what I think about you, do I, John?' she asked and my heart sank as I feared what she was going to say. She leaned towards me and I took her in my arms as she lay against me, weeping. I didn't want to lose this woman in my life but at the same time I knew I was asking too much of her; she was too young to be subjected to this sort of degradation and the risk that she had endured this night.

If things had gone badly wrong and we had been caught fair and square, she would have received short shrift from her gaolers. She would have had it very hard compared to me. Our 'crime' would have featured in every rag in the Republic and every sordid detail of the evidence would have been printed – and we would certainly have received stiff prison sentences.

But Cynthia clung to me desperately and said between sobs, 'God didn't let us meet to see us torn away from each other. He was here protecting us tonight, I am sure of that, and we must stick together no matter what.'

I sat holding her, just thinking. As a rather hard-boiled advertising man I had met all types of people during my life and experienced all manner of things. I regret to admit that so far I had seen more of the worst side of human nature than the good, and as a result I had become cynical. My early-taught Christian beliefs had long since been chipped away by the harsh realities of life, and if prior to this anyone had spoken such words I might have smiled disdainfully at the best or, at the worst, laughed aloud in contempt.

Now as we sat there clinging to each other I thought very seriously about what she had just said, and a flood of emotion welled up inside me. Perhaps we were not so alone in our trials after all. I too had been through a very testing time and the combination of what had taken place tonight plus the strains imposed on me over a now very long period was almost too much for me; I had to fight desperately for a while to prevent myself from breaking down. Cynthia needed a rock at the present time, not a blancmange. However, from that night on, while we remained in South Africa, I always had this strange feeling that someone 'up there' approved of our association and would cover us with a 'divine mantle' of protection.

It was almost four-thirty in the morning and dawn was not so far away. I told Cynthia to stay where she was while I made my weary way back to the front bedroom where I once more peered steadily across the road, using the monocular this time. I studied the window carefully but there was no sign of enemy activity. Nevertheless I still felt 'funny' and wasn't at ease at all. To the right of the house was a small tree and I moved the monocular over to the shadowy area beneath it. Just as I was about to move it away, more or less satisfied that we were no longer in any danger, I froze as I saw the glow of a cigarette. I probably wouldn't have noticed it if the smoker hadn't been taking a draw at that moment.

The cunning bastards, I thought. My instincts were right after all. The truck had driven off and they had left an observer behind in the hope that we might leave together, in which case we would have been arrested.

I went back to the kitchen and closed the door behind me and put on the light. For a moment my eyes were dazzled by the brightness having been in the dark for such a long time. Cynthia could tell that something was wrong by the look on my face. I sat down and told her what I had seen.

'Well, love, we'll now find out how much Ramona loves you. You have no option but to go to her and ask her to put you up for a few days until we have found somewhere safe for you. You can't stay here a moment longer. I know now that those buggers across the road have twigged on to what we are up to, and I won't allow you to end up in Roeland Street, especially not in your condition.'

We were now faced with the problem of getting her out of the cottage without our friend across the road spotting her. I had already worked out something that I thought would get her away safely. I explained carefully and made sure that she understood quite clearly what she had to do.

'I'm afraid you will have to climb over the fence one more time, love,' I said ruefully.

She just shrugged and said, 'I'm getting quite used to it now.'

I hoped my plan would work. The chapel gardens extended

over a wide frontage and were protected by a chain-link fence. The gate leading to the chapel was in the centre of this fence. The police observer across the road would be able to see the complete frontage of these gardens if he were to look that way but he wouldn't be able to look at two places at the same time. If Cynthia were to climb over the chain-link fence in the front corner furthest away from the cottage while I distracted the observer, she would stand a good chance of escaping unseen. She listened to my plan carefully and nodded in agreement and assured me that it was a good idea. It was the only one I had.

Before she disappeared over the fence again, we agreed to meet that night at nine as I felt it was time that Ramona and I met. Cynthia wasn't very keen on this last idea but she agreed that it was silly for us to carry on like this as Ramona would find out sooner or later in any case.

Once more I assisted her over the fence and we agreed to wait for five minutes to give her ample time to reach the corner of the chapel's chain-link fence before I started my performance in the bedroom. I watched over the fence as she carefully made her way to the other side of the garden. Returning the chair to the kitchen and once more hiding all traces of our activities in the garden, I impatiently looked at my watch. When the five minutes had elapsed I went through to the front bedroom. Pulling the curtains open, I put the lights on and sat on the bed and waited for what I thought would be more than enough time for Cynthia to have climbed the fairly low chain-link fence and made her way through a small lane to the main road, where she would be able to catch an early bus to Athlone.

Satisfied that she would have made good her escape by now I walked over to the window and gave the hidden observer a deliberate two-fingered salute before closing the curtains again and going back into the kitchen. By this time it was early dawn and I was physically and mentally exhausted after what could only be described as a traumatic night. I decided not to go to work and I showered and went to bed instead.

When I woke later, I telephoned the office to let them know that I would not be in as I was feeling a bit under par, which was quite true of course. During the day I thrust Cynthia's suitcases up into the cock-loft and made sure that there were no traces of her former presence in the house – just in case the police decided to pay me a routine call.

At about half-past-five I heard a knock at the back door and metaphorically pulling myself together I walked through to the kitchen and prepared myself for a spot of cross-examination by Marie. I knew that she and Dan must have heard the commotion during the night.

'Hello, you old bugger,' she greeted me cheerfully enough. 'You're looking a bit rough.' She told me that she had noticed my car on the verge and had knocked at the back door a couple of times, thinking I was sick. She must have knocked while I had been asleep. I explained that I had been out very late and had a bit of a skinful and still had a lousy hangover. She grinned and told me that I had missed all the fun. I tried to look suitably mystified and asked what she meant.

She and Dan, she said, had been woken up at about one-thirty when Spot started barking his head off. She got up and found a couple of uniformed policemen fiddling around with her side gate. When she asked them what they wanted, disturbing people at that time of the morning, they replied that they must have come to the wrong place. Apparently she told them to bugger off before she set the dog on them, and gave them a mouthful of Afrikaans abuse. 'They won't come messing around here again in a hurry,' she laughed. After their misfortune in meeting the ebullient Marie, they left shortly afterwards with a flea in their ears.

She asked if there was anything I needed and I thanked her and said I was perfectly OK. I went back and flopped down on the settee and began to prepare myself mentally for the forthcoming, dreaded meeting with Ramona. How would she react? Well, whatever she said or even did, could not be any worse than what we had gone through during the night.

An almost pathetic *mreeouwl* from the direction of the front door reminded me that Fred had been shut out for most of the day and was probably very hungry. When I opened the door he trotted in, clearly pleased to see me, with his abbreviated tail thrust high, and he went through his customary ritual of ankle-rubbing and purring. I gave him a pat and he scampered off happily towards the kitchen looking for his food.

I lounged around going over the previous night's events and

wondering what pleasure the people across the road had gained from tipping off the police. I also wondered why the police had called last night. Cynthia had not set foot outside for weeks so she couldn't have been seen entering the house. The curtains were always drawn so they could not have seen her through the window. It puzzled me. The only thing I could think of was that Cynthia must have glanced out of the window one afternoon while I was at the office, from sheer boredom, and the Watcher might have caught sight of her.

I wasn't hungry so I went off to the bathroom and enjoyed a hot shower. I shaved carefully and took extra special care with my selection of clothing and my grooming. After all, it was going to be a big night – I was going to meet the family. I had a good look at myself in the mirror. Although I was past forty years of age, I still managed to look no more than thirty, despite having drunk enough vodka and brandy to put twenty years on me. I always feared that one morning I would peer into the bathroom mirror to discover that my face had done a 'Dorian Gray' on me, and I would be terror-stricken to find myself staring into the eyes of a haggard old wreck.

After dressing I decided that despite my lack of appetite it would be wise to eat something, so I had a bit of smoked fish with a poached egg flopped on top of it. Still with time to spare, I tidied up the kitchen a bit and mooched aimlessly round the house casting an eye at the brandy bottle. However, I felt sure that if I rolled into Ramona's presence smelling like a distillery it would not be a good start to what could anyway be a very shaky relationship, so I forgot the brandy.

I left the house in good time to meet Cynthia, and as I started the motor of the little car I cast a glance across at the enemy lines. No action there; perhaps a spot of wound-licking was taking place, accompanied by muttered threats, of course. Cynthia was waiting at our rendezvous but I could tell by the fact that she didn't move when she recognised me that someone else was around, and this was her warning for me to continue driving, which I did, without delay. I made a couple of diversionary trips around the block and finally parked a little way up the road from where I had seen her earlier.

I switched off the motor and lights and lit a cigarette. Shortly afterwards a silent figure walked past my car from behind and cast a look inside as he went by. When this person had gone Cynthia appeared by the passenger door and I let her in.

'Turn round,' she said. 'Don't go that way.'

I started the engine and did a U-turn and as we drove off she told me that the man had walked past her three times since she had been waiting for me: 'I think he is suspicious about you, too.'

I asked her how she had got on after leaving the cottage that morning. She said that a white man had approached her as she was waiting for the bus and had asked where she was going. She told him that she was on her way to her sister's home. When he asked where she lived she told him to mind his own bloody business, but he warned her that he was a police officer. 'He wanted to know where I had been,' she said, 'so I told him that I had been visiting relatives in Malmesbury and some friends had dropped me off by the bus stop.' Apparently the man had stared at her suspiciously for several minutes before nodding and walking away.

She went on to tell me that Ramona had suspected that something of the sort had happened and had been more understanding about the situation than Cynthia had expected – until she mentioned my racial classification. That did it and Cynthia was subjected to a good hour of sisterly lambasting until Ramona finally ran out of steam and burst into tears. However, she became calmer when Cynthia told her about the way I had stuck by her and been kind to her. When Cynthia told Ramona that I was going to take her away from South Africa and marry her, Ramona just gave her a look and said, 'If he does he will be the only one that has that I know of.'

The forthcoming meeting didn't sound very promising but it had to be faced as a lot now depended on Ramona's willingness to extend a little goodwill towards us.

We had now driven past the coloured township of Athlone and were making our way along Klipfontein Road which passes through the main non-white areas of Cape Town, such as Nyanga. Cynthia directed me down a left turning which led directly into the bleak suburb of Kew Town with its scruffy, sand-blown streets. I was a bit nervous because I had no right to be in this neighbourhood but I gritted my teeth and remembered the 'mantle of protection' that I felt was hiding us from our enemies. We stopped at the entrance to a courtyard of small houses.

'It's down there, John,' Cynthia said. 'I'm going in first and you follow a few minutes later. If you watch you should be able to see where I turn in and in any case there will be three orange lights in the window.' She got out of the car and spoke to me through the window. 'Knock on the door three times and Ramona's father-in-law will let you in,' and with that she was gone.

Here we go then, I thought, adjusting my tie for the possibly thousandth time. For this special occasion I was wearing a lightweight dark-blue suit as Cynthia wanted me to look my best when meeting Ramona. I felt a bit overdressed, actually. I had been well briefed by Cynthia while making our way here. 'Be polite and watch your language,' she had told me. A rabid-looking cur sidled past the car, oblivious of my presence; its ribs stood out pathetically as it trotted beneath a street light. The road seemed to be littered with bits of brick and broken glass.

I felt rather vulnerable, knowing that police patrols cruised around these areas at regular intervals. At last it was time for me to make my appearance and getting out of the car I closed and locked the door with great stealth before creeping into the court. Towards the end of the little street of houses I could see a bonfire. Its orange glow lit up the faces of children standing staring at it. I guessed that this was diverting their attention from me and I was grateful for the fire. The distance from my car to the house was no more than fifty yards but it felt a lot further to me that night and I was thankful when I opened the gate leading to it and knocked three times on the door, as instructed.

The dark windows nearby seemed to be staring at me in a hostile way, and a movement from the entrance to one of the houses betrayed the presence of two young coloured girls who had noticed me. My knowledge of the Afrikaans language was not very extensive but I understood the murmured 'Wit bastard' that came across to me. They didn't know me from a bar of soap so I could hardly blame them for being vindictive towards me. I might have been a policeman for all they knew.

I just hoped that they would not tip off a band of local

skollies – muggers – to wait for me to emerge again. At this point the door in front of me opened and a short, thickset coloured man with close-cropped white hair faced me. He seemed ill-at-ease but he was doing his best to welcome me politely. 'So you're Mr John, are you?' he asked, inviting me in. He held out his hand and I shook it and said, 'Yes, and I'm very pleased to meet you.'

He introduced himself and showed me into his home. The front door opened directly into the parlour, as they called it. It was bright and cheerful and gleaming with cleanliness. There was the usual big, family table in the middle of the room, covered by a yellow plush tablecloth and with a vase of plastic flowers standing in its centre. In a corner was a small fireplace and on the mantelpiece above it stood lots of family photographs in individual frames. The principle photograph was mounted in a heavy frame, on the wall above the fireplace. It was slightly faded and had been rather crudely hand-tinted. It showed a man in army uniform with several medal ribbons on his chest. I looked closely at it and identified the gentleman who had opened the door to me.

It was my chance to open a conversation. 'I see you did your bit during the war, Mr Du Plessis.' He smiled, pleased that I had recognised him in the photograph. He had been a driver with the South African army in the Western Desert and had been wounded twice. I thought how kind it was of his grateful country to stick him and others like him in dumps like this and treat them like second-rate citizens.

I mentioned my own wartime experiences and he flattered me by telling me that I looked too young to have been in the war, fighting. Shortly after this he excused himself and disappeared behind a beaded curtain suspended over an open doorway which led to the kitchen and bedrooms. A moment later a young coloured man entered the room, obviously to give me a once-over. This turned out to be Leonard, Ramona's husband. He was wearing a white shirt and tie, black trousers and a maroon V-necked pullover. He was smoking. He appraised me carefully but was very pleasant and explained that Ramona was busy with their small son and would be free in a moment. I put my hand in my pocket to pull out my cigarettes but Leonard produced a packet and offered them to me. I lit up and we stood together smoking and making small-talk.

After a while he too excused himself and disappeared behind the curtain, no doubt to give Ramona a quick run-down on me.

Shortly after another young chap came in and gave me a shy nod before sitting down on an old settee and picking up an even older magazine. He looked remarkably like Sammy Davis Junior but I thought it would not be prudent to mention this to him. I lit another cigarette and offered 'Sammy' one as well. He reached out and took it without looking up, and then produced a lighter which he lit and held out to me but without actually looking at me. A definite sign of friendship, I thought, as I leaned down and accepted the light.

The next person to enter the room for a quick eyeful of the new European prospective family member turned out to be the old man's wife, a little dumpling of a woman with grey hair. She was wearing a flour-covered apron and her arms seemed to be covered to the elbows in flour. Whenever I saw her after this, she always looked the same. She was a kind old lady who always made me feel welcome whenever I visited them. We talked for several minutes and when I made complimentary remarks about the cosiness of her home, she was genuinely pleased. So far so good, I thought, but I still had Ramona to face.

A few minutes later Leonard thrust his head through the bead curtains and said gravely, 'You can come through now.' I felt my confidence oozing away as I walked towards the curtains. Leonard was waiting for me outside a partly open door at the end of a corridor. He nodded me through into the room beyond and when I walked in Ramona was sitting on a large double bed while Cynthia perched nervously on the edge of an armchair in the corner. It wasn't a very big room and in addition to the bed and the chair, there was a large wardrobe beside which stood a dressing-table covered with family photographs and perfume bottles. A number of suitcases were piled neatly on top of the wardrobe and in a corner was a cot in which a small boy of about two years of age stood staring at me with large, dark eyes. He had a thumb stuck in his mouth.

Ramona didn't look a lot like Cynthia; she was at least ten years older and was inclined to be a bit plump and motherly.

Her pleasant face was rather sombre at that moment. She gave me a thorough good looking up and down and I felt myself being carefully assessed. Cynthia said something in Afrikaans and giggled nervously but a sharp retort from Ramona quickly wiped the grin off her face and she sat quietly twiddling her fingers. Ramona wanted to know everything: how had I met her sister, how long had I known her and what were my intentions regarding her condition? I told her the truth but I said nothing about the police raid as this would have upset her needlessly. I said that I was prepared to do anything that would protect Cynthia during her pregnancy and I wanted to take her out of South Africa as soon as reasonably possible after the child had been born.

She listened carefully without interrupting and when I finished she said, 'Obviously you have good feelings for my sister but I don't believe that you will take her with you when you go. This town is full of coloured girls with bastard children because of white men. Why should you be the exception?' She wasn't being nasty or deliberately unpleasant; she was merely telling me what she believed. I looked at Cynthia and asked her if she trusted me.

'You know very well that I do, John. I know that you will never let me down. You are the only man I trust – white or black.'

I turned to Ramona and said, 'I respect your point of view, Ramona, and also understand your concern about your sister. I'm glad that you care that much about her but I hope that you will learn to trust me. Believe me, I love Cynthia and I have only her best interests at heart.'

Ramona told me that if she had known about our relationship earlier she would have made efforts to stop it, even to the extent of going to the police to charge me with pestering her sister and inciting her to commit immorality. I told her that I was sorry she felt that way and what could we do now about Cynthia's immediate problem as it was not safe for her to continue living at my cottage. I pointed out that I was not a rich white man by any means but I would be able to provide for Cynthia's comfort and safety. 'She's my responsibility now, after all, and as far as I am concerned I'm her husband.'

Ramona spoke quietly to Cynthia and Leonard in Afrikaans

for a few minutes and excused herself for not speaking in English. 'It is easier for me to find the right words when I speak in my natural language,' she explained.

They finished talking among themselves and finally Ramona gave me a little smile and said, 'Well, I suppose we mustn't be inhospitable. Would you like some coffee and apple pie?' I nodded gratefully and felt more confident at this change in her attitude. It hadn't been such an ordeal after all. After Ramona and Leonard went out of the room, Cynthia looked a bit anxious. I stepped across and gave her a little kiss. 'Cheer up, darling, it's going to be all right, I can tell now.'

Ramona returned with a cup of coffee and a piece of pie and both were delicious. After a moment she said, 'We know of a place where Cynthia might be able to stay. It's a bit of a rough street but the people are all right. But I must warn you that if you decide to visit Cynthia while she is staying there, you will be taking your life into your own hands.' I didn't like the sound of that but Cynthia's safety was of paramount importance just at that moment. Ramona continued, 'It is the only place we can suggest but I will see that you and Cynthia are able to meet each other from time to time, so don't worry about that.' I agreed to go along with her on any arrangements as long as Cynthia would be OK. She made me give her my word that I would not try to call there to see Cynthia unless she had made the arrangements herself.

Leonard came into the room and said, 'Shall we go over there now and see what they think?' Ramona nodded and said, 'Yes. Let's go now while you are here. It will be safe enough at this time of night, especially if we are with you.' They went out to the car and I kissed Cynthia and told her to take care of herself. I gave her some extra money to tide her over until I saw her again and went out after Ramona and her husband.

When we arrived at Cynthia's next refuge I wasn't very impressed. In appearance it was only a shade better than the place where Beattie's mother lived in Elsies River. Banks of sand swept up into verges on either side of the heavily potholed street. Most of the street lights were not working and the few that were hardly threw down any useful illumination. It was a real cut-throat's paradise. As we bumped and lurched along in semi-darkness, Leonard told me to park at the end of the street next to a church. They felt it might be safer for me to leave the car there as the lighting was a bit better.

We got out and walked back down the grim-looking street and I thought that no one in their right mind would hang around in a place like that, which probably accounted for the fact that there wasn't another soul in sight. At last we reached a small gate which Leonard pushed open. It had a loud, agonising squeak and I made a mental note to oil it at the first opportunity in case nocturnal visits became necessary. We walked up a short, sandy path and Ramona knocked on the front door. It was opened almost immediately by a small, dark woman with black hair neatly parted in the centre. This was Leila, the wife of Kerim, who was going to be our genial host. They were Muslims and there were various extracts from the Koran mounted on the wall of their lounge.

The walls of the lounge were painted sky-blue and the customary table in the middle of the room was covered by a maroon cloth. There was a large, old-fashioned radiogram against one of the walls and four dining-room chairs ranged neatly alongside. To the left was an opening that led to the kitchen and Kerim and Leila's bedroom, and to the right was a door which opened into the small room that Cynthia would inhabit.

A short, slightly-built coloured man came out from the kitchen to greet us. This was Kerim, the master of the household, and after much shaking of hands we got down to the purpose of our visit. Kerim agreed to allow Cynthia to rent the room and it was agreed that he would decorate it. Leila would put new curtains at the window and would clean and polish the composition floor. I was quick to point out that I would pay for all the materials that they would need and also for Kerim's labour. On hearing this, Kerim's rubbery lips peeled back in a smile of real enthusiasm. I soon discovered that money motivated Kerim very quickly, and to mention it was to bring a smile to his face.

When the subject of monthly rental arose I proposed what I knew to be a very generous sum, which I regretted later. They readily accepted my offer and I gave them a month's rent in advance and enough extra to enable them to buy paint, curtain material and whatever else they needed to make the room habitable. Leonard said that he would organise the collection and delivery of the furniture from Rosanna's and that was that. On the way home Ramona chided me. 'You offered them far too much money, John. They would have been happy to have accepted half that amount.' I knew she was right but I thought that they would make sure that Cynthia was well looked after and wouldn't want to jeopardise losing their income. How naïve I was.

I couldn't see Cynthia liking it there very much but we had no choice as things stood. Any port in a storm, I thought. Leila seemed nice but I was not very taken with Kerim. There was something rather unctuous about the little fellow and I felt that he would need watching.

Ramona agreed that I should bring Cynthia's suitcases from the cottage the next night and we could take her to her new hiding-place. I arranged to collect them at nine and Leonard said he would meet me at the end of the courtyard because I had confessed that I felt nervous about walking along their street in case people started gossiping.

Just as we were about to cross the road to reach my car a prowling police truck thundered past, flinging sand behind it. I kept my head down and wasn't noticed as being white by the crew. 'Do they patrol this area very often?' I asked.

'The buggers are always sniffing around here, man – at all times of day and night.'

This news disheartened me more than I was already. I wasn't happy about recent developments and didn't like the idea of Cynthia staying in that dangerous neighbourhood, but what could I do?

I drove them back to their house and they invited me in for a coffee but I felt that I wanted to reach the sanctuary of my own home. I knew that Cynthia was safe and that was all that mattered: I had had enough for one night. I thanked them and promised that I would return as arranged.

The following night Leonard was waiting for me and he walked me back to the house. Cynthia was ready and Ramona was sitting on the bed with her coat on prepared to leave. I was not allowed to go anywhere until I had had a cup of coffee and sampled mother's apple pie again, which was no hardship to me.

We arrived safely outside the church at the end of the road in which Cynthia was going to live and I could see that she was not at all happy about the prospect. I squeezed her hand. 'It's not as bad as it looks, darling, and it is safer than the cottage,' I said rather lamely and I heard her sigh. Poor kid, I thought. On this occasion there were a few more people around than on the previous night; they were mostly children who stopped and watched us silently as we trudged along through the sandy wastes, occasionally stumbling on a half-brick.

Some of the children had run off calling out excitedly. That's right! Tell the whole bloody neighbourhood, I thought. They were obviously rushing home to tell their parents that they had seen a white man walking along the street. I hoped that they might think me a doctor.

We received a loud, squeaky welcome from the gate which had me wincing in the dark and I was glad to get inside the house. Kerim and Leila had worked hard on the little room and it looked quite nice. Cynthia seemed a bit happier at the prospect of staying there and Leila was very kind to her and made her feel welcome. Kerim was hovering in the background wearing his oily grin.

While Ramona and the others went off to the kitchen I remained with Cynthia in her little room and as soon as they left she came up to me and put her arms around me. 'It's not so bad, is it, love?' I asked, kissing her. She smiled and told me that I wasn't to worry about her. I felt rather easier in my mind but I still didn't really like the set-up there, and Cynthia was a bit upset because Ramona had warned her that I would not be able to just call around when I felt like it because I would be taking dreadful risks.

Ramona put her head around the door. 'We'd better be on our way in a minute,' she said, and I kissed Cynthia quickly and told her that I would be back again soon. I asked her if she needed any more money but she seemed to have enough. Leila said, 'Don't worry, Mr John, I will look after her like a daughter for you.' I thanked her and Kerim and we left. I gave Leonard my cottage address should any emergencies arise.

THE LETTER

Bob was busy in the kitchen of my former flat when I paid him an unexpected visit. He smiled with pleasure when he opened the front door with a tea towel in his hand. 'Come in, you old sod,' was his greeting as I walked in and plonked myself down on the bed.

'Give us a drink, then,' I said, 'or I won't tell you what's happened to us.' His mobile eyebrows worked overtime as he started ferreting around in the wardrobe. He emerged holding a bottle of Oude Meester and with a smirk of satisfaction on his face.

'I thought you weren't supposed to drink that stuff any more,' I said with a shake of the head.

'It's Beattie's,' he replied with his customary crafty leer. 'She'll play buggery when she finds out.'

Beattie's or not, I gladly accepted the half-filled tumbler that he handed to me and waited until he came back from the kitchen with a small jug of water.

He sat down on the bed with eager anticipation on his face. When I told him about our terrifying experience during the night of the police visit his eyebrows rose and fell in accompaniment with his jaw as his face registered one emotion after another: fear, suspense, astonishment, horror and anger. For once he was almost lost for words. He sat dumbfounded when I finished my narrative. Realising that he had to say something, he did. 'Fuckin' 'ell!', which was not entirely unexpected. He looked very concerned until I told him what had taken place between me and Cynthia's family, and he exhaled a breath of relief when I assured him that Cynthia was now safely ensconced in another hiding-place.

'How are things working out between yourself and Beattie?'

I enquired. He replied that he and Beattie also intended leaving the Republic together as soon as they could raise the necessary money for travelling expenses.

'How are you going to do that, Bob?' I asked, knowing that it was fundamentally impossible for him to save money, no matter how little. It was rather sad sitting there listening to him. Nevertheless, he believed unshakably that that was what he would do and it was not for me to disillusion him.

'Give me a bit of paper and a pen and I'll show you how you can get the money together in six months if you set your mind to it.' Glad that I was showing interest in his plans, he did so, and I drew up a budget based on figures that he provided, which showed clearly that he could achieve his target by cutting out all unnecessary items. He was excited about the idea and swore that he would start following the budget as from tomorrow. 'Cor! Beattie will be pleased. She'll see that we stick to it, just you see,' he said enthusiastically but I knew in my heart that there would be no way that Bob could cope with any sort of budget, no matter how simple. He simply lacked the character to achieve such an objective.

He still owed me the money that I had lent him to get himself off his prison sentence. I told him that if he could save 120 rand in the first month, I would write off the outstanding debt, to encourage him. 'There you are,' I said, 'that's a hundred and twenty rand for a start.'

He leapt to his feet with delight and seized my hand in a firm grip. 'Done, mate!' he cried. I smiled at his obvious pleasure and said nothing more on the subject. I just knew that the poor chap wouldn't make it.

He made a couple of cups of tea for us and as we sat silently sipping them, the door burst open and Beattie came in. She seemed pleased to find me there and even more pleased to see cups of tea in our hands instead of glasses of grog. She was nicely dressed and had improved a great deal in her personal appearance since she had been shacking up with Bob. They were good for one another, that was plain to see. She nagged Bob incessantly but only for his own sake. He pretended that he hated it but I could see that he was happy to have someone caring for him and in his own rough way he tried to please Beattie too.

Before I slipped away, Beattie asked me when the baby was

due. 'Just a few more weeks now, Beattie,' I said and Bob chipped in. 'Cor! We'll 'ave a real piss-up that night!' he said, rubbing his hands with gleeful anticipation. On this cheerful note I wished them goodnight and drove home to Rondebosch.

There was a note pinned on the front door from Terry saying that he and Di had called and would try again the next evening. I opened the door and Fred came bounding out with something in his mouth. He dropped it at my feet and when I bent forward to see what it was I was annoyed to see that he had caught and killed a fat chameleon. The hedge beside the house was full of these harmless and friendly little lizards. I often saw one clinging hopefully to a small branch while waiting for lunch to fly past in the form of a nice, juicy airborne beetle, or failing that at least a plump bluebottle. I picked one carefully off his perch on one occasion and he sat quietly on the sleeve of my jacket watching me with those marvellous, swivelling-gun-turret eyes that they have. He wasn't a bit scared and when I took him off my sleeve and placed him back in the hedgerow his swivelling eyes followed me as I walked away.

Fred blinked up at me with a look of pride on his whiskery face. 'You're a nasty piece of work,' I said as I looked down at him. On the other hand, no mouse with half a brain would have set foot in our cottage, and being a true-blue moggie Fred had to catch something, I supposed. I patted him and deposited the poor chameleon in the dustbin at the side of the house.

It was still relatively early and I dug out a bottle of brandy from my emergency supply and made a mental note to replenish the stock. As I sat in my favourite boozing chair in the kitchen with my reflection facing me in the mirror, I poured myself a generous measure and raising the glass to the reflection, wished it 'Good Health' and began a light conversation. At a party that I had attended at a nearby nurses' home some time before, I had found myself chatting to one of the hospital psychiatrists. During the conversation I let it be known that I often enjoyed a little chat with myself in the mirror when I had been knocking back the hard stuff, and I asked him if this was a bad thing. He grinned at me, probably not believing me in any case, and said, 'That's perfectly OK, but if you ever lose the mirror and you find yourself chatting to the wall, that's the time to come and see me.'

AN ACT OF IMMORALITY

The nights were becoming a bit chilly and Fred had ceased his roof-hopping activities and seemed to have settled for nights at home. On retiring to bed after polishing off several large brandies, I would lie in the dark listening to late-night music from Springbok Radio and, as often as not, a furry body would slither lithely down inside the bed and curl itself up against my cold feet, an arrangement which seemed to satisfy both Fred and myself.

The following evening, after a steady and productive day behind the typewriter, I decided that I ought to socialise a bit more, and strolled down to the very pleasant main bar at the Toolbag Hotel hoping that a few of my advertising associates might be there. I liked to keep an ear close to the professional grapevine as one never knew what one was going to hear.

When I walked in, to a slightly raucous welcome from a few chaps that I had known for some years, they were enjoying, if that is the correct word, a selection of the usual sick 'Kaffir' jokes. One short, dapper, English-speaking South African, employed as marketing director for an old-established UK distributing organisation, was in extraordinarily good form that evening and one of his contributions was as follows:

'This crowd of Jaapie [yokel] farmers up in the Free State had nothing to do one Sunday afternoon so they made a big circle in the sand and built a strong fence around it made from old railway sleepers.' His captive audience listened intently, ice cubes rattling gently inside large glasses of gin and tonic. 'Then they got hold of a Kaffir and buried him up to his neck in the sand in the centre of the ring.' Polite silence as he paused for effect. 'They then chucked into the ring an old lion that hadn't eaten for a week and stood back and watched the fun!

'The lion couldn't believe his good fortune and he made a savage rush at the Kaffir's exposed head but somehow the bloke managed to dodge the beast's charge.' Glazed eyes, as the listeners prepared for the punch line.

'The frustrated lion made another charge, and as it leapt over the African the bloke managed to snap with his teeth and got the old lion right in the nuts. The watching Jaapies cheered excitedly and a voice bawled in Afrikaans, "Fight fair, you Kaffir bastard."'

Followed by much curling-up by the audience.

A large, red-faced Afrikaner made the next contribution. He had arrived in Cape Town from Johannesburg earlier in the day and obviously wished to establish himself as one of the lads, and so we came to:

'This nervous little Jewish bloke who ran a shirt factory in Germiston, up on the Reef, was driving to Jo'burg one morning when he accidentally hit two Kaffirs who stepped out from some bushes. The bloke was driving pretty fast and one Kaffir went right up over the bonnet and through the windscreen into the back of the Chevvie. The other African was clouted in the hip and he managed to hobble and crawl off into the bush.'

The audience stood enthralled by this and waited patiently for the rest of the story.

'Police truck stopped and a big cop asked the driver what had happened. He, the driver that is, was dead worried about it because he expected to get ten years for manslaughter. He told the tough Afrikaner cop what had happened and after listening sympathetically to the white driver, the cop took out his notebook and as he started jotting down the details, he said, "Don't worry, man, we'll 'ave this bugger for breaking and entering, and when we catch up with the other sod we'll do him for running away from the scene of a crime." '

This brought a roar of approval from the audience.

I left.

Back at the cottage I found a letter waiting for me on the floor of the hall. As I walked through to the kitchen I noticed that the postmark on the white envelope read Beaufort West. I was puzzled because I didn't know anyone in Beaufort West which is a town in the Cape Province almost five hundred miles from Cape Town.

Curious now, I took a knife from the drawer and slit the envelope open. Inside was a single sheet of paper folded neatly once. I read the cryptic message hand-written in bold capital letters, and a chill ran through me.

It read as follows:

JOHN · WHITE + CYNTHIA · COLOURED = HARD LABOUR

Just as I had started to feel reasonably hopeful again now that Cynthia was in a safer home, the sudden arrival of this mysterious letter flattened my spirits and I immediately headed for the brandy. I was so upset that I simply unscrewed the metal cap and swigged it straight from the bottle – neat: unheard of for me. I must have swallowed the best part of a quarter of a pint of the scalding liquor which burned its way fiercely down my throat. Instead of soothing me it seemed to make me feel more desperate than ever.

I paced from one end of the kitchen to the other for some time, casting glances at the innocuous-looking sheet of white paper lying there on the table. I stopped only to replenish my glass. Then I shrugged and said to myself, 'It's no good getting into a panic. Use a bit of logic. Apply reason to the problem, not this bloody stuff.' And I flung the contents of the half-empty tumbler into the sink and went to find a note-pad and pen.

I sat down at the table and began to think. The first thing was to write down the names of everyone I knew fairly closely. It wasn't a very extensive list of names, but it was a start. I studied the list for some time and began to strike out the names of those people who I felt could be eliminated from my list of suspects.

First there was Bob – not forgetting Beattie, of course. It was far too subtle for either of them. They both knew about my relationship with Cynthia and they could have told me their thoughts without this melodramatic performance. Apart from this, I could hardly imagine Bob, or Beattie come to that, doing such a despicable thing. But was it so despicable? Was it a threat, or a warning from someone anxious not to see Cynthia and myself in serious trouble but not wanting to become openly involved, or who didn't want to embarrass me by identifying themselves?

If it was a threat or a straightforward nasty bit of poison-pen activity, could it be Chopper? After all he had no cause to love me, not that I had done him any real harm or presented any threat to him. How could he have found out about Cynthia and me? Had Bob foolishly opened his mouth too wide while having a drink too many with Chopper? But the more I thought about it the less inclined I was to suspect him.

So I struck out Bob and Beattie and also Chopper from my list and looked thoughtfully at the next two names, Basil and Brenda. First of all they didn't know Bob or Chopper so there could be no leakages there. Secondly, I had never told them that Cynthia and I had become lovers.

Next came Terry and his wife Di. I thought it highly unlikely that either of them would have approached the subject in such an oblique way; they had struck me as being too straight forward for tactics such as these. Of the few remaining names, none were worthy of serious consideration with the exception of Marie and Dan.

Dan's work took him all over the Cape Province which is the biggest of all the provinces, and it was possible that he might have been in Beaufort West on business when he could easily have slipped the letter into the nearest mail box. This line of thought was worthy of deeper research and I promised myself to make some discreet enquiries of Marie as soon as the opportunity presented itself. I remembered too that Dan had a relation up in Beaufort West; that opened up some interesting possibilities as well.

When I returned home from the office the next day I decided to take a bottle of brandy into Marie's kitchen and invite them to share it with me. They were obviously delighted by the offer and as the little boy had already gone off to bed we were able to relax and enjoy our drinks together. Dan brought glasses down from the cupboard and when I asked him how things were going he said, 'Ach! Not so bad, man, but a bit slow.'

We chatted lightly about nothing in particular and our topic of conversation for at least twenty minutes was Marie's handiwork in the garden. She had recently chopped down a fairly large fruit tree and had carried out the rather tough task as well as any man could have done. I told her that just watching her through the window had given me pains in the back. They both laughed at this and I got straight in at that point by asking Dan if he ever managed to get up to Beaufort West during his work. 'It would be nice for you to spend a night or two with your brother, wouldn't it, Dan?'

If Dan had been the person who had sent the letter, he

certainly hid his feelings well. He glanced over his glass at me, appearing quite unconcerned. 'No such luck. It's a bit of a drag from Cape Town and I think they have a bloke in Jo'burg who makes the rounds up in Beaufort.' That seemed to bring that line of enquiry to a shuddering halt, and after a few more drinks and a slice of cake that Marie insisted I should eat, I thanked them for a nice evening and made my way back into my own cottage.

I cooked a fair-sized piece of stockfish for Fred and decided to look in on Basil and Brenda. It was a pleasant drive across to Green Point and Basil was quite surprised when he opened his front door and found me grinning on the doorstep.

'Well, well well!' he said as we trudged up to their lounge. 'You'll never guess who's here, darling,' he called out as we reached the top of the stairs. Brenda's head appeared around the kitchen doorway. 'Blow me down if it isn't the man from Rondebosch,' she sang gaily, but seeing the expression on my face said, 'Hey, man. What's the matter? Hang on a minute, let me wipe my hands and I'll come through.' I flopped down into a low chair and told them that it had been one of those days when it would have been better if I had stayed in bed. A drink appeared in my hand as if by magic and I relaxed a little in their friendly company. I badly wanted to tell them about the letter and other things but it would have meant revealing too much and I held back.

Brenda poked me with a long finger. 'Had any supper yet?' I shook my head and told them that I wasn't very hungry. Basil stood up. 'Come on, we'll take you to a new place that opened recently, it's not very far from the Pavilion. You'll like it there.' He paused for a moment, then: 'Just a minute, there's something I'd like you to hear before we leave. You might find it interesting.'

Brenda said, 'If it's what I think it is, you might as well sit down again.' So I did and Basil came back carrying a new-looking cassette recorder and turning to me enthusiastically, said, 'Just listen to this, man. I recorded it the other night at Green Point.' He and Brenda had told me about a concert they had been to at the stadium where one of the Republic's up-and-coming pianists had been the main event. Apparently his style was considered by some to be slightly eccentric. Just the sort of thing that Basil was keen on – he liked to be different. At least I got another drink out of it and I sat politely waiting for him to stop fiddling around with the recorder.

A moment later the discordant, jangling notes of a piano echoed and re-echoed around the room. I sat listening attentively while Basil reclined on the settee with eyes closed and a look of rapture on his face.

He turned to me, snapping his fingers gently in time with the rhythm. 'Great, isn't it?' he said.

I looked pointedly at the gleaming, silvery cassette recorder and said, 'Yes. It looks a nice little unit. Where did you buy it? Stuttafords?'

He opened his eyes and stared at me. 'The music, you ignorant, uncultured sod.'

'Oh! Sorry,' I replied, helping myself to another drink.

When I asked him if he would like a refill he shook his head irritably at being disturbed while in ecstasy. The spastic, jerky notes continued to twitch their way into the room and I couldn't stand it any longer. 'What the hell is it supposed to be? It sounds like a bloody loonie at large in a music shop.'

At this, Basil sat up slowly and gave me a dreadful look which made it clear that he was in the presence of a cretin. I quite liked needling Basil when he was in one of his 'cultured' moods.

'I mean, just listen to that,' he said.

I listened and no sound came from the recorder at all.

'Just get that crazy break, it lasts twenty seconds.'

'Why? Is he knackered?' I enquired.

'No! you stupid idiot, that's to allow the audience to participate.'

I sat up at this. 'You mean they've taken their pianos along as well?'

Basil ignored this. 'The guy's a genius!' he said, shaking his head in wonder.

'He must be if he managed to get silly buggers like you to pay to listen to him.'

He gave up at that and stood up. 'Let's go and eat, for Christ's sake.'

Later, through a mouthful of lasagne, Basil asked, 'Want to come to a party on Saturday?'

I couldn't remember the last party I had been to and the idea appealed to me. 'Who's throwing it?' I replied, cupping my ear because of the background noise in the restaurant.

Basil refilled my glass with a very nice Chianti. 'The whole bloody intelligentsia of Cape Town will be there,' and he mentioned the name of a well-known artist. It was a bright, tight community and from the little I had seen of some of these people, the general impression I had was that they seemed to dislike each other intensely. However, as I enjoy studying human behaviour patterns I readily agreed to attend.

It was difficult for me to sleep that night. That damned letter had upset me more than I realised and I lay awake thinking about it. On top of all my other anxieties it was almost the proverbial last straw, and I began to feel the effect all these worries were starting to have on me. I wasn't the same person I had been a year ago, I knew that. Although I was in quite good physical shape, my nerves were in shreds and I knew that it would only be a matter of time before my physical condition would be affected. I was still eating quite well and stuffing myself with vitamin pills every day, especially Vitamin B-complex pills to help counteract the excessive amounts of alcohol that I was now consuming.

Vodka had more or less replaced brandy because I had done a bit of research and discovered that vodka contains fewer toxic substances than any other spirit – gin being apparently the worst. I had to admit that my hangovers were less severe after drinking heavy amounts of vodka. Despite all this, I knew I was heading for disaster and just prayed that I would hold together long enough to get Cynthia and our forthcoming baby safely out of South Africa.

Not far from the cottage was a small general store owned by a friendly Indian. I had struck up a cordial relationship with him and his family and we never failed to spend a while in general conversation whenever I called in for a few things. Next time I went to see my Indian friend in his shop I filled a couple of paper carriers with various items such as fruit, eggs, magazines, sweets, coffee, sugar, milk and toothpaste. On the spur of the moment I decided to take these things over to Ramona for her to take to Cynthia, whom I hadn't seen for a few days.

THE LETTER

I reached Ramona's home without causing any reactions among the neighbours. 'How is she?' I asked anxiously when Ramona opened the door to me.

'Come in, John,' she invited though she sounded a bit edgy. Len had gone over to visit Cynthia and Ramona seemed to be a bit ill-at-ease alone with me.

She led me through to the cosy kitchen where I shared coffee and cake with the rest of the family. They seemed pleased enough to see me and made me feel welcome.

'When can I see Cynthia again?' I asked Ramona.

She looked perturbed and said something in Afrikaans to her mother-in-law who shook her head with a smile and replied, also in Afrikaans. Ramona turned to me and said, 'Leonard and I will bring her here on Friday evening at seven. Can you get over here then?'

I thanked her and got up to go. 'I'll be here, Ramona. See you then, eh?' I was in a brighter mood as I drove out of Kew Town onto the main Klipfontein Road and turned for home.

Cynthia and I sat alone in Ramona's bedroom that Friday evening and talked for just over an hour. I placed my hand on Cynthia's bulging tummy and felt the baby moving. It was a fantastic experience and I was overjoyed to realise that this little bundle of love, still safe and secure inside her beautiful mother, was my daughter. I was absolutely convinced that she was a girl. No doubts whatsoever. Cynthia agreed with me on this point.

We had coffee and Ramona appeared to collect the cups. 'I think Cynthia should get back to Leila's now, she looks a bit tired,' she said. I agreed and taking Cynthia's hands in mine I hoisted her to her feet. 'Come on, Mum, this is no time for you to be larking about with a man.' We kissed and I left the house unnoticed.

Saturday, and in the morning I drove into the city to buy a few things in readiness for our offspring. Cynthia had told me that she was superstitious and didn't think it was a good thing to buy clothes for an unborn baby. I wasn't troubled by such superstitions and I spent some time happily poking around in the baby department of a large store. My purchases were mainly nappies, baby-powder, oil, safety pins, feeding bottles and such like. I kept darting furtive glances around in case any of my friends appeared. There would have been a considerable amount of speculation at the Toolbag if I had been nabbed buying baby items.

Basil's party wasn't scheduled to begin until nine that evening and as I had time to spare I went for a swim and a couple of hours of sunbathing on the prickly lawn of the Pavilion. I had lunch alone and afterwards decided to pay Bob a visit. I found him with Beattie and Chris, and when I joined them the flat was overcrowded as it had not been designed to accommodate four people at the same time.

I had no sooner arrived when there was a resounding knock-knock at the door. Bob peered through the frosted-glass panel in it and turned to me. His moustache twitched with dismay and his eyes were as round as marbles. 'It's the bleedin' police,' he gasped.

'Well, open the bloody door, man. They obviously saw me entering and in any case, we're not doing anything wrong. Let me do the talking.'

Adopting a nonchalant air, Bob turned the latch and swung the door open and a suspicious-looking white police constable entered, looking around hopefully. By this time I was carefully studying an open magazine lying on the dressing-table while Beattie and Chris had done a discreet bunk into the kitchen, taking their glasses with them and, no doubt, hurriedly emptying them down the sink.

'Wot's goin' on 'ere, then?' he asked. 'Wot are those girls doin' 'ere then, hey?'

I peered casually into the kitchen. 'Hopefully doing the washing up and the laundry, Constable,' I said with indifference. Ignoring the policeman I said to Bob, 'So is that all right then? We'll meet there in about fifteen minutes?'

Bob caught on and nodded as he lit a cigarette. As I walked towards the door I smiled at the slightly confused constable and said, 'He's English, y'know. I told him that he wasn't supposed to allow his maid to bring any of her friends in. As a matter of fact I was just mentioning it to him when you knocked.' I turned to Bob. 'You must be careful about things like that here, Bob; people can easily get the wrong impression if you don't.'

Bob stared at me with his jaw sagging but the girls picked it up quickly enough. They stepped into the little living-room and headed for the front door.

'We were just leaving anyhow, Constable,' Beattie said. 'Sorry if we caused any embarrassment, master Bob,' and with that they had gone. I heard them going up the iron stairs leading to the servants' quarters on the roof.

The police constable, robbed of his initiative, gave one last look around the place and nodding sternly said, 'Better watch it, man! You can get into big trouble with these girls. Listen to what your friend here tells you,' and he clattered off down the steps.

'Cheeky bastard!' Bob snarled, safe in knowing that the constable was now out of earshot.

'*Stupid* bastard!' I said quietly as I pointed an accusing finger directly at him.

Flopping back on the bed I lit a cigarette and blew out the smoke wearily. 'How much longer can I put up with living like this?' I said, more to myself than to Bob who told me to cheer up and have a drink. I stayed talking to him about this and that and the future, and he suddenly tugged two five-rand notes out of his trouser pocket. 'Oh! yeah, before I forget,' he said, 'there's ten rand off that money I owe you.' I thanked him and asked him how his savings drive was shaping up and received the answer that I was more or less expecting: 'Well, I 'aven't 'ad a chance to get goin' yet, really.'

He walked with me down to the car and as I drove away I gave him a wave through the window. Through the rear mirror I saw him turn and walk slowly back up the steps towards the flat. He looked a sad, lonely figure and I wondered whether he would ever fulfil his great, almost overwhelming desire to return to his beloved England, with Beattie. It had become an obsession with Bob lately and all he ever talked about was his desire to see his elderly father again and Hastings where he used to live.

Back at the cottage I had a hot bath which I thought would help to relax me as I was tense and apprehensive about the coming major event in my life – and Cynthia's: the arrival of Hanna. My mind set off on another of its agonising journeys of self-torture. What if the baby was abnormal? What if anything should happen to Cynthia during childbirth? If

Cynthia died and the baby survived, what would become of it? I couldn't claim it as my child; they would place me in a mental institution at the suggestion, and I would never know what our baby looked like. Tears began to roll down my cheeks at the thought of such things, and I forced myself to pull out of the mire of self-pity in which I was wallowing.

I had a stiff pre-party drink and shook off the morbid feelings that had overcome me. 'This will never do,' I said to myself. 'If you allow yourself to crack now, Cynthia and Hanna won't stand a cat in hell's chance of making it alone. Now go to that party and have a smashing time.'

I dressed in what I considered to be something suitably cultured. In some respects I would be the odd-man-out at the party. I would probably be the only single man there without a female partner, neither would I have any claim to fame in artistic circles. I was a writer of sorts, certainly, and I couldn't help smiling at the prospect of some member of the local literati asking me politely what my latest work was. I could imagine the expression on his face if I said, 'An advertisement for used cars in this evening's *Argus*.' That would have gone down like a lead balloon. I brightened at the thought and began to look forward to the evening. Perhaps it would do me good after all.

By the time I turned up, most of the guests seemed to have arrived. I knew a number of them through my association with Basil. I managed to find a seat on a settee and wedged myself between a tall, thin woman and a short, stocky man. The woman wore a dark grey dress with a very low neckline and I was intrigued by the golden key which dangled between her flat breasts from a heavy gilt chain. I wondered what its purpose was.

The short, stocky man turned out to be her husband, a Canadian with a dome-like bald head surrounded by long, wispy fringes. He was an artist and he talked quickly, in short bursts, like a machine-gun. He stuck an olive into his mouth and asked me what I did for a living. When I told him he said, 'Oh! Great! Just great! I have a friend back home in Toronto. Writes copy for an ad agency. Makes a bomb apparently.' He was a nice enough bloke who punctuated most of his conversation with the word 'horseshit'. Every time he said it, his wife said, 'Watch it, Rossy!'

I was soon enjoying the evening and the sumptuous buffet meal served on the host's large stoep. Afterwards I leaned against a supporting stanchion and looked out towards the dark sea. Tiny lights flickered here and there and as soft music drifted out from the lounge I thought of Cynthia. We lived in two worlds and it seemed so wrong that I should be standing here, full of good food and drink, while she had to stay in that shitty little room in the ghastly street in Kew Town. I cheered myself by thinking that it wouldn't be like that for ever and eventually she would be able to share everything in my life.

I made up my mind that I would sneak over to Kew Town after leaving the party and on the way I would buy some nice things for her to eat. To hell with the skollies and the cruising police trucks. Looking at the groaning buffet it occurred to me that most people had eaten and there was still enough food left to give a modest army a reasonable snack. Why shouldn't Cynthia eat from the rich man's table tonight, I thought. Surreptitiously I filled a paper bag with tit-bits and sloped off to the car where I put the bag under the front seat. I strolled down to the main road and bought a large bottle of Coke and also a large bottle of milk and put these into the car too before returning to the party.

The guests had filed back into the lounge and I saw Basil doing something with his cassette recorder which he had with him. I thought that he wanted to tape the party, but I discovered his true purpose when he looked over at me and with a wicked grin said, 'Ah! Here he is now. Got a little surprise for you, John.'

I frowned, puzzled, as I had no idea what he was on about. I sat down on the carpet close to the Canadian chap and his wife when, to my horror, I recognised the voice coming from the recorder. It was my own and I realised what Basil had done.

In the past I had composed one or two limericks and discovered that I seemed to have a natural talent for these useless odes. I became ambitious and wrote two very long ones in a similar mould to the famous Eskimo Nell classic. One was called 'The Cascara Kid' and the other 'The Man from Down Under'. I suppose they were funny enough in their own way, but decidedly rude and I didn't stay to see what the reaction of the listeners would be. I disappeared before the tape reached the naughty bits. Basil phoned the next day to tell me that they had been a great success and everyone had been disappointed by the author's modesty.

After leaving the party I drove back to the cottage because it was far too early for me to attempt to visit Cynthia, especially with it being a Saturday night when the streets of Kew Town might be filled with shebeen patrons and other revellers. I judged that one-thirty a.m. would be a reasonably safe time to depart.

What worried me a bit was the possibility of a cruising police truck or car spotting me and stopping me in which case I would be in trouble. I decided that if this should happen I would tell them that I had been homeward-bound after a party and someone had given me wrong directions and how relieved I was that they had come along. That would have been accepted – once, that is – but if I were to be seen creeping along the sandy roads bearing gifts as it were – well, that would take a bit more explaining. Dismissing these negative thoughts from my mind I went out to the car and noticed that the hall light was on in the house across the road. I could not see anyone's silhouette nor any movement inside the room but I knew that I was being watched again. I felt a flush of anger wash over me and I was tempted to stride across and have it out with them. Fortunately, common sense saved me and I merely ignored the Watcher.

It was now exactly one-thirty and I started the motor of my little Beetle and set off, in the opposite direction, for the benefit of the Watcher. I am sure they must have been wondering where the hell I was going at that time of the morning but I wasn't breaking any laws – at least not yet – and I drove off in a reasonably good mood.

As I passed Athlone and entered Klipfontein Road it was deserted and I drove carefully across the intersection leading towards Kew Town, casting a cautious glance over the road at the grim façade of Athlone police station. A pair of vans were standing in the foreyard of the station; one of them had its headlights on in readiness to depart on patrol. I kept an eye in the rear-view mirror to make sure that the van wasn't taking the same route that I was, but it still hadn't moved and gradually it fell out of sight and I relaxed a little.

THE LETTER

I took a rather devious way to the church at the end of the road in which Kerim's house stood. Instead of parking in the main road directly opposite the church as I had done when with Ramona and Leonard, I turned into a dark side-road adjacent to the church, as I felt that the car would be safer there and would not be readily seen by a police cruiser. I switched off the ignition and sat for a minute or two to prepare myself for a trip across no-man's-land. My mouth was dry and I felt apprehensive which was natural enough under the circumstances. At last I opened the door of the car, and taking the goodies from beneath the seat and slipping them into a carrier bag which contained the drinks and other things from the cottage, I got out and closed and locked the door as quietly as possible.

Apart from the noise made by occasional gusts of wind it was as quiet as the grave, and looked about as cheering, and I cast anxious glances around me before setting off across the road. A mangy cat glided past about five yards ahead of me and it gave me a quick look and broke into a run. I plodded along through the sand and grains struck my face as the wind gusted and picked up handfuls of it to fling at me as if warning me to get away from there. Odd pieces of paper bowled along and I side-stepped broken bottles and larger pieces of brick and masonry. Although my destination was only another two hundred yards along on the right, it seemed to be about two miles to me. I kept my head down but my eyes and ears were straining to detect anything that might have meant danger. Every sense I had seemed to be on 'war-alert' and the slightest movement of bits of paper, a cat or a dog was mentally recorded and registered and sifted as I navigated that dangerous stretch. As I neared the gate I heard the revving of an engine back somewhere along the road which I had recently crossed. I turned and saw the beams of twin headlights making their way towards me. Throwing discretion to the winds, I did the last few yards in three leaps and scuttled through the gate, which happened to be wide open, thank God. I stepped quickly behind a crude trellis made of wood which luckily stood a few feet away from the window of Cynthia's room. I stayed still watching for the vehicle but it didn't turn into Kerim's road and disappeared leaving everything in darkness. The string of the carrier-bag handle was now cutting into my fingers and I felt as though I were participating in the production of some low-budget thriller movie.

Cynthia's window was in darkness which was hardly surprising at that time of the morning. I hated the idea of disturbing her but I wanted to see her and give her the things I had brought. I tried our coded knock and watched the curtain for movement. There was no sign of life so I knocked again. A moment later the curtain parted slightly and Cynthia's eyes were staring at me. She looked scared but when I gave a silly little wave, waggling my fingers at the same time, she recognised who it was and grinned happily. I raised my finger to my lips and shook my head to warn her not to speak. She opened the window carefully and I whispered urgently, 'Don't speak, darling; here, take this,' and I handed through the carrier bag.

She smiled and stood up on the bed so that she could lean out to kiss me. 'Thanks, darling,' she whispered as I pushed her gently back into the room.

'There's a letter inside the bag,' I told her. 'After you've read it, burn it in the stove in the kitchen and don't let Kerim or Leila see it. They mustn't know that I have been, OK?' She nodded that she had understood and after making a motion to her indicating that she should close the window, I waved again and turned back to the trellis and that awful street.

The wind whistled angrily around my ears as I made my way back to the car. The streets were deserted and no one appeared. I thanked God as I silently pulled the door of the car shut after climbing in. The reliable little engine started at the first turn of the key and I moved out. I held my breath until I turned onto the main Klipfontein Road and let it out with a long sigh as I headed safely for home. No one could bother me now.

Fifteen minutes later I was back outside my cottage and a few minutes later I was peeping cautiously through the front-room curtains to see if the Watcher was on duty. There was no movement and I went through to the kitchen to make a cup of tea before going to bed.

A few nights later Bob and I were discussing future plans and he told me that he had written to his father in Hastings to let him know that he would be returning to the UK as soon as he could and would be bringing with him a coloured woman whom he intended marrying. His father had written back to say that as long as she was a good girl, he didn't care what colour she was, which pleased Bob immensely.

I was happy for Bob but I warned him that it was a well-known fact that letters in and out of the Republic were often opened and read by security agents. 'Be very careful about what you write, Bob, and don't over-criticise the country either. Remember that since you and Beattie were taken in for questioning, they will have a dossier on you and will be taking a great interest in you.'

He looked thoughtful when he heard this. 'Cor! I never thought of that,' he said.

'Well, from now on I would if I were you,' I cautioned him.

I carried out another hair-raising visit to Cynthia, unbeknown to her family or, as far as I knew, Kerim or Leila. This time, Cynthia handed me a letter which I could hardly wait to read. When I reached home and was sitting in the kitchen with a cup of tea in front of me, I opened it but it didn't make very pleasant reading and my stomach sank as I read on.

It seemed that Kerim, good Muslim as he presented himself, was a drunken little bugger whose favourite pastime consisted of knocking the unfortunate Leila around. He had not bothered Cynthia in any way – luckily for him – but she obviously felt insecure and unhappy where she was. 'Here we go again,' I said aloud, clapping my hands to my head in despair. We had run out of time now and our baby was almost due. There was nothing that I could do. Although Ramona and the family were sympathetic, about both of us I suppose, they felt that if Cynthia stayed with them it might lead to serious trouble because of talkative neighbours, especially if the baby was extraordinarily light-skinned. Apart from this, the little house in the courtyard was already overcrowded.

In her letter Cynthia begged me to allow her to spend just one last night with me at the cottage before the baby arrived. She was dreadfully unhappy where she was and she just wanted to be alone with me because she felt safe when we were together. I agonised over this for some time as I knew that if we had visitors there would be no way that she could do her famous fence-climbing routine again. On my next visit she almost pleaded with me to allow her to come over to the cottage just once more. She missed Fred too, apparently. That did it. Against all my instincts I gave in to her request and worked out an elaborate scheme to enable me to get her over to the cottage and safely into it. If Ramona found out she would blow a gasket, that was for sure, and the goodwill that I appeared to have built up between her and myself would blow away like thistledown in the wind.

Cynthia said she could bribe Leila not to say anything so I gave her a five-rand note to slip to Leila. It was agreed that I would pick her up around the corner where it was nice and dark, the next night at eleven o'clock. I impressed on her that she should be absolutely on time. I would not wait around in that neighbourhood a second longer than was absolutely necessary and I didn't want her hanging around on her own either. I also made it perfectly clear that she would not be allowed to stay the night under any circumstances – it would have been asking for serious trouble and I felt that we were taking too many risks as it was. She promised that she would just stay for a couple of hours and then I could take her home again. On the next night, she was on time and bulging madly. She heaved herself into the car, and as there was no question of her lying down on the back seat she propped herself up in the corner and tried to keep her head away from the rear window. I shrugged and hoped for the best.

It was about eleven-fifteen when we arrived in the vicinity of the cottage. I told her that I would enter the house first and suggested that she should follow about ten minutes later. I stressed that if she saw the front-room light come on she was not to come in and should return to the point where I had dropped her. Fortunately there was no enemy activity at all and she entered safely.

She was absolutely delighted to be at the cottage again and Fred made a big fuss of her, too. We had a salad meal which I had prepared earlier and afterwards I insisted on doing the washing up. We sat talking happily in the lounge, but I began to feel edgy and wasn't particularly cheered up when Cynthia told me that Leila's daughter, Jinja, who lived a few streets away from Kerim's house, had become jealous of her. From what I understood, not only did the daughter know about our relationship but half the bloody street had found out, thanks to that loud-mouthed drunken little sod Kerim. I thought, This is just the news I need on the virtual eve of the birth of our baby. Our situation was now extremely vulnerable and I just didn't want to think of the consequences, should Jinja inform on us.

Cynthia told me that Jinja had borrowed some of her clothes and hadn't returned them. I told her not to make an issue out of it. 'Just let sleeping dogs lie,' I said, 'and don't worry too much. You'll be going into hospital in a few days and while you're there I'll find some way of solving our problems, so be a good girl and don't worry.'

I was badly rattled by the latest development and I said I would take her home at about three a.m., but I would slip over to Sea Point for an hour or so now to see Bob. I felt that if the Watcher was around it might look less conspicuous if I was seen leaving, as I had often gone off for a drink at this time of night and he knew it, and in any case, if he saw me returning later I would be entering the cottage on my own.

Cynthia wasn't too keen on the idea of my going out but she could see that I was extremely restless and like a cat on hot bricks, so she only said, 'Don't be too long, love. I get worried when you're not here.'

I bent and kissed her several times. 'Have I let you down yet, sausage?' I asked, using one of the silly names I often called her. She smiled and shook her head and I blew her a kiss as I left the room. No need to explain the security drill to her now.

Bob was pleased to see me even though it was rather late, but after I told him Cynthia's news and how it made me feel, he agreed that it was probably a good thing that I had come over for a chat. We sat and listened to Springbok Radio over a couple of brandies and we picked holes in various items of news. I couldn't help smiling when I heard the words: 'And here is the world news coming to you from Springbok Radio'. According to the commentator, the world began just south of the Zambesi and ended at Cape Town harbour. At about one o'clock, I got itchy feet again and had an urge to get home. I didn't like the idea of leaving Cynthia alone too long in such an advanced stage of pregnancy. Bob walked with me to the car and asked me to give Cynthia his love and best wishes. I promised to do so and drove off with a wave.

I was now rather tired and drove slowly home along the National Road with Table Bay and the busy docks on my left and the bulk of Table Mountain on my right, now shrouded in darkness.

When I turned into our road I sat up behind the wheel with a cry of 'Oh! My God!' A small crowd of people was standing in the road near a police truck and an ambulance. The whole sickening tableau was right outside my cottage. Someone was directing operations with a torch and there were lights on in Marie and Dan's windows. I pulled in to the side of the road and was almost physically sick with shock and fear.

Cynthia had obviously gone into labour and must have staggered out into the road instinctively to find help. Under those circumstances man-made laws don't count for very much. Whatever she had done, it was the end of everything now. I dared not go anywhere near the cottage. I would have been arrested on sight and that wouldn't have helped Cynthia or me at that stage.

It suddenly dawned on me that Marie and Dan could recognise my car from where they were standing, and I started the motor and swiftly reversed around the corner out of sight. I sat there trying to think of what to do. I was worried sick about Cynthia but as long as she was being taken proper care of there was nothing I could do for her, and I tried to shut my mind from thinking of her in the hands of the police. What about the baby? What a sad and miserable way for our little child to start her tiny life, in the hands of the bloody police.

Taking stock of the situation I discovered that I had little more than ten rand on me. I was wearing a pair of white beach trousers, a long-sleeved sports shirt and a pair of rope-soled sandals – without socks. I made up my mind. I would go back to Bob and hope that he could lend me about fifty rand to enable me to drive up to Johannesburg. I had a few friends there and would be able to find somewhere to stay; getting a decent job shouldn't be too hard.

I would just have to start from scratch again and I would have to leave all my possessions in the cottage. What about Fred? I hoped Marie and Dan would take care of him for me.

It was a terrible decision to have to take but I really couldn't think of anything more logical under the circumstances and at such short notice. I would be able to get money to Cynthia through Ramona as I had the postal address of the little house in the courtyard. I didn't see how the police could charge Cynthia with immorality if there was no consenting white male around. Perhaps Marie and Dan would cotton on and come up with a likely story.

Time was running out and I set off to Sea Point. Bob's flat was in darkness and I hoped that Beattie wasn't there as I wanted to speak with him alone. I also felt that I had had enough of Immorality Act risks for one night.

I tapped on the frosted glass of his front door and heard the bed-springs creak as he sat up. There was a pause. He was thinking: Oo the bloody 'ell is this at this time? I tapped in our usual way and the bed creaked again as he stood up. The door opened and he looked startled. 'Wot's up?' he asked.

When I told him what had happened he shook his head and said, 'Christ, man! You can't just bugger off and leave the girl in a mess like this!' He looked quite old and drawn and I knew that he was sincerely concerned about us.

'Bob, do you think I'm not aware of my responsibilities?' I went on to explain that if I was not available to the police it was possible that the only thing they could charge Cynthia with would be trespassing. On the other hand, if I went rolling up it would be a different kettle of fish. 'I have no intention of deserting Cynthia or our baby, Bob, I'm sure you know that.'

He nodded slowly and was obviously crushed by this latest development. 'Poor little bugger,' he muttered time and again, shaking his head.

The poor chap obviously didn't want to lose my companionship either, I could see. I was the only friend he had and he was very upset. 'Let's 'ave a cuppa tea,' he said, pulling himself to his feet wearily. I needed more than a cup of tea to cheer me up but I sat and waited patiently while he shuffled around and muttered to himself.

He came back with two cups of tea and went off again for a plate of biscuits. We sat in silence drinking the hot, sweet tea. I didn't want any biscuits. I wondered what everyone would think. What would Marie and Dan have to say about it all? The Watcher and his spouse would be delighted and would no doubt look upon our misfortune as an act of Divine Providence. I imagined them at that moment telling the police about the strange ways of the *rooinek* living across the road – 'He looked the sort of person who would associate with, er . . . coloureds, Officer.' That sort of chat.

Yes, I could just imagine the scene but at that moment I was worried sick about Cynthia. She had been so happy about our coming baby but what a horrific ending our sad little story was having. I prayed that she would be all right and that they wouldn't take the baby away from her: that would kill her, I was sure.

I wondered what Ramona would think, and Cathy and the other members of the family. I would hardly have blamed them if they cursed me for this happening to their family. What a dreadful, bloody mess it all was. I had considered going to their house to tell them but I thought it unwise as things were – perhaps I could make some personal contact later when things had settled down.

'What about all your stuff at the cottage?' Bob asked. He looked a bit forlorn sitting there in his baggy old Marks and Sparks pyjamas, clasping his teacup. I looked at my watch; it showed a little after two a.m. and I wondered if they would still be at the cottage. I told Bob to leave things for a few days and then he could call on Marie to see if she would release any of my belongings to him. I also assured him that I would write to him on arrival to let him know what my plans would be. He had 'borrowed' fifty rand from Beattie who had left a wallet with some money in it for emergencies. 'This is a bleedin' emergency, ain't it?' he had said with a faint image of his crafty leer on his lined face. He looked miserable now as he slipped on his old jumping jacket. 'I'll come and see you off,' he said. I put my hand out of the car window and gave him one final handshake before driving off, and a wave as I turned the corner into Beach Road.

Before setting off on the long drive to the Highveld I decided to have one last glance at the cottage. What made me decide to do so? Perhaps it was the sixth sense at work again. When I turned into the road it was deserted, and the cottage looked the same as it had when I had first set off from it earlier in the night. I drove past on a recce and continued on around the block and stopped round the corner from the house. I switched off the motor and sat in silence for a few minutes.

I decided to take a risk. To hell with it, I thought, I'll go inside and grab a few things, and Fred if he's there, before leaving. I climbed out of the Volksie and started to walk quietly towards the cottage. My mouth was dry and I had an ominous feeling that as soon as I entered the house, lights would be flung on by triumphant police lying in wait and I would be dragged away in handcuffs – much to the joy of the Watcher and his lady.

I was literally shaking with fear as I unlocked the front door and stepped inside. To my surprise the house remained in darkness and it was very quiet. Before I had time to close the door gently behind me, Fred shot out from his hedge and bounded inside, purring with pleasure at seeing me. He appeared to be safe enough, I thought, as I tiptoed along the hall in the darkness. I dared not put the lights on as I didn't want to reveal my presence to either the Watcher, or to Marie and Dan who might have still been awake and wondering what to make of their tenant.

I thought about what I should take with me but first I took Fred into the kitchen and gave him what was left of the topside in the fridge. He would be travelling a long way and would need a good meal in his tummy. I tiptoed back into the lounge, and leaning behind a door so no one would see the light, I lit a cigarette. I was about to remove it from my lips when I heard a voice. The cigarette fell to the carpet and I stood stock-still with shock. It sounded like Cynthia but it couldn't be.

'John, man, what are you doing? Where have you been?' It *was* Cynthia. I picked up the cigarette and went through to the spare bedroom where her voice had come from. The room was in darkness and I closed the door behind me before I switched the light on.

She was lying in bed and drew the covers up to hide her eyes from the brightness. 'Christ! Are you all right? What the hell was all that nonsense outside in the road earlier on? I nearly had a heart attack.'

Hastily stubbing out the cigarette I knelt beside the bed and took her in my arms. 'Oh, God! Darling, I thought I had lost you – and Hanna.' I kissed her many times on her lips, cheeks and eyes. 'I thought you had been taken off by the police. I was just on my way to Jo'burg, I couldn't think of anything else to do.'

She hugged me and seemed pleased that I had been so concerned about her. Then she told me what had happened: it was incredible and afterwards it seemed as though fate had played a cruel practical joke on me. 'I was lying here in the dark,' she said, 'just waiting for you to return, when I heard a lot of voices from outside in the road, so I crept down the hall and into the front bedroom and peeped out through the curtains.' I hugged her gently and waited.

'There were lots of people outside our house and a police truck and an ambulance arrived and for a moment I thought they were coming here. I was frightened to death, I can tell you.'

I kissed her. 'I'm sure you must have been, love,' I said encouragingly. 'Go on, tell me all about it.'

She snuggled closer. 'There was a lot of shouting of instructions going on and Dan had made himself the master of ceremonies and was waving a torch all over the place.' So he was the sod with the torch, was he? I thought. She told me that someone was lying on the grass and was taken away in the ambulance but apart from that she knew nothing. I would find out from Marie in the morning, I thought.

'Come on, my girl!' I said, helping her up. 'You've had enough excitement for one day and I can take a hint. You're going home this minute before something else horrific happens.'

After scrutinising the enemy stronghold across the road I decided that it would be safe. I told Cynthia where the car was, and watched her depart safely ahead of me. Just as I was about to leave I remembered Fred and the topside. I tiptoed through to the kitchen and yanked it away from him and put it back in the fridge, leaving him looking around in puzzlement, licking his whiskers.

'Sorry, lad,' I said. 'There's always another day, you know. See you later.'

THE BABY

I called at Ramona's home with bulging carrier bags containing fruit, soap, tins of baby-food, baby-bottles, nappies, safety-
pins, towels, baby-powder, cotton-wool buds, slippers for
Cynthia, magazines, baby vests and some baby clothes – and
a large jar of Horlicks.

Ramona had heard from Leila that I had taken Cynthia out
of the house, and she was not very pleased with me and gave
me a telling-off. I felt bad enough after what had happened,
in any case. I still found it hard to believe that another pregnant
woman, a white lady who lived a few doors along from the
cottage in Rondebosch, had decided to take a breath of fresh
air and had collapsed on the grass verge of our cottage and
delivered her baby there.

Ramona told me that Cynthia was well but was weary of
carrying the baby and wanted to get it over with as quickly as
possible. Cynthia had been to the clinic again and had been
told that she should report for her confinement on July the
third. Only three more days, and not long after that I would
become a father. I was already showing symptoms of imminent
fatherhood which were noticed by some of my colleagues at the
office. One moment I would be worried about the possibility of
complications arising at the birth, and the next minute I would
be grinning inanely to myself. It was frustrating because I
wanted to tell them but couldn't. Every time I walked into the
Regency bar I wanted to tell Reg that I was going to be a dad
shortly but I couldn't.

There was Bob, of course. Thank God for Bob. He had been
overjoyed when he heard about the fiasco of the 'early delivery'
outside the cottage, and that I was not doing a bunk to Jo'burg
after all. He was almost as excited about the baby as I was

and I had to put up with a lot of good-natured banter from him during the days before the baby's arrival. He did his best to bolster my morale which tended to go up and down like a yo-yo.

Because here I was at the age of forty-four, having written off the prospects of ever being a father, and now that I had reached what must surely be one of the major high spots of a man's life I was not able to celebrate my happiness like other dads throughout the world. I consoled myself with the thought that it wouldn't be like this for ever, and one day I would be able to make up for everything we were now suffering. In the meantime I promised that I would muster up every bit of love that I could find to give to Cynthia and our baby, when she arrived.

Of course I would not be able to visit Cynthia while she was confined, nor could I make direct enquiries. That would have been looked upon with the gravest suspicion. I was tortured now by wondering what would happen if there was some sort of an emergency. Perhaps Cynthia would call for me and want me near her but I wouldn't be able to go to her because of the heartless system. I comforted myself with the thought and knowledge that Cynthia was a strong, healthy young woman and the likelihood of any complications arising at childbirth was probably remote. Nevertheless the possibility was still there and I was uneasy in my mind.

She would receive the best possible attention; after all she would be in one of the world's leading hospitals. Groote Schuur had become a world name due to the dedication and great talent of Dr Chris Barnard. There were plenty of things I could find to criticise about South Africa but I had to give credit where it is due. At one time I had a very close friendship with a South African operating-theatre sister and I learned a good deal about the medical services in the Republic. As far as I could tell, they were second to none.

During a long, animated discussion I had with my friend I had challenged her on the impartiality that she claimed was shown as between white and non-white patients at the hospital where she was then working. It is a children's hospital and a very busy one. She accepted my challenge and told me that I should visit the outpatients' department where she was on duty at that time, during any night of the following week.

I accepted her invitation and called in at the hospital at three a.m. to see for myself just what the procedures were regarding black and white outpatients. I found myself in a long wide corridor with a queue of anxious mums and dads of all colours, waiting to have their children treated. Many treatment rooms led off this corridor and in each of them I could see white nursing sisters and nurses busily attending to their young patients.

One white couple tried to jump the queue ahead of a coloured family, and I was pleasantly surprised when an Afrikaner sister told them that some of the people had been waiting there for hours and 'Would you mind taking your turn in the queue with the others'. Not *all* is bad in South Africa and not *all* white South Africans are bad.

A few weeks before this I had driven over to Sea Point one day to see if Bob was around and found him in his customary spot at the Regency. 'Ah! Just the bloke I want to see,' was his greeting. He told me that he had something special for Cynthia at the flat and he would give it to me before I went home again. We enjoyed an hour of speculative conversation about our respective futures, then made our way to the little flat where he began to rummage around in his capacious wardrobe. Eventually he re-emerged, red-faced and successful, clutching a small, red-velvet box, threadbare with age.

He handed it to me with an air of conspiratorial benevolence and said, ' 'Ere! Give this to Cynthia with me love. Tell 'er it's for Hanna when she grows up.' I opened the little box and found a heavy silver medallion of uncertain age. I asked him where he had got it from and what he might know about its origin. He looked at me silently and merely tapped the side of his nose, and I had to be satisfied with that. I knew that he had skippered a few ocean-going cruisers around the Med in his younger days, and from what he had told me over several brandies during earlier conversations I suspected that he had dabbled in a bit of contraband from time to time, but I never pressed him on this point and I didn't press him about the gift. However, it looked too valuable for him to just hand over like that, and I thanked him and told him so as I held it out for him.

He was very indignant at my refusal to accept it and I had no choice but to accede to his kindness. I must have looked a bit worried because he said, 'There's no need for you to get suspicious about it, John. I bought that little bauble in Beirut years ago – paid for it fair and square.' I thanked him and said that Cynthia would be very touched by his generosity. He busied himself with the brandy bottle and said, 'Forget it, man.'

Days later, I was walking through a large store in Cape Town called OK Bazaars when my eye fell on a display of the identical baubles that Bob had 'picked up in Beirut'. The old bugger had told me that it was made of genuine Arabic silver. I never said anything to him because I knew that he meant well and wanted to do something extra special for Cynthia.

On the night of the second of July, the eve of Cynthia's departure for the hospital, I visited Ramona and asked when I might be able to see the baby and the proud mother. She warned me not to go anywhere near Leila's house immediately after Cynthia's discharge from Groote Schuur because neighbours would be popping in to see the baby.

I was fed up. 'Christ, Ramona, I *am* the father, after all! How do you think I'm going to feel not being able to see my own child?'

Leonard was listening to our conversation. He had turned out to be a decent bloke and I think that he trusted me even if Ramona didn't entirely. 'Why don't I take the baby round to John's cottage so that he can spend a few hours with it?'

I rubbed my chin thoughtfully for a moment. 'Sounds like a good idea, Len,' I said. 'But don't you think that the neighbours might be a bit suspicious if you appear on my doorstep and hand over a new-born baby and then leave again?'

He grinned back at me and said, 'What if they didn't know it was a baby?'

I sat up and took more interest. 'What do you have in mind, Len?' I asked eagerly. His plan was to pretend he was delivering groceries to me. A friend of his, who could be relied on, would drive Leonard to my cottage with three corrugated-cardboard cartons. He would carry them to my front door and hand them in. The top carton would have some sticks of celery and so forth protruding conspicuously out of it; the middle carton would contain things that I would need for the baby; and the bottom one would contain the baby. It was a brilliant scheme and I couldn't thank Len enough. Even Ramona said, with a smile, 'Are you sure you haven't done this sort of thing before, dear?'

I was given a verbal course on baby-care and shown some highly technical operational techniques in the art of nappy-changing and making up baby's bottles. Armed with this information and excited at the prospect of being able to see my child after all, for a brief moment I was happy and carefree. Then: 'What if she should cry and Marie hears her?' I fretted.

'Just put the radio volume up a bit and stick a bottle in her mouth. Don't worry, man, it'll be all right!' said Ramona, who thought that it was all very romantic.

'But how will I take her back to Cynthia? I won't be able to drive the car and look after the baby at the same time, will I?' I persisted.

Ramona laughed at this. 'Good Heavens! You're talking about a newly-born baby; she's not going to start climbing all over the car, you know. Just make sure she is cosy and warm in her little box and she will be perfectly happy and she will go to sleep.'

I chewed that one over for a while and, at last satisfied, I made my way home again. I arranged to call round the next evening to find out if anything had happened.

All during the next day I was on edge wondering how things were working out with Cynthia. I couldn't really concentrate on my work and found myself making all sorts of silly typing errors until in the end I gave up. I could hardly wait for the working day to finish. At last I got away to Ramona's house, fully expecting to find that I was now a father. Instead she told me that nothing had happened as yet and if there was no sign of the baby during the night, the hospital planned to induce the birth the following day. I had taken a bottle of Scotch around with me to wet the baby's head, and while Ramona and her mother-in-law tut-tutted from behind the bead curtain and made other disapproving noises, Len and I shared it and were joined later by the old man. An hour or so later I said my goodnights and returned home, feeling a bit flat.

I knew that I wouldn't get much sleep that night so I decided to go for a drive. All I could think about was Cynthia and that I should have been with her. She would understand of course, I knew that, but I still felt guilty because I was not there. De Waal Drive went past the hospital so I drove along it until I reached Hospital Bend, curiously enough a notorious accident spot, and pulled in briefly and tried to imagine which lighted window represented the room in which Cynthia would be lying. I felt sad that I couldn't go to see her, loving her as much as I did, and in great depression I drove back to the cottage to the vodka – and Fred!

The following day was even worse but I made a serious effort to concentrate on my work to try to keep my mind off what might be taking place in that architecturally beautiful building lying beneath the bulk of Table Mountain. At five o'clock I was away like a flash and pulled up outside the cottage twenty minutes later. As I walked up the short path, Fred bounced out of the chameleon-riddled hedge. He had obviously been sleeping because he stretched and yawned before heading for my ankles. I picked him up and took him to the house and as I entered the hall I noticed a white envelope lying on the floor. I ignored it as I thought that the butcher had dropped it through the letter-box. He always delivered my meat to Marie who kindly put it in her fridge until my return from the office. I assumed it was his bill and I would look at it later. After filling Fred's water bowl and putting on the kettle I strolled back and picked up the envelope and opened it as I returned to the kitchen. Inside was a brief note which read:

Congratulations DAD, Hanna was born this morning, 7 pounds 8 ounces, she and mum are fine.

I leapt out of the chair I had flopped into. Seizing the startled cat, I waltzed him around the kitchen and cried, 'What do you know, Fred. You're a bloody uncle!' I longed to rush next door to tell Marie and Dan. The way I was feeling I would even have given the Watcher a cigar. Instead I had a hot bath, and changed, and proceeded to pace impatiently around the cottage waiting for dusk as I wanted to get across to Ramona as quickly as I could that night.

Leonard opened the door and grinned when he saw my own grinning face.

'Hello, Len, where's Ramona?'

He nodded over his shoulder and said, 'There's a family gathering in the kitchen. Come and join us.' I didn't need any second bidding and dashed through the bead curtains anxious to find out what had happened.

'Here he is!' the old lady cried as I entered the crowded little room.

'Tell me *all* about it and don't leave a single word out,' I said excitedly. 'What does she look like? The baby, I mean. How's Cynthia? Is she all right? Is the baby dark or light?'

Ramona told me to cool down and have a drink. Yes, she actually produced a bottle of brandy from somewhere and gave me a large glass. She couldn't bear the stuff near her as a rule. I sat down and looked expectantly at Ramona. 'She's absolutely beautiful. A real chip off the old block. She has a full head of straight, chestnut-coloured hair and grey eyes and she is whiter than you!'

I couldn't take all this in at one go and asked her to tell me again, only more slowly. She did and then, to my surprise, she walked around the table and kissed me shyly on the cheek. Cathy and the old lady did too and I shook hands with the men. What a moment that was.

'What about Cynthia?' I asked. 'How is she after all this?'

Ramona said, 'She's fine, man. They had to cut her a bit but she's all right.'

I was shocked. 'Cut her? What do you mean?'

She made a patting motion with her hand as much as to say: Sit down, man, relax. 'Take it easy, man, it was just a little cut and she only needed a couple of stitches. It's quite normal in cases like this, you know.' She told me that Cynthia should be out and about again in a few days but I knew it was going to try my patience waiting to see her again – and Hanna for the first time.

'Give me another tot, Ramona,' I said with a laugh of delight at the good news, and with a little mock-frown she refilled my glass.

We had a bit of supper, and Len and I, assisted by the old man, made short work of the brandy. As we chatted happily somehow we got onto the subject of occult affairs. I have always been interested in such things, and this would be a splendid opportunity for me to learn a little about supernatural matters from a Cape Coloured point of view, as I had heard that Cape Coloured people are extremely superstitious.

Leonard was a believer in ghosts which he called *tokoloshe*, actually a Bantu name for an imp or mischievous spirit.

'Have you seen such a thing?' I asked and he assured me that he had, on at least two occasions. I nodded encouragingly.

'One night,' he started, 'I was walking towards the main Klipfontein Road from here and as I walked along I started to get a funny feeling. I was scared!' I said nothing and poured another tot for each of us. He told me that although the main road was still a fair way away, he could hardly wait to reach it. I realised that I would be taking the same route on the way home that night and decided to keep my foot well down on the accelerator. 'You won't believe this, but a man walked past me on the inside.'

'I bet you were glad of his company,' I said. He looked up at me and said in a quiet and sincere way which made me feel a bit uneasy, 'He wasn't making any sound because he was about three feet above the ground!' That *was* a bit disquieting, I had to agree. I lit a cigarette and offered one to Leonard. He nodded thanks and leaned forward as I flicked my lighter. He sat back and drew on the cigarette, then removed it from his mouth and examined it for a moment before continuing.

'*Tokoloshe* are afraid of fire, you know. As long as you have something burning nearby they won't come near you.' I looked suitably impressed and asked if the one that had overtaken him three feet off the deck had threatened him in any way. He shook his head. 'No! But I didn't look at it, I just kept on walking towards that main road and I was so relieved when I got there and other people were around me.'

I had no reason to doubt that Leonard actually believed what had happened on his eventful walk. I had heard of stranger things than that. No doubt a lot of rubbish had been passed down to coloured folk by their forefathers but there is always a percentage of happenings which defy any scientific or rational explanations.

There was more to come. 'Another night I was walking past that very same spot when a black dog leapt right over my left shoulder and vanished before my eyes.' Any person who has some knowledge of the occult and ghostly legends will confirm that practically every country, and Britain is no exception, has its favourite black-dog ghost stories.

'What did you do, Len?'

He sipped from his glass and said, 'I looked over my right shoulder immediately.' I must have looked puzzled for he continued, 'If a black dog jumps over your shoulder, you must look over the opposite one straight away.' When I asked him to explain the reason he said he didn't know, but that was what his father had told him to do if ever such a thing should happen to him.

We then got round to talking about legendary treatments for various disorders. This proved to be amusing as well as interesting if not very educational, and reminded me of several that Leila had passed on to Cynthia which were guaranteed to cure infants' ailments. For example, should a baby develop a protruding navel – a common enough occurrence from what I had seen in my travels through Africa – the mother should place a penny over the navel and then bind a cloth around the baby's body to keep the coin in position. Another classic was if the baby becomes constipated, tickle its anus with a hen's feather – not a duck's, mark you – and should the unfortunate child survive long enough to develop dysentery, the thoughtful mother should take seven lice and ensure that the baby ate them at once. I had warned Cynthia that if I caught her giving our baby any of these treatments, I would tickle her bottom with the back of a hairbrush – and Leila's too!

On the way home after a cheerful evening I thought over the conversation and was reminded of a tale that Cynthia had been told by Leila. According to the story, Leila's mother saw pictures in the fire and when Elizabeth, her other daughter, told her that someone had stolen her false teeth, the old lady said that she would watch the fire that very night and would quickly learn who the thief was. When asked next day if the fire had revealed the identity of the thief, the old lady had replied smugly, 'Ah, yes, dear, I know now who stole them but the fire also told me that if I reveal the name of this person it will lead to serious trouble,' and no one ever did find out who had stolen Elizabeth's false teeth. I liked the sound of the old lady, who had apparently prophesied that our baby would be a boy. When she heard that we had a baby daughter she immediately blamed the coal she had used and said that the person she had borrowed it from must have had a wicked soul! To me this seemed a very practical and well-thought-out answer and I wondered what the old dear was doing outside the advertising profession.

I took a turn around the garden before going to bed that night, and from the corner of my eye I saw a figure walking seven feet above the ground. It was Fred taking a nocturnal stroll on top of the fence. So much for *tokoloshe*, I thought, and returned to the kitchen to have a friendly little chat with myself in the company of a more tangible spirit.

The big moment of my life was almost due – the delivery of Hanna to the cottage – and in readiness for the occasion I bought a film for my Polaroid camera. This notable event would have to be recorded, if not for posterity at least for my old age. Marie and Dan had left for a brief visit to Port Elizabeth which was a definite advantage.

On the afternoon that the delivery was to take place I could hardly remain in the same position for more than a few minutes. I was wildly excited though I rejected all temptations to drink any booze. Strictly no way. I sat in the front room looking at my watch every two minutes and waiting for the sound of the van's engine. At last I heard a vehicle approaching and I stood up quickly and looked through the net curtains. It was them. Len stepped out, removed three cartons from the back of the little vehicle and carried them casually towards the gate. I held my breath as he rested them against the fence so that he could unlatch the gate with a free hand. He walked towards the stoep and I waited for him to knock. When he did I forced myself not to rush madly to the door. I counted ten slowly before walking out to open it.

He smiled broadly and said, 'I've brought your groceries,

master!' I sensed that we were being observed by the Watcher or his delightful spouse, and without smiling I took the cartons from him and said, 'Thanks a million, Len. I'll see you later, OK?' He turned to leave and said quietly, 'Look after her, she's lovely,' and he was gone. I carried the cartons carefully through into the lounge and placed them gently on the settee, then hurried back and closed the front door. Taking a deep breath I walked calmly back to the lounge and looked down at the cartons for a moment.

What a way for a human being to have to see his own child, I thought, and I lifted off the two top cartons, and gazed in rapture at the beautiful little creature who lay there cocooned in a soft, white fleecy blanket. A small pillow had been stuffed down in the bottom of the carton to provide a comfortable bed for her.

Her lobster-red face peeped out from the folds of soft material and when I lifted her out I was amazed at the lovely, full head of hair that she had. I sat down on a chair and held her close and said, 'So you're our little act of immorality, are you, darling?' and I am not ashamed to admit that I couldn't hold back my tears. She was absolutely divine and I sat talking softly to her for such a long time that I suddenly realised that it was beginning to get dark.

Pinned to her blanket was a list of instructions and a short, loving note from Mum. I examined the contents of the middle carton and found everything necessary to give Hanna a feed. She was asleep on the settee so I went through to the kitchen to read Cynthia's note properly, and the instructions. I also put the kettle on to make myself a cup of tea. Then I sat down at the table and read everything carefully. Cynthia told me that she loved me very much and missed me but that she was well and I shouldn't worry about her. I re-read the feeding instructions and learned that Hanna needed to be fed every four hours. According to the time of her last feed another one was imminent and as I knew that babies yelled their heads off if they were hungry I wasted no time and got cracking on making up a bottle.

When I had finished and tested it for the proper temperature, I went back into the lounge and looked down at my adorable little offspring like any doting dad would. I marvelled to think that she was a combination of Cynthia and myself – a product of our love for each other; there had been no lust involved, just love. I was proud of Cynthia too and mentally thanked her for giving us this delightful little creature whom I could only gaze at in wonder.

I had already loaded my camera and placed it on the settee ready for action. Suddenly Hanna's eyes opened; they were the colour of slate and I wasn't sure whether she was seeing me or not. Her tiny face wrinkled and she began to show signs of distress. I grabbed the bottle and placed the sterilised teat against her quivering little lips. She clamped herself on to it at once and the wrinkles and look of panic subsided, much to my relief. I managed to get one shot of her by holding the bottle with one hand and the camera with the other. She seemed to enjoy her feed. Cynthia's instructions had stated two measures of baby food but I thought this was a bit niggardly so I had made it three. Perhaps this accounted for the look of contentment on the baby's face as she sucked away happily.

I suddenly remembered the bit about 'windies' and I removed the teat of the empty bottle from her still-sucking lips, lifted her up carefully and placed her over my shoulder as instructed, patting her back and saying encouraging things such as, 'There's a good little girlie for her loving dad. Do nice windies for daddy,' and so forth. After a little while she did her stuff and I felt very proud of myself and by now an experienced father, of course.

During the course of her 'windies' she had vomited excess milky curds all over her dear old dad so I laid her down and wiped her with some tissues and gave myself a wipe at the same time. After this nasty experience, I realised that a clean nappy would now be required and I dithered around for a few minutes almost wringing my hands in gutless anxiety at the prospect of what might lie ahead.

It wasn't as bad as I had expected. I prepared for this operation by getting a clean towel from the bathroom and folding it to form a blanket. I made up a bowl of warm water which I carried through to the lounge where all the action was and placed it on the floor. I then laid my offspring on the towel and unfastened the large safety-pin and opened the package.

Oh boy! I thought as I hauled her clear of the nasty-looking yellow gunge that she was warmly lying in. I put her back on the clean towel and got rid of the dirty nappy in the dustbin, returned, bathed her wrinkled little bum carefully with cotton wool and eventually, after powdering her, managed to re-wrap her in a clean nappy. She lay there seemingly content, with her two little legs sticking out like rhubarb. They looked a bit bandy to me and I made a mental note to ask Ramona to have her checked for rickets or something. I need not have worried. When I told Ramona she burst out laughing, and assured me that all babies have bandy legs.

It was dark enough now to take Hanna back to Ramona's place and I tucked her lovingly back into her carton and made sure that she was well wrapped in her fleecy blanket for the journey home. She certainly seemed to be a well-behaved baby. Apart from a few tentative squeaks when I was changing her nappy, she had been as good as gold and now lay in her box quite contented. I smiled down at her and blew her a kiss and said, 'Don't worry, darling. You'll soon be back with Mum again.'

I strolled down to the gate and casually looked up and down the road as if waiting for someone. Seeing that the coast was clear I returned to the house and collected the carton containing the diminutive but extremely precious little bundle. As I carried it out to the car I couldn't help thinking what a strange nation of Christians these people were, that harmless citizens such as Cynthia and I, not to mention the baby, were compelled to act out our lives in such an un-Christian way. It seemed to me to be not only sad, but sick, and I shook my head in wonder as I placed the carton gently on the passenger seat. We had an uneventful journey to Ramona's and while I was driving I was thinking about Hanna's future. If I had deserted her mother what sort of a future would the baby have had? It would have been near impossible for Cynthia to have supported her properly and that would have led to dreadful problems for a start. Hanna would have ended up with her relatives at Malmesbury, running barefoot amongst the chickens, and whatever her education might be it would be third-rate compared to that of a white child in South Africa. She would probably have grown up to work in a sweat-shop factory in the Cape earning peanuts, or as an ever-smiling maid or nanny to some fat idiot too idle to wipe her own child's nose.

We had a minor incident at the cottage a few days later while Marie and Dan were still away. The butcher was not able to deposit my meat in her fridge and he very thoughtfully telephoned me at the office and asked what he should do. Without thinking I told him to leave it on the window-ledge inside the bedroom. When I arrived home and entered the cottage, moggies flew out of the house from every possible opening. I think every cat within a radius of two miles had enjoyed a topside feast, thanks to my stupidity. When I entered the front bedroom I found the host, Fred, standing over what was left of the topside, plus various scraps of paper. It looked as if they had dragged the joint all round the bedroom, across the bed and halfway up the wall. Although it wasn't Fred's fault I wanted to kick a cat and as he happened to be the most convenient one, I stepped towards him purposefully. Fred, who was nobody's fool, could clearly see that his beloved master wasn't feeling very well and a discreet bunk out of the bedroom window might be in order. Obeying these moggie instincts with alacrity, he left me to clear up the mess as best I could.

It would be pilchards for Fred for the rest of the week. He hated them. However, I relented later on as it wasn't Fred's fault and normal relations were established between us once more.

That evening I set off for Sea Point to track Bob down. He had changed his venue and I found that he was giving the Sea Point Ritz the benefit of his patronage. With all due respect to the Sea Point Ritz, the only thing that it had in common with the Piccadilly Ritz was its name. It seemed to suit Bob admirably for I found him chomping his way through their famous bar supper which consisted of a large plate containing chicken, lamb, beef, curried something, peas and mashed spuds – all for the princely sum of twenty-five cents which in those days of not so long ago was the equivalent of today's twelve and a half pence. This service was intended to attract solid drinkers to the bar and consequently the Sea Point Ritz was always packed with cheek-bulging patrons.

Bob's eyebrows twitched when he saw me forcing my way through the guzzling customers and he greeted me with a glutinous word or two; his mouth happened to be stuffed with mashed potato at the time. I managed to order a round and while I was waiting for the barman to deliver I watched in wonder as Bob rammed great forkfuls of lamb, chicken and curried something into his cavernous mouth – all at the same time. If his heart was not too good it made me wonder what state his stomach was in. He appeared to find difficulty at times in swallowing the enormous loads but solved this by glugging down huge mouthfuls of frothy beer between cheek-bulging mouthfuls. I nudged him, and pointing at his still well-laden plate said, 'Nobody's going to nick it, you know. You'll kill your bloody self if you eat like that. What are you trying to do? Commit suicide?' He tried to sneer but it wasn't easy with a mouthful of gravy.

When Bob finally ended his gargantuan meal, signified by a cataclysmic belch, he proceeded to tell me of his latest idea to make a quick killing. He sidled close and told me that he knew of a bloke who would pay up to five thousand rand for drivers to collect loads of dagga – marijuana – smuggled over the borders of Swaziland, and then to drive the loads down to the Cape. I replied that it would be easier to try to sell the Voortrekker Monument, the Afrikaner shrine in memory of the Great Trek, to some wealthy Texan. I told Bob that I had managed to take a photograph of Hanna and I would show it to him after we left the Ritz. He was immediately full of questions about the baby and Cynthia but I suggested that we should talk about it later as 'You never know who you are standing next to in these places.'

He had been chatting to an elderly Irishman when I arrived and the latter was deeply immersed in conversation with another bloke to his right. The Irishman, known as Paddy – of course – eventually turned his attention back to Bob who introduced him to me. He proved to be a great conversationalist like many of his countrymen are, and we had an amusing chat for a while. He seemed to have a great predilection for an Irish liqueur whiskey known as Tullamore Dew and proudly stated that he had a bottle back at his hotel, not too far away from the Ritz. When he invited us to share this treasure with him, we readily accepted his kind invitation. We were to follow him down after a little while as he said he had to meet someone there and would have to leave immediately.

Accordingly, Bob and I made our way to what turned out to be a slightly seedy residential hotel near a place called Rocklands. Paddy was waiting on the stoep behind a small table on which stood his bottle of Tullamore Dew. 'Pull a chair up, lads, and sit down,' he cried with genuine pleasure at seeing us. We joined him and a few minutes later a balding immigrant from England glided up and Paddy introduced him as a fellow guest of the hotel.

His name was Jack and he was a rather sad character in his early forties. He looked as though he needed a shoulder to cry on and after a couple of Tullamore Dews out came his unhappy story. Jack had arrived in the Republic just a few weeks ago and he was disconsolate because he had not been able to find a decent job. He had paid his own fare to South Africa and had bought a return ticket. 'If I can't find a reasonable job by next week I'll get the first mail-boat back,' he threatened sulkily. When I asked what he did for a living he told me that he had spent most of his life working as an assistant in his father's bike and pram shop in a village in Essex. I realised that this was his one and only great adventure; a desperate bid to escape from what must have been mind-numbing boredom. He was trying to shake off the shackles of a totally wasted life, and his round, slightly fat and petulant face told a story of weakness, lack of character and despair. I pitied him. He rattled off an embarrassing monologue of sordid tales of his sexual conquests with the girls of his village which quickly indicated that he had never enjoyed the charms of a woman in his life.

It was pretty obvious that the force that had driven him into setting out on a long ocean voyage to try to find an exciting new life in a new world had not been courage or a sense of challenge, more the anxiety of the desperate, and fear of what might lie ahead when his ageing father died. His mother had already passed on and it was fairly certain that he had been greatly influenced by her.

'What have you done so far about trying to find a job, Jack?' I asked, and with a nasal whine which was five points against him for a start, he said, 'I've tramped the streets of Cape Town trying to find anything. I don't speak Afrikaans and that's why I can't get a bleedin' job,' he whined on.

I pointed out that I didn't speak bleedin' Afrikaans either but it hadn't stopped me from obtaining a few highly-paid and responsible jobs since I had been in the Republic. I told him that I didn't think he had really tried seriously to find a job and he strenuously denied this. 'I mean,' he blathered on, 'I thought I'd get a job as a supervisor or something like that.'

I sniffed my Tullamore Dew and mentally applauded Paddy on his good taste. 'Supervising what?' I pressed Jack.

'Well.' Pause. 'I mean, I thought that all the niggers did the work 'ere and we whites sort of supervised them.'

I could hardly believe this and swallowed some Tullamore Dew. 'You mean to tell me that you thought it was all plantations here with the faithful niggers, as you call them, trudging home, singing, to their shacks, dutifully tugging their forelocks as they march past kindly old massa standing with his whip behind his patriarchal back?'

He looked a bit baffled for a moment. 'Er . . . Yer. Summat like that.'

I told him that he had obviously come to the wrong country as South Africa wasn't quite as he had envisaged it. 'You should have done a bit of research on the country before you bought your ticket, Jack,' I said. But despite his feeble-minded approach to life, I couldn't help feeling sorry for him and I began to see him as a product that had to be marketed. 'I tell you what, Jack,' I said, filled with inspiration.

'What's that?' he asked, looking at me blearily.

'I will write a letter to a local newspaper and I'll guarantee to get you a job, but you will have to extend your stay for one week to enable the newspaper to have proper time to publish your letter.'

He looked mildly interested. 'How do you know they'll publish the letter?' he asked.

'They'll publish the letter, you see if they don't. It'll be such a bloody tear-jerker you might end up with the Pulitzer Prize!'

Jack began to make all sorts of excuses to avoid staying but we persisted with our arguments and in the end he rather reluctantly agreed to put his departure off for another week.

The following day I was as good as my word, and I skipped lunch to work on Jack's letter. It got off to a promising start with the heading: 'Must I leave your beautiful country?' I knew that would grab the editor's attention. I followed with a touching leading paragraph which read as follows:

I have only been in your beautiful country for two weeks but I have fallen in love with it. Sadly though, despite strenuous efforts on my part, I have not been able to find a job. Although I do not have any special qualifications I am hard-working, sincere and I am prepared to tackle anything. I had to scrimp and scrape to find the fare to come here which I will never regret, but now it seems that I must return to England on the next mail-boat. I had hoped to find an exciting new life here and, who knows, perhaps a charming South African wife etc., etc.

Although the latter was a nice touch I felt a bit unscrupulous, but on the other hand, I had promised results.

For several days after delivering the letter to the *Argus* by hand, I scanned its columns hopefully. In the meantime, Jack had chickened out on his word and had hopped aboard the mail-boat a week earlier than he had said he would.

The day after he sailed, his letter appeared in the paper and the results were staggering. I discovered that the manager of the hotel was desperately trying to find out where Jack could be contacted because he was being inundated with offers of remarkably good jobs for him. The newspaper also received several letters from good-hearted people willing to help. The truth of it was that Jack didn't really deserve such kindness and I honestly felt ashamed of myself and still do.

One letter which was published by the newspaper read touchingly as follows:

When my husband and I arrived in South Africa many years ago, neither of us could speak a word of English or Afrikaans but he didn't give up and eventually he started his own business. Later he lost the use of his hands due to a fire at the factory but he still refused to give up and has made a success of his life. Jack X sounds just the sort of man we would like to give a chance to as my husband is thinking of retiring in a few years and Jack could possibly take over the business.

This letter really moved me and I was glad that Jack had gone: he would have been a dreadful disappointment to the lady and her brave husband.

Apparently when Jack arrived at Southampton a representative of the Cape Town newspaper was waiting to meet him with the job offers but Jack hadn't the guts to follow any of them through.

During my next visit to Ramona I demanded to see Cynthia as I was fed up with this business of exchanging notes through windows and receiving messages from third parties. I wanted to see her and the baby for myself and find out how she was and how she was being treated. Ramona said she would ask Kerim and try to arrange for us to go over one evening with Leonard and herself. It was agreed that two nights later I would be able to go over to see them, but fairly late as they were anxious that as few people as possible should know that they were receiving visits from a white man. As it was, too many neighbours were making snide remarks about Cynthia and the baby living with them.

The evening came and once again I found myself driving into that depressingly ugly area. After a couple of abortive attempts to leave the car without being observed by passers-by we eventually managed to climb out of the car into the now deserted street and after braving no-man's-land we reached Kerim's house without, as far as we knew, having been observed by anyone.

Cynthia was in bed and looked a bit run-down. There was a coloured girl sitting simpering in a chair and I took an instant dislike to her. She made no attempt to get up and leave the room as we entered and although I wanted to kiss Cynthia and give her a warm hello, I refrained in the presence of this stranger who turned out to be Leila's daughter Jinja, and a thoroughly sneaky bitch she looked too. I gave her a brief nod and a cool but polite 'Good evening', and she seemed to get the message because she rose and left the room.

Hanna was asleep in her mother's arms and I leaned over and kissed them both. Cynthia clung to me with her free arm and wouldn't let me up. She began to weep and my heart sank. I was upset by her state and also realised that we had more problems ahead. She told me all about it. Apparently Kerim hadn't paid his electricity bill and the local board had threatened to cut off the household supply unless he coughed up. On top of this, they were refusing to supply Cynthia with hot water to bath the baby and herself, and I discovered that quite a few of the things which I had sent over for Cynthia had never reached her. I felt like going through to the kitchen and banging the greasy little man's head against the wall, but that would be the way to disaster. We would have to pay him more money if necessary until we could find a solution to the problem.

I asked her if Kerim had ill-treated her in any way and she swore that he hadn't. She said he was a bit scared of me and wouldn't have dared lay a finger on her. I called him into the parlour and asked why Cynthia could not have hot water for herself and the baby. He gave me his blubbery smile and waved his arms around like feelers and started whining about the high cost of living, blaming the luckless Leila for his present problems as he had given her the money to pay for the electricity bill but she had wasted it.

He was lying, that was for sure, but I kept my opinions to myself. I asked how much the electricity bill was for and he mentioned a few rand. I gave the money to Leila and told her to pay the Electricity Board the next day and show me the receipt when I next visited them.

Kerim looked at Leila and then at me and I knew what was going through his mind. There was nothing that he could say or do but I knew Leila was going to cop it again as soon as I left, and I badly wanted to lay a bunch of fives on his slimy teeth.

I went on to ask why Cynthia had not been receiving all the things I had been sending over for her, things which she needed badly for the baby. Leila twisted her gnarled fingers in embarrassment and Kerim looked intently at the wall and shrugged. 'I don't want it to happen again, OK?' I said. They nodded and I said goodnight, and went to have a few final words with Cynthia before leaving with Ramona and Leonard. I told Cynthia that she would have hot water the next day and none of her things would be stolen again. I made a fuss of her but she didn't look well or happy and I knew that she would have to leave this place somehow. I managed to coax a little smile out of her before leaving and assured her that she had nothing to worry about and that I loved her very much and would always take good care of her. She held my hand for a few moments, reluctant to let me go, but I gently disengaged it and went out after one last peek at Hanna who was oblivious to all our problems, thank God.

On the way back to Ramona's, Leonard offered to buy a bottle for us to enjoy over supper with them but I thanked them for their kind offer and declined. I just wasn't in the mood and wanted to get home to think.

On our next visit to Kerim's house Cynthia assured me that she felt better but she still didn't look too good to me. I sat on the bed and nursed Hanna while Cynthia told me that Jinja was becoming a nuisance.

'In what way?' I asked.

Jinja had been looking at some of Cynthia's clothes and appeared to be extremely jealous of her and our relationship. She had asked Cynthia to lend her one of her dresses to wear at a party and Cynthia had been too nervous to refuse; the dress had never been returned. Jinja also 'borrowed' the medallion that Bob had given me for Cynthia, and that had gone missing as well. I knew we had a serious problem. I felt a sickening chill run through me when Cynthia went on to tell me that Jinja had been dropping hints that two of her friends who were policemen – coloured policemen they would be – must have been told about us because they had been asking her a lot of probing questions.

There was only one person who could have told them as far as I could see and that was Jinja herself. I tried to reassure Cynthia that it was just a lot of bullshit and not to worry about it, but I was very worried myself. In fact I learned later that about twenty minutes after I had left the house, the two 'friends' had called to talk to Jinja.

Kerim had been hanging around like a bad smell and wanted to say something to me before I left. He insisted that Cynthia was costing much more than he had expected and when I asked how much he said, 'About ten rand'. I gave him the money and told him that I would increase the monthly rent by this amount. I would have given anything to have woken up the following morning to read in the newspapers that the Immorality Act had been abolished: I would have slowly strangled Kerim and enjoyed doing it – and got away with it too.

As I was leaving, a delicious odour wafted through from the tiny kitchen and I learned later that Kerim had enjoyed a tasty supper of broiled pigeons. Kerim had been entrusted with the care of his uncle's racing pigeons and for some unaccountable reason they had 'failed to return' after he had released them. If I had known where his uncle was living I would have cheerfully told him what had happened to his beloved pigeons.

THE LIVING NIGHTMARE

Cynthia's health worried me. Although the coloured midwife was calling in to see her, I was given to understand that her visits were irregular. She had already received her money, after all, and Cynthia was not in a condition to complain, even if she had known who to complain to.

At my next visit I was concerned to find that she seemed to have rather a high temperature and had not been eating proper meals. It seemed that apart from the fruit and packets of biscuits that I was sending to her, she received little else. She also complained about the incision that the doctor had had to make during her delivery, which should have been receiving attention from the so-called midwife, but wasn't.

I told her to leave her window unlocked as I would return again very early in the morning. She looked worried at this and when I asked what was the matter she admitted that she was very concerned in case Kerim found out. I told her it could prove to be very unfortunate for him if he did.

Realising how unwell Cynthia was played havoc with my overloaded nervous system and when I got back to the cottage I flopped down on a chair in the kitchen almost in a state of despair. No one could help me or console me, apart from Bob, and it was wearing me down, this constant anxiety. I pulled myself together and started making a list of things to take to Cynthia. Antibiotics, antiseptic and cotton-wool meant a drive to an all-night chemist at Sea Point. It had been cold in the little concrete box of a room in which she and the baby were incarcerated so I added a hot-water-bottle to the list. Two Thermos flasks, one for boiling water and one for pre-mixed baby feeds, enough to last the night. An electric fire, and above all a damned good hot meal.

Roast beef and Yorkshire pudding ought to put a bit of life into the lass, I thought, and as I busied myself in the kitchen preparing this bizarre banquet, I smiled and bet that I was the only man in the world who had cooked roast beef and Yorkshire pud at 2 a.m., south of the equator. Deciding to make a real job of it I included roast potatoes, creamed potatoes, cauliflower – and gravy. When the meal was ready, I put it on a tray and covered it with aluminium foil and then carried it out very carefully to the car. I glanced across the road but there was no sign of enemy activity so I returned and collected the rest of the stuff I had got together.

By this time it was about three-thirty in the morning and I sat behind the wheel of the Beetle praying that my mission would be achieved without any hitches or interference. I can't remember all the disjointed things I said to our Maker on that occasion, but I do wonder what he thought of me. Despite my many shortcomings, he continued to throw his 'protective mantle' over me, no doubt while shaking his head.

I drove carefully and fairly slowly because I didn't want the roast beef and Yorkshire pudding going straight on whenever I turned left or right. There was perspiration on my forehead and cheeks as I drove agonisingly past Athlone police station, and when I made the turn into Kew Town I saw the funny side of the mess I was in.

What if a patrolling police truck or car stops me now? I could imagine their faces at finding a tray full of hot food on the floor of the car at that time of the morning. What possible explanation could I have given? Apart from pleading insanity there would have been little else I could have thought of in the circumstances.

What fun the newspapers would have. I could see the headlines in my mind's eye as I drove furtively on: 'Secretary of the Cape-Coloured Pudding Club caught in the early hours delivering the goods', or 'Eccentric white man found wandering around the Cape Flats at three-thirty in the morning in possession of a hot roast beef and Yorkshire pudding dinner. Gourmet's mobile cornucopia.'

My already tortured mind boggled at the thought. There was no limit to the possibilities. I could almost see the bifocal glasses of the judge gleaming in astonishment as he peered down at the red-faced police officer giving evidence at my trial. 'You say you found the accused driving around the unsavoury areas of Kew Town with a hot dinner in the car – at three-thirty in the morning? Surely, Officer, you can't be serious. What did the accused say when you stopped him?'

'He asked me if I had any salt on me, Your Honour.' Thank God for my Yorkshire sense of humour, I thought, as I pressed on with grim determination.

The streets looked bleaker than ever when I reached the church. Reversing the car carefully into the side-street next to the silent building I switched off the motor and sat quietly for a few minutes, watching for any movement or lighted windows. The houses remained dark and nothing stirred. It was a bit eerie sitting alone in that little vehicle with the wind singing a mournful dirge around it, and I could think of several other things that I would rather have been doing.

Reassured that it was safe enough to set off for the house, I got out of the car and placed the tray of hot food on the ground while I reached inside for the carrier bag containing the other things. Lifting the heavy bag in my teeth and the tray in my hands, I pushed the car door shut with a knee and set off across no-man's-land. Not a thing in sight, not even a moggie attracted by the smell from the contents of the tray.

The bag was becoming uncomfortably heavy in my teeth and the journey seemed to take hours instead of minutes, but I eventually reached the gate and nudged it slowly open to minimise any squeaks. I tiptoed painfully up the little path. The string handle of the bag was really hurting my gums and lips by this time and when I lowered the tray to the ground and removed the bag from my teeth the relief was immediate – and sublime.

With an aching back I rose and tapped softly on the window. Cynthia must have been awake and waiting because she reached up and pushed the window open. I put my head into the room and whispered, 'Shhh! It's me, Dad! Stay where you are and keep Hanna quiet.' I handed the bag through first and she took it from me. I leaned in and whispered, 'Sit up and take this from me, there's a good girlie.'

When she saw the loaded tray entering the window her eyes opened wide in astonishment and she said, 'Oooh! What's this?' The aroma was delicious, I had to admit. My own share of the meal was waiting at the cottage, in the oven.

'Move your legs, darling, I'm coming in,' I whispered and grabbing hold of the window ledge I managed to heave myself up. With a lot of panting and muttering I made a rather undignified but quiet entry into the little room. After closing the curtains and drawing the curtain that covered the entrance to the room I switched on the bedside lamp, and raised a finger to my lips to remind Cynthia to be very quiet. I nodded towards the tray and gave her a thumbs-up signal and a wink. I dug down into the carrier bag and found a knife and fork, also pepper and salt and a jar of mustard, and soon she was staring down in awe at the plate of steaming hot food.

She was hungry and I sat quietly watching her enjoying the meal, probably the first decent one she had seen for some time. When she finished the lot she lay back against the pillows and blew out her cheeks. 'The best meal I have ever had,' she said, smiling contentedly at me. This cheered me up. Baby Hanna was snoozing contentedly inside a drawer that I had sent over for that purpose on an earlier occasion. She didn't wake when I reached down and tickled the tip of her tiny nose.

I filled a bowl with hot water from one of the flasks and set it aside for the water to cool a bit. I then tore open the packet of cotton-wool and pulled a hunk out. There was a small tumbler on the window shelf and I poured a little of the antiseptic into it and diluted it with some of the water from the flask. Dipping the cotton-wool into it, I said, 'Right, my girl! Let's have a look at that cut.' Cynthia tittered and said, 'Don't be silly.' I waved the piece of cotton-wool and said, 'Come on, just pretend I'm a doctor and keep your eyes shut. It's got to be cleaned and looked after or you'll end up with a bad infection.' She looked embarrassed and shy but she turned her head away and I gently drew up her nightie. She winced as I bathed her carefully. There was no sign of infection but she was a little bit inflamed there and swollen. When I finished and tucked her up again she took hold of my hand and said softly, 'You're a good man, John.' I smiled down at her and whispered, 'I'm a bloody fool – but I love you.' I gave her two antibiotic capsules.

Before leaving I showed her the things I had brought and

when I plugged the electric fire into the wall socket and switched it on, it soon warmed the small room and brightened it with a cheerful glow. 'If Kerim complains, tell him I'll give him extra for the electricity,' I told her, and made my way out of the window again after kissing and hugging her and reminding her to tell Hanna that her dad loved her.

I peered carefully through the trellis outside, and the street was silent and deserted. I was lucky and I reached the comparative safety of Klipfontein Road without any trouble and was soon back at the cottage. I was too tired to eat but went straight to bed and must have fallen asleep at once. When I woke, I felt as though I was smothering and found Fred sleeping on my face.

This was the start of a series of pre-dawn visits which still haunt my memory. If I had left Cynthia and the baby to the tender mercies of Kerim and Leila they might have become very ill and undernourished. I had no choice but to make sure, in my own way and by my own efforts, that they were well cared for and had everything that would be required. I began ferrying food and other essentials to Cynthia and the baby at different times of the early mornings. It would have added to the danger to have established a regular time-pattern and for Cynthia and Hanna's sake I dared not risk being caught. This daily programme was double hell because it affected my own metabolism. My built-in time clock, which we all have, simply didn't know what the blazes was going on. One day I would set off at 1 a.m., the next at say, 4 a.m., the day after that 2.30 a.m., and so on. As a result I felt rather worn out during this nightmarish period. I discovered that it was best for me to go to bed at the cottage, after a quick snack, almost as soon as I arrived home from my day's work. I would then wake at midnight to prepare the hot meals to take to Cynthia, often delivering them at some unearthly time of the morning.

During one of our clandestine meetings while she was busy eating a particularly tasty casserole I had cooked and brought over, Cynthia told me about her experiences in Groote Schuur Hospital. She had been treated very well there and had been attended by white doctors and nurses who had been kind and considerate. She had been given an injection to bring on the birth, and in due course the baby made her appearance. Hanna

239

was made a great fuss of by a white nursing sister who had been attending Cynthia at the time. After marvelling at the baby's colour and European appearance the sister had waggled an admonishing finger at Cynthia and said, 'I think someone has been a naughty girl around here, you know.' Cynthia told me that she had felt herself going red and she didn't know where to look, despite her attempts to appear innocent.

On that occasion, as I was driving back through Kew Town towards the main road shortly before three in the morning, I became aware of a pair of headlights approaching from behind, and when I glanced into my rear-view mirror I saw the familiar outline of another Volkswagen Beetle. My nervous system and all my senses immediately locked into a defence mode and my long-suffering stomach knotted into a ball of tension as I realised that the vehicle now apparently following me must be a police car.

When I reached the main road I turned left instead of right and drove in the direction of Nyanga, a black township, with the headlights of the car behind almost burning the back of my neck, or so it seemed at the time. My mind was in a whirl as I desperately tried to think of some credible reason for driving around at this time of night, but I knew there was nothing sensible that I could come up with and I was left with prayer. It seemed that there was something in praying after all, for the solution to my rather nasty dilemma came quicker than I had expected. I pulled in to the side of the road as casually as I could, and pretended to be looking for something in the glove compartment.

The other Beetle slowly overtook me. I studiously ignored it as it went slowly by and I could feel the driver staring with curiosity into my car. It was a most unpleasant moment and I just wanted to be sick with fear instead of putting on this ridiculous pretence of ice-cool self-containment. I lit a cigarette with deliberate slowness and a wild idea was born.

I did a U-turn and started heading back towards Athlone and, as I had suspected, the driver of the other Volkswagen did the same and started following me again. As I drove across Jan Smuts Drive I made a bold move. I swung the car into the forecourt of Athlone police station and stopped right outside the entrance. Glancing back I could see that my pursuer had slowed almost to a stop and was obviously puzzled by my action. Taking my courage into my hands, I climbed out of the car and giving him a slight wave, strolled casually into the police station, hoping that he would assume that I too was a policeman.

When I entered the dismal atmosphere of the enquiry room with its institutional finish of green and cream, a short, stocky sergeant with a sun-reddened face stepped from behind a partition and said, 'Can I 'elp you, sir?' in a strong South African accent. I told him that I had been visiting friends at Stellenbosch and had taken what I had thought was a short cut on my way to Sea Point, but had found myself driving through what appeared to be a native township. He went to great trouble explaining how to get to Sea Point from Athlone and I managed to keep our conversation going for the better part of twenty minutes. Although it was a fairly cool morning, I could feel sweat trickling down my ribs from underneath my arms, and after thanking him profusely I walked out to the car and was relieved to find that the other Volksie had gone.

I drove home quickly and fell into bed, exhausted, and must have fallen asleep at once but I was woken by a nightmare. I dreamed that I was lying on my side in the dark and my eyes were open. In the dim light from the window I saw the head of an African rising up from below the level of the bed and his black, gleaming eyes stared directly into mine. He was unshaven and there was a look of insanity about him. It was so realistic and frightening that I screamed aloud and in one movement lashed out with both feet straight at the face but found myself kicking at nothing.

It upset me so much that I sat up, knowing that I wouldn't dare go to sleep again. I was still trembling when I heard a loud knocking at the kitchen door. It was Dan; he and Marie had been woken by my blood-curdling yell and he had come to see what was up. He was dressed in pyjamas and was grasping a Zulu knobkerry which he normally kept on the wall of his lounge as a memento of a trip he had made to Natal. He stared anxiously at me. 'Christ, man, are you all right?' I told him what had happened and he drew his arms across his chest to ward off the morning chill. 'God, man! You yelled loud enough to wake the bleddy dead!' Relieved to find that I was alive and well he returned to his house and I closed and re-bolted the back door and made a cup of tea.

My erratic and nerve-wracking visits to Cynthia with home-cooked meals ranging from steak-and-kidney pie and vegetables to Lancashire hot-pot followed by rice pudding paid off and she soon recovered her normal health and vitality. It was impossible for me to consider having her at the cottage again because I wasn't prepared to take the slightest risk of our being arrested – we had a baby to think about now, not just our own safety. Recent events had done little to improve my own state of health and well-being and I felt that a short holiday would improve my general condition.

I decided to drive up to Johannesburg where I had one or two friends. I always enjoyed the drive through some exciting and beautiful parts of the Republic, and the prospect of getting away from Cape Town – and Kew Town – cheered me considerably. Cynthia was pleased that I was going to have a break but she was also anxious that nothing should happen to me, and I assured her that I would take great care of myself and would drive carefully.

I made special arrangements with Ramona and Cathy to make sure that Cynthia and the baby would be well looked after during my absence, and I left them with plenty of food and money for this purpose. I also asked Ramona to keep a closer eye on her sister and to make sure that she was not left alone too much at Leila's.

Fred and I set off in the early hours one morning and were soon buzzing steadily along the National Road in the direction of Sir Lowery's Pass which offers spectacular views of False Bay, the Cape Flats and distant Table Mountain, known affectionately in the sentimental Afrikaans ballad as 'Die Oude Tafelberg'. I drove on past Somerset West and turned northeast at Grabouw towards Worcester where I joined National Road number 1 and headed towards the Karroo Desert.

It was a beautiful morning and although the winter months were still with us, the sun was warm, and I wound down the window of the little car as we hummed happily on our way. The Karroo is a vast area of arid, sun-baked red earth, broken

here and there with occasional vivid green patches of vege-
tation. Elsewhere nothing but dried-up bushes dotted the
harsh landscape. Whenever I drove through the grim territory
of the Karroo it made me think of Mars, the red planet. It was
a great place to make a science-fiction film, the Karroo.

The National Road ran in an almost straight line for the
better part of three hundred miles through the desert. Tall
chain-link fencing separated the road from the desert terrain
to prevent wild animals from straying into the path of speeding
vehicles, especially at night. Every so often one would come
across a twisted, burned-out shell of a car that had run out of
road or overturned, possibly due to a burst tyre or a wild dog
getting in the way.

One had to drive with great care on this particular route as
sitting behind the wheel while travelling at high speed along
a perfectly straight road, shimmering in a heat haze, could
have a hypnotic effect on a driver. Many tragic and devastating
road accidents in the Republic have been blamed on this effect,
which could cause a driver to fall asleep while travelling at
speeds of over eighty miles per hour. It had actually happened
to me once when I was driving to Durban, when the car struck
the central dividing section that ran between the dual motor
lanes. Luckily for me the car did not overturn and I awoke
with a shock to find myself careering along on the wrong side
of the road. It was as well that it was early in the morning and
there were no other vehicles about otherwise I might not be
sitting here now typing this account.

As we buzzed along, the temperature was rising and I
estimated that inside the car it must have been in the nineties,
even though the windows were open. During winter in the
Karroo, solid ice can form during the night but the days can
be sizzling hot. Fred, who was in his customary place on my
lap, looked a bit unhappy. His spiny little tongue was hanging
out due to the excessive heat so I removed my foot from the
accelerator where it had been firmly pressed to the floor and
pulled in to the side of the road for a break.

I had brought with me a small white plastic bottle which
contained water and had a spray attachment fitted to the
bottle cap. When Fred was obviously uncomfortably hot I
would spray him with this useful little gadget. Although it

must have produced the desired effect, Fred hated it and whenever he saw me reaching out for the dreaded spray, he would dive under the seat and spit and swear as I hauled him out again unceremoniously. Fred was a long-suffering little mogulator and he must have had great affection for his eccentric master or he would have left home a long time ago.

I noticed a falling-off in engine power as we climbed upwards in the direction of Johannesburg. On arrival there I would have to re-tune the motor to enable it to cope with the thinner atmosphere of its six-thousand-feet altitude – and again on returning to the sea level of Cape Town.

Before leaving Cynthia I had given her a telephone number where she could contact me in the event of any emergencies while I was in Jo-burg. I told her *not* to use the number unless it was absolutely vital as it could represent a danger to our security. Two days after my arrival I was visiting a friend's business address in the heart of the great metropolis and a call came through for me. It was Cynthia; she was all right but panicking a bit because she thought that I might not return. I quite understood her insecurity and I managed to put her mind at rest without saying any words of love. I knew there was a good chance that the conversation could have been tapped; this practice on the part of the State was not entirely unknown at the time. When she told me that she missed me and loved me I sweated with fear and apprehension; the sixth sense was working overtime again. I tried to tell her as cryptically as possible to be careful what she was saying over the phone but she obviously didn't understand what I was talking about. The conversation lasted for only three minutes but they were the longest three minutes of my life. Although I was pleased to hear that she was well and it was good to hear her voice I was mightily relieved when the conversation came to an end.

About five minutes after she had rung off I was sitting chatting to my friend when Betsy, the telephone operator and receptionist, came into the office. She had an expression of puzzlement on her face and we both looked at her with interest, waiting for her announcement. 'That was funny,' she said. 'Guess what, John?' I had an uneasy feeling and preferred not to. 'The long-distance operator just rang me to ask me if

Meneer Carr is a European or a Non-European.' I had that urge to vomit again and developed the shakes. Laughing nervously I said, 'Christ! I've lived in the Cape for so long, I'm beginning to sound like a Capie' [a word used by whites to describe a Cape Coloured], and they grinned – a little uneasily, I thought.

As I left the office I felt really upset and all my anxieties which I thought I had left behind in Cape Town surrounded me again. Oh, God! I thought as I walked into the high-speed lift, is there ever going to be an end to this nightmare? Even a thousand miles away from Cynthia I couldn't escape from the effects of the Immorality Act. I walked back to the flat where I was staying but couldn't unwind; my mind was working overtime as it did when under acute stress and it began exploring the possible results of that telephone call.

The government operator, of course, would have recorded where I had received the call; through her colleague in the Western Cape, she would have been able to locate where the call had been made from – probably from Athlone post office. She might have written down some of the details of the conversation that had taken place and although I had been notably discreet with *my* choice of words and expressions, Cynthia, bless her naïve little heart, had been pretty liberal with the 'darlings'.

It was no good blaming Cynthia for the present situation: she didn't understand the finer points of telephone tapping and all the other little dodges the regime foisted on its long-suffering citizens – to preserve their particular brand of Christianity and democracy.

I could imagine the telephone operator telling her story to the officers of the Special Branch – probably at this very moment – and my blood ran cold when I realised that the receptionist at my friend's office in Johannesburg knew where I was staying while here. It would only be a matter of time before the Special Branch men would be calling in to ask for my whereabouts. I began lacing myself with brandy as I considered the consequences.

By the time I had finished taking the situation to what my tortured mind considered to be the logical conclusion, I was totally convinced that I could expect a visit from State security

agents at any moment, and I lost no time in packing my belongings and moving to another place of refuge, with Fred of course.
The following day after a sleepless night I considered selling
the car for what I could get, finding someone to take Fred in
and then jumping on a 707 to London.

How did I let all this happen? I wondered. If I had been so
badly in need of female affection and companionship, why
hadn't I found the daughter of a wealthy farmer and settled
down to a cushy life here, without all this mind-bending
intrigue? Why did I have to do it the hard way? I thought of
all the people I would be hurting and letting down, which
aggravated my already unhappy state of mind even more
unbearably. I felt myself sinking lower and lower into a great,
enveloping mass of dark despair.

One very close friend of mine lived in Jo'burg. I could trust
Ron, who was an Australian businessman with very little
affection for the South African political system. I needed to
talk to someone about my troubles and I decided to get in
touch with him. When I rang his office he was there and
seemed to be genuinely pleased to hear from me. 'Hello, you
old bastard,' was the typical affectionate Australian greeting
that buzzed into my ear. I smiled. It was good to hear his
quiet, friendly voice again and I readily accepted his kind offer
to have a meal with him that night.

He had booked a table for two at a smart restaurant not far
from the Stock Exchange and I found him at the bar. He
grinned broadly when he saw me and he held out his free hand
in welcome as I walked up to him. Short, thickset, fair-haired
and fresh-faced, he looked me up and down with exagger-
ated wonder and said, 'Jesus Christ! How the hell do you
manage to always look about ten years younger than your
age?'

I gave him a playful punch in the midriff and offered my
standard reply: 'By smoking eighty a day, drinking a bottle a
day, and worrying *all* the time.'

Within minutes of being in Ron's company, I relaxed and
felt cheerful once more. After a couple of drinks we went into
the restaurant where we were conducted to a table by a
flamboyant *maître d'* who clearly had a great deal of respect for
my companion. During the course of the meal I told Ron my

story and to give him credit he didn't choke on his carpetbag
steak or criticise me. He just sat quietly and chewed steadily
at his food while I gave him the full story.

By the time I had finished he was halfway through a large
peach melba and without looking up he said in his pleasant
'strine twang, 'You really love this little Sheila, don't you?' I
nodded. 'If they do track you down you ought to be able to
give them such a load of bullshit that they wouldn't have a leg
to stand on. You're worrying too much, mate. They're too
busy hunting saboteurs to worry about the likes of you and
your bit of coloured crumpet!' There was no offence intended
in his description of Cynthia and I merely smiled at his choice
of words.

He convinced me that my fears were groundless and then,
fixing me with a penetrating stare with his shrewd blue eyes,
said, 'If you do shoot through to the UK and leave Cynthia
and the kid here, how are you going to feel about it in a few
years' time?' He paused to reach for a toothpick and looking
at me again said, 'There's no bloody future here for them, you
know.' He was right, of course, and I didn't need to be
reminded of this unpleasant fact.

I showed him a photograph of Cynthia and Hanna and he
looked at it surreptitiously and told me to tuck it away in case
the wrong eyes saw it. 'They look terrific, John. Take her and
your kid out of this bloody country as soon as you can. She's
obviously nuts about you, too.' He patted me on the shoulder
as we walked out of the restaurant. 'You're a real bloody
character, John, I'll give you that, and I wish you all the luck
in the world, mate.' We ended up in a cheerful Greek nightclub
where he seemed to have many friends and I finished the day
on a happier and more confident note dancing 'Zorba' with
an elderly Jewish lady.

On the way back 'downhill' to Cape Town I made the
mistake of giving a lift to a middle-aged hitchhiker who turned
out to be the worse for drink. He had been lolling against the
petrol pumps of a garage that I had stopped at for a refill. He
was trying to get a lift to Beaufort West where he lived, and
the Bantu pump attendant looked relieved when I rather
reluctantly agreed to take the fellow home.

During the journey he tried to put the bite on me for money

and I didn't care much for his attitude. He suddenly spotted Fred who was curled up on my lap staring at him with unblinking green eyes; I suspected that Fred didn't like our passenger either.

The drunk said, 'Whassat?' and reached out to stroke Fred.

'Don't touch him, for Christ's sake!' I cried. 'He'll have your bloody eyes out, I'm warning you.'

He sat back and leaned as far away from Fred as he could. 'It's only a bloody cat,' he said shakily, trying to focus his gaze on Fred, who blinked innocently and remained blissfully unaware of the terror his presence was arousing.

'Only a bloody cat, hey?' I said, warming to my game with sadistic pleasure. 'Just look again, my friend. See those unnaturally large, round. eyes, and you obviously haven't noticed that he hasn't got a tail like an ordinary cat.' The drunk peered closer and said nothing as I continued, 'Furthermore, what sort of a cat travels by car sitting on the driver's lap?'

By this time I was becoming alarmed in case Fred started purring. 'Wosortacatisit?' the passenger croaked, watching Fred with slightly bulging eyes.

I played my trump card. 'He happens to be the only Royal Nepalese Fighting Cat in the Republic,' I announced proudly.

'Fighting cat?' he almost squawked.

'The only cat in the world that a Dobermann Pinscher flees from. And loyal and faithful to only one master.' I was really enjoying myself now and as my obviously worried passenger cowered as far away as he could from Fred and myself, I finished him off with, 'Actually I was heavily fined not so long ago in Cape Town for being a bit careless with Te-Ta-Nus [which I pronounced as Taytarnus] here. I left him out on the stoep one evening without thinking and a neighbour's prize Alsatian mistook him for an ordinary cat. Very sad really; the owner had to have the dog put down, you know.' The passenger's eyes were goggling now. I glanced across at him quickly and said, 'If anyone were to lay a finger on me, it would be their lot, I can tell you. Old Te-Ta-Nus here would have their jugular out before you could say "Voortrekker Monument"!'

This was too much for the drunk and as soon as we reached the outskirts of Beaufort West he insisted on being let out to walk the remaining distance, but I insisted on dropping him close to where he lived and he had opened the door and almost stepped out into the road before we had stopped moving.

I bet the story of Te-Ta-Nus, the Royal Nepalese Fighting Cat, went the rounds of the bars in that pleasant little town for some weeks afterwards. As we drove out of the town again I patted 'Te-Ta-Nus' affectionately on the head and he purred contentedly and blinked up at me. I did the rest of the journey without stopping for any extended rest periods and consequently I was tired out by the time we reached the grass verge outside the cottage. Fred was overjoyed to see his chameleon-loaded hedge once more and I left him happily scrabbling around beneath it as I trudged into the house and flopped down onto the bed.

Marie's banging on the back door woke me up some time in the afternoon and when I tottered through to open the door her sun-tanned face was creased in a welcoming smile. 'Enjoy your trip, man?' she asked and when I told her about the Te-Ta-Nus incident, she howled with laughter and wheezed, 'Oh, Christ! Wait till Dan hears about this.' She told me that Terry and Di had been asking after me and would I please give them a ring. I did and we arranged to meet at a well-known restaurant which specialised in superb steaks.

My first call that evening was at Ramona's home and she seemed to be pleased to see me. Knowing what she was thinking I said, 'Surprised I returned, Ramona?' She turned aside with a smile and a shrug and said, 'Well, let's just say that I'm glad to see you again.' While I had been away, the two police friends of Jinja had been calling at Leila's house almost every night and were obviously up to no good. 'You couldn't have gone away at a better time,' she told me. Cynthia was well and so was Hanna and that news cheered me up a little. But she also told me that Cynthia was unhappy there and felt very insecure.

It appeared that Kerim, on the strength of his new-found source of income – me – had decided to retire from working for a living, and spent most of his time playing a weird sort of billiards in the covered yard behind the house with numerous scruffy individuals. From what Ramona said, it seemed that they spent much time drinking cheap wine and smoking dagga.

This was bad news, but as things stood then there was nothing I could do about it, other than add the knowledge to the rest of my worries.

During the early hours of the following morning I was on my way to Kew Town carrying a load of recently cooked chicken curry which was sliding around on the floor of the car on a large plate, along with some other items I had bought for Cynthia and the baby. As I turned into Kew Town and was making my stealthy way to the church where I would find dubious sanctuary for a few minutes, I saw the unmistakable outline of another cream Volksie cross an intersection directly ahead of me. The driver had obviously spotted my lights and would more than likely turn and make a bee-line for me to find out whether I was friend or foe.

With no thought for the curried chicken I did a spectacular U-turn and the curry went one way while I went the other. I drove back to Rondebosch as though the hounds of hell were after me and aborted any efforts to get food across to Cynthia that night. She hadn't been expecting me so I guessed I would be forgiven and decided to try again the next morning.

Next time I saw Cynthia she told me that the police had been carrying out a series of surprise raids in the area while I had been away, which was very considerate of them, I thought. From time to time the police would, for no apparent reason, select a township or a part of a township, and would make a series of spot raids or put up road-blocks. Reports in the press revealed that they often made a rich haul of petty criminals but they were obviously on the look-out for arms caches.

On one spectacular occasion, much to the acute embarrassment of the Government and many leading families in Cape Town, our friendly police made an unexpected raid on a certain establishment in the Cape Town area and netted a haul of eminent local worthies of high position. Despite frantic efforts to keep this event under wraps, it leaked out and became common knowledge and police raids subsided for some time after that. It must have been a fun-night for all concerned.

Terry and Di were waiting outside the steak restaurant in Woodstock when I arrived with two minutes to spare. They had with them another couple, Bill and his attractive fiancée, charming young South Africans of English origin. Our table was decorated with flowers and was covered with a homely check tablecloth. The atmosphere was pleasant and conducive to good eating.

The opening conversation was easy and relaxed. Terry asked me about my trip to Jo'burg and I said that I had enjoyed the change but was glad to be back in Cape Town once more. After the meal we ordered another bottle of wine and sat talking for some time. I remarked that this was the only restaurant I had been to in the Republic that seemed to know how to cook a 'blue' steak, and related an amusing incident that had happened in a very popular and expensive restaurant in Johannesburg some years before. I had ordered a rare steak from the beaming *maître d'* and when it arrived at my table it was overcooked. I like my steaks almost dripping with blood. I complained to the *maître d'* that his chef must have misunderstood his instructions and I went on to explain exactly what I meant by a 'blue' steak. Twice more the steaks were overcooked, and finally the *maître d'* in sheer exasperation said, 'Perhaps Sir would care to come through to the kitchen and cook his own bloody steak.' Which I did.

When I returned to my table flushed with success and followed by a red-faced *maître d'* carrying my steak, I received enthusiastic applause from the other diners, but after that never dared to show my face there again.

Midway through coffee and liqueurs, Bill put a question which I had been asked before on a number of occasions. 'Tell me, John, why is it that people overseas seem to hate us so much? You've lived here for some years now and can see the problems we are faced with. Do *you* blame us for the way we do things here?'

I didn't particularly wish to get involved in what could turn out to be a long and heated argument so I gave my stock reply. 'Look, Bill. As you say, I have lived here for some years but I still look upon myself as a visitor – a guest, if you like, in someone else's home. Do you expect me to be rude enough to criticise your wallpaper after I have just enjoyed your hospitality?'

He laughed at my excuse. 'Oh! Come now! It isn't quite the

same thing really, is it?' He persisted in wanting my honest opinion. I wouldn't be drawn until he made the mistake of trying to justify South Africa's treatment of its non-white citizens. That seemed to get under my skin and I put down my coffee cup and looking directly at him I replied, 'Look here, Bill! You and your charming fiancée are typically nice South African people and I really have enjoyed this meal and your company so let's not spoil it by bringing up the fact that you're troubled by uneasy consciences.' I didn't want to talk politics as I am not really a political animal. The others looked a bit startled at my sudden outburst but I was steaming a bit by this time.

'If we *are* going to discuss the problem that seems to bother you and so many of your fellow countrymen so much, let's start by cutting out the bullshit of trying to justify something that is beyond justification. Neither you, nor Mr Vorster, nor anyone else here could justify the way you treat your fellow human beings in this country.' Terry and Di sat listening without comment, and Bill and Joanna looked a bit uncomfortable but I was determined to finish what I wanted to say.

'It is perfectly simple as I and millions of others outside South Africa see it. You, the whites, are sitting on top of the cake and, apart from the crumbs, there is no way that any of the blacks are going to get a slice. Right?' A stunned silence so I continued: 'To some extent I can quite understand your feelings. The way you South Africans see it is that you baked the cake and even produced the ingredients so why should the Kaffirs have any of it. But you see, the black people have been providing you with cheap labour for centuries and they have watched you prosper while they and theirs have suffered because of your greed. There is much that you could have done to improve the lives of the poor devils – but haven't.

'The Africans are not all that much different from us, you know. They have their worries just as we do. On Sundays, African parents like to see their children wearing nice clothes and eating decent food, and they want to see their kids making some progress in life. What have they got to look forward to as things stand? Do you honestly think that this state of affairs is going to last for ever, Bill?' I shook my head and took a drink of brandy. Looking straight at him I said, 'One day, you and your people are going to have to run for your lives because you made the mistake of not being kind enough and not sharing at least some of your spoils with a rapidly growing mass of black citizens who will make the changes for you. You will eventually run out of bullets, my friend, and that is when you will see the moment of truth staring you in the face; so make the best of it while you can!'

Bill looked quite shocked when I finished what I wanted to say. I wondered what Terry and Di, who knew of my relationship with Cynthia, must be thinking, but they kept tactfully quiet. We lit cigarettes and Bill said with some feeling, 'Well, I did ask what you thought of us.'

I drew on my cigarette and said, 'Look, Bill, there was nothing personal about what I said, but in any case, it is not important what *I* or other outsiders think, it is what *you* think of yourselves that matters. You claim to be a Christian nation. If you truly believe that what you are practising *is* Christianity, as preached by Jesus Christ, you're either cruel hypocrites or totally and incurably mad! And what is more, I think you know this.'

We dropped this topic of conversation and got back to light-hearted generalities, and the atmosphere lifted again. They were decent-enough young people but underneath their façades of conviviality they were desperately unhappy about the image of South Africa overseas and they so desperately wanted to be liked, as a nation. Nor could they understand why other countries failed to appreciate their problems, which they always claimed to be unique.

The situation at Kerim's had now deteriorated so much that he was beginning to show signs of hostility towards Cynthia. He removed the electric fire from her room and made it fairly clear that he wanted the money from me, but not Cynthia's or the baby's company in his house, though I had been as good as my word and had never visited his home at times that would have invited unwanted attention or gossip. Jinja had now become a thorough nuisance and was almost openly stealing many of Cynthia's things – on the pretext of borrowing them, of course.

253

We were in an intolerable position and I sensed that blackmail would be the next ploy of the little so-called Muslim whose brown teeth I longed to ram down his throat. I tried to find alternative accommodation but it was not possible and it could only end in disaster the way things looked then.

I hadn't seen Basil and Brenda for some time and I arranged to take them for supper one evening. During the meal I suddenly found myself telling them about Cynthia, Hanna and myself. They were stunned and listened intently as I droned on with my long tale of woe. And I told them about the time when I had even suspected that they knew all about it and had been against me, like everybody else.

When I finished, Basil looked at me sympathetically and said quietly, 'You poor bastard,' and I could see that Brenda had been deeply moved by my confession. 'Why didn't you tell us about this before, John?' she asked me. 'At least we could have given you a bit of moral support.' In some ways they felt responsible for having introduced Cynthia and me in the first place.

'Don't!' I begged them. 'I have no complaints. I don't regret meeting Cynthia, it's just this bloody awful situation we are in at the moment that's causing me so much concern.'

What seemed to stagger them more than anything was that Cynthia and I had not been caught, despite the arrival of Hanna and that we had now been associating for over two years. Basil shook his head in wonder. 'I could never have done it, John.' They were relieved when I told them that I intended taking my little family out of South Africa as soon as possible, and said that they would help in any way that they could. Regarding my immediate problem, they agreed that somehow I would have to take Cynthia and the baby away from such a potentially dangerous situation without delay.

I was glad that I had confided in my friends. Confession is good for the soul, I said to myself as I drove home after a celebration to wet the baby's head, which Basil had insisted on. They both wanted to meet Cynthia again as soon as I could arrange it. I had to explain that as things were at the moment it was out of the question, but I would organise a meeting as soon as I could.

The next night, laden with two carrier bags full of things

for Cynthia and the baby, I arrived at Ramona's. As soon as I saw her face at the door I knew she had bad news. She asked me to go through to the bedroom where we could talk and my legs began to get that rubbery feeling once again as I walked in carrying the heavy bags.

We sat on the bed and with a very worried expression she said, 'We were at Kerim's last night and Leila told me that Cynthia and the baby must get out.' I felt myself sagging as I listened to this further announcement of bad news and I lit a cigarette with shaking fingers. Kerim had been warned by Jinja's police friends that he was in danger of becoming involved in an Immorality case by keeping them under his roof. Apparently they knew all about it from Jinja and they were determined to get me sooner or later. Ramona's face registered her own fear and I was finding it difficult not to panic.

'I hate to ask you this, Ramona, but has the old man got a drink in the house by any chance?' She left the room and returned a few minutes later carrying the best part of a tumbler of brandy. I drank it as if it were Coca-Cola but it didn't seem to do much good. Leonard came quietly into the room. 'It's bad, isn't it, man?' he said glumly.

'You can say that again, Len,' I sighed as I stood up. 'I want to go home now to see what I can work out.' I drove back to Rondebosch and the loneliness of the kitchen – and the bottle.

THE EARTHQUAKE

I decided to have it out with Kerim the following night. By this time I had had enough of him and his threats and bullying tactics. I went to his house not caring whether Jinja's friends or the whole of the South African police force were there. For a change, I parked my little Volksie in front of the house. The street was quiet and apart from a small group of youths kicking a tin around further along the road, there was no one in sight.

Leila went pale under her natural colour when she opened the door and saw me standing there grim-faced. 'I want to speak to Kerim,' I said as I stepped inside. Leila looked nervously across the street to see if any neighbours were watching. I went into Cynthia's room and greeted her cheerfully. 'Hello, love! Dad's here. I'm going to have a word with Kerim. Don't look so worried, it'll be all right.' She did look very worried and told me that Kerim had been in one of his drunken rages earlier in the day. Although he had not had the guts to speak directly to her, he had been yelling and screeching at Leila to make sure that Cynthia would hear every word.

He wanted her and the baby out immediately, although I had already sent him the next month's money in advance. I was simmering with anger. I told Cynthia to pack things that she would need and to wrap the baby up as well, as I was taking them out of that house tonight.

'He'll send for the police!' she gasped in alarm.

I shook my head. 'I've met gutless wonders like Kerim before,' I said. 'He'll keep his mouth shut after I have spoken to him, and this time, I shall be the one doing the yelling.'

At that moment Leila came into Cynthia's room and I asked to speak to her husband. She said he was not well and was lying down in their room at the back. I was glad to hear it and felt like telling her that there wouldn't be any improvement in his condition after I finished with him. She looked so forlorn that I felt sorry for the woman; she suffered dreadfully at the hands of her rat of a husband.

I gave her a couple of rand and told her not to give it to her husband. 'Go and tell him I want to see him and I am not leaving until I have.' She looked scared but turned and went off towards the back of the house. I followed, and when she opened the bedroom door I walked in behind her. Kerim was lying on his back staring at the ceiling. When he saw me he sat up with a start and gave me his blubbery grin.

'Get off that bloody bed, I want to talk to you,' I snapped.

He cowered and his lips curled back over teeth almost the colour of his skin. 'If you lay a hand on me I'll send for the police,' he squawked.

'Never mind all that crap!' I answered. 'I understand that you want Cynthia and the baby out tonight?' He shuffled uncomfortably and looked everywhere but at me. 'OK! She and the baby are in the car and we will be leaving in a minute. But before I go I want that thirty rand off you – now, man.'

He put on an air of bravado that didn't quite come across. 'I've got friends in the police, they'll put paid to you and your game,' he blustered.

I looked bleakly at him and said, 'I have gone through hell for that girl and our baby and if you do anything that might endanger them in any way – or me – I promise you I will come back here and I'll kill you. You had better be very careful, Kerim, or you may not have very much longer to live, my friend.' There must have been something in the way I spoke that had a salutary effect on him. He was terrified and looked as though he might faint. I held out my hand and rubbed my thumb and forefinger together. 'The money, Kerim!' He tugged some notes out of a trouser pocket and held them out. When I counted them I found only twenty-two rand but I didn't bother about the missing eight. As I was leaving I turned and pointed a finger at him, saying, 'Ramona and Len will be over tomorrow to collect Cynthia's things. Tell that thieving bloody daughter of yours to keep her fingers out of them – and one more thing: if you knock Leila around after I leave, I'll find out and I'll come back and kick shit out of you, understand?' He stood looking sulkily at the floor as I walked out into the corridor.

Before I left the house I told Leila not to worry. 'He won't hit you, love,' I said. 'But he'll scream blue murder when I've gone so you'd better bung cotton-wool in your ears.' I don't think she understood everything that I had said but she wished Cynthia and me happiness and good fortune, and I kissed her on the cheek before walking out to the car, and to God knew what.

'Where are we going?' Cynthia asked nervously from the back seat, where she lay cuddling Hanna.

'We're going home, love,' I said as cheerfully as I could under the circumstances.

'To the cottage?' she asked in surprise.

'Where else?' I said. 'Don't worry, darling. It's the only place I can take you to. We'll work something out I'm sure – and furthermore, it's about time that you applied for a passport, young lady.'

There was a silence from behind me; then, in a small voice, 'You really are going to take me away with you, John?'

I laughed aloud. 'You silly little bitch. Do you think I've gone through all this lot because I have nothing better to do with my time?'

She laughed too and there was real happiness in her laughter.

Strangely enough, although we were in one hell of a mess at the time, I felt curiously elated, euphoric might be a better description. 'Have you got anything dark to wear in one of your bags?' I asked.

'Why?' she said.

'I think you should wrap something dark around Hanna; the little sausage is going to be a bit conspicuous in her white blanket and we must be absolutely dead sure that we're not seen entering the cottage.'

I would go into the house first and take the baby with me. Cynthia was to wait for at least five minutes before going through the usual undignified routine; I would bring in her things later. 'I tell you what,' I said, with sudden inspiration, 'You lie low and I'll come out again in a few minutes as if I've decided to park the car in a better position. Then when I open the door you crawl out and keep on your hands and knees all the way into the house, OK?' I drove around the block and had a good look at the enemy camp but all was still and there were no signs of light or life. It was now or never.

I pulled up on the grass verge from the direction opposite the one I normally came from, so that when the car stopped the driver's door was dead in line with the gate. It was a daft place to park but I had done it deliberately. I was going to put on an act just in case I had an unseen audience. I pretended that I had been drinking and reeled a bit when I got out of the car. I had Hanna under one arm as though she were a bundle of laundry. She was now shrouded in a navy blue jumper which her mother had wriggled out of.

I staggered carefully up the path and, convinced that I was being watched, I paused to make a seemingly drunken fuss of Fred who had appeared from his favourite hedge. Once inside the house I walked quickly through to the spare bedroom and placed Hanna gently on the bed. She was fast asleep, thank goodness. I returned to the car after a few minutes during which I lit the stove and put the kettle on for a hot drink. When I reached the car I opened the door and took a piece of mutton-cloth from the glove compartment and began wiping the windscreen. I moved around the car and began to wipe the side windows and, for good measure, peered thoughtfully at the front fender for some time.

I hoped that my antics would keep occupied whoever might have been watching, long enough for Cynthia to make good her entry to the house. I heard an urgent scrabbling noise and knew that she was moving, hot-kneed as it were, towards the cottage. Giving her plenty of time to get safely in, I flopped back drunkenly into the driving seat and switched on the main beams of the car's headlamps, which was the sort of thing that I felt a slightly tipsy person might have done. Switching them off again, I started the motor and slipped into reverse gear, taking what seemed an endless amount of time to reverse about three feet. It was a sterling performance and I prayed to God that it hadn't all been for nothing.

In view of the fact that I now had the infant in the house I thought I had better not go to bed, and suggested that Cynthia should lie down fully dressed – just in case. When she and the baby were lying quietly on the bed, I sat in a chair fantasising and imagining what I would have said if the police were to raid us and catch the three of us together. 'I was on my way home from a party, Officer, and I have to admit that I was a bit the worse for drink. I saw this woman walking along carrying what looked like a baby. She told me that she had nowhere to go and like an idiot I said she could stay at my place on condition that she leave again tomorrow morning.' It seemed feeble so far. 'Of course, if I had been completely sober I would never have been so stupid, but I couldn't see a baby on the streets all night, not even a coloured baby, could I, Officer?'

Knowing exactly how much sympathy Cynthia, Hanna and I would have received, I gave up and tip-toed off to the kitchen to make myself a cup of coffee. A moment or two later I was joined by Cynthia who couldn't sleep either, and I stood with an arm around her as the kettle began boiling. We could hear some noises outside and Cynthia tugged the kitchen curtain slightly open. When we peeped out we could see that something was happening on the roof of the shebeen at the other side of the wall behind the chapel. A couple of coloured chaps were doing a wild fandango on the roof and it was quite obvious that they were both drunk. Some of the patrons below were shouting and yelling. Suddenly a flicker of orange flame ran up the side of the old building and the shouts and yells turned to screams and hoarse cries as pandemonium broke out.

'Christ! It's on fire,' I said needlessly as the rickety old building went up in flames. The dancers, realising that they were now in real danger, gave loud yells of alarm and leapt off the roof. We heard them crashing to the ground as they landed among the screaming crowd below. There was a fearful racket coming from behind the wall; great orange flames licked hungrily into the night sky and blazing orange sparks flew upwards from the inferno below.

The shouts and excited screams of the onlookers faded as they made their way towards the front of the building which faced onto a main road. Soon we heard the clanging of bells as the fire brigade drew near and not long after this the fire was brought under control. As we stood with our arms around each other watching the flames subsiding, I felt relief. The diversion was a blessing, although I wished no harm to the owners of the shebeen and its patrons. At least we could go through the rest of the night without fear. In the middle bedroom, Hanna began to stir in her sleep. Cynthia already had her feed ready and before the child could come properly awake, she slid the teat gently into the baby's mouth and peace reigned supreme. If Hanna had cried she might have been heard by Marie and Dan – especially at that time of the morning when it was still and quiet. Very little traffic drove past during the night. Satisfied that baby was asleep again, we crept back to the kitchen and had a cup of tea as neither of us could settle down.

I lit a cigarette and smoked in silence for a few minutes while Cynthia watched me quietly as much as to say, Where do we go from here, Dad? I looked across at her and said, 'We must make plans to get away from this country as soon as possible, Cynthia. I'll tell you what you have to do to obtain a passport but you must do exactly what I say. If you follow my instructions carefully and don't panic, we shall be all right. Do you understand?' She nodded. We were too weary to go into details then but we agreed that a discreet departure from the scene of the crime, as it were, would be a very good thing for our continuing safety.

Before I left for the office that morning I reminded Cynthia of the familiar and explicit instructions for the day. No cooking, though she could boil hot water for the baby's feed, no flushing the toilet, no moving the curtains or running the taps or walking too near the glass panels in the front door, and – above all – no crying from Hanna. I always felt dreadful at having to enforce such awful restrictions but Cynthia was as aware of the dangers as I was, and with a baby to consider was even more sensitive about the situation.

Cynthia and the baby remained in the cottage for the next ten days and it was murder for all of us. I was frightened to death in case Hanna cried, especially during the night when it was so quiet. I insisted that she should sleep next to me so that, if she should cry, I could grab her bottle and stuff it into her mouth without giving her a chance to really howl.

Consequently I found myself trying to sleep with one eye open and both ears alert. I was so finely strung now that within seconds of Hanna uttering the slightest of bleats, I was fully awake and had the teat in her mouth before she could fill her lungs for a really good blast. No baby got quicker room-service. The grotty jobs such as changing mucky nappies were left to mum who snoozed innocently next to me. I began to look as bad as I felt, and my well-meaning boss, referring to the bags under my eyes, suggested that I ought to have a break from living it up. 'What are you – some sort of sex maniac?' he asked jokingly.

Every evening after supper Cynthia and I would sit in the kitchen running through the procedure for obtaining a passport. It might be a simple enough thing for most people to do in many other countries but in South Africa at that time it was a tricky operation for a non-white person.

In the first place a non-white requesting permission to leave the country had to have a very good reason for doing so. Then a non-European wishing to settle in another country was normally given an exit-only visa which meant that he or she would not be able to return to the mother country, unless deported. A coloured person, at that time, had to deposit the sum of three hundred rand with the Department of the Interior before being allowed to leave the country. This was to minimise the expense of their return should they be deported by their new host country. And a coloured person seeking a passport could only do so by showing the Department of the Interior a return ticket. As far as I knew, these rules applied only to non-whites in the Republic.

We had to think of an acceptable and verifiable reason for Cynthia wanting to go to Britain for a holiday, and this was where my brother came in. I had written several very cryptic letters to him and in an early one had indicated what had happened and that I intended bringing home a coloured potential wife. I asked him what his feeling would be about this. His reply assured me that whatever I chose to do was all right with him and he would welcome Cynthia like a sister on our arrival.

'We'll find you a nice pen-pal,' I told Cynthia, and I concocted and typed several letters, supposedly from my brother's daughter to Cynthia. I explained that when she went to the Department of the Interior for the interview at which she would have to give a convincing reason for wanting to leave the Republic, she should tell them that she had noticed a pen-pals column in an English Sunday newspaper and she had written to an English girl whose address had been printed in the column.

This had been the beginning of a friendship by letter which resulted in her pen-pal's father and mother inviting her to spend a holiday with them in London. It seemed a reasonable explanation to me and I ran through it with Cynthia until she was word-perfect. She would also be expected to show some evidence of her story so I typed a letter of invitation in which I added what I thought was a nice touch. I knew that she would need to satisfy the Department of the Interior, and the Passport Control Officers in the UK, that she had sufficient funds to provide for herself during her stay in Britain, so I included the following paragraph:

> The sums of money which you have been sending to Isobel during the last two years have mounted up to quite a sizeable amount now. I don't know if you have been keeping a record of the amount you have sent but we now have almost one hundred pounds so you will be quite rich when you arrive. You don't need to worry about your living costs because you are coming as our guest for as long as you would like to stay. Isobel would like you to stay with us for at least three months as you might not get another chance for a long time.
>
> We were sorry to learn about your boyfriend deserting you and leaving you with Hanna to look after but we are dying to see the little child, she looks beautiful in the photograph you sent to us . . .

'That ought to convince the buggers,' I said as Cynthia read it carefully. I addressed an envelope to Cynthia, using Ramona's address, and sent it to my brother in London, asking him to mail it back to me with a phoney letter inside, so that Cynthia would be able to produce an authentic-looking letter, properly postmarked in the UK.

My brother became intrigued by the drama that was taking place six-and-a-half thousand miles away and he joined in with the cryptically written letters so enthusiastically that half the time I didn't know what the hell he was trying to tell me. He kept referring to a mysterious person 'up North who will smuggle you-know-who out with the small parcel [Hanna?] if things get too bad'. I wasn't sure who this mysterious person 'up North' was until after I had returned to Britain. At one time my brother had been on very friendly terms with a now-dead African leader and his wife, whose country was not all that far from the Republic. I thought he had been referring to someone 'Oop North' in Yorkshire where we had originated from.

As soon as Cynthia was able to leave the cottage and move around, she would have to call in at the Department of the Interior and ask for a passport application form which I would help her to complete. Then we would have to wait and see. She was very excited about the situation now and made quite a fuss of me.

Things looked a bit more promising now that we had actually decided to do something positive about getting out, although I knew that we still had a long way to go and many problems to cope with. Cynthia had spent six days incarcerated in the cottage and after some rather heavy hints from Marie during our now rare conversations, I decided to take the bull by the horns and tell her our secret. I was aware that I would be taking a risk but I had known Marie for some time now and felt that I would be able to trust her. I imagined that at the worst she would tell me to find another place to live as soon as possible. I said nothing to Cynthia about my plan because she would have had a fit on the spot at the very thought of me telling an Afrikaner woman.

I based my judgement on the fact that Marie was married to a fairly liberal-minded bloke and I had heard her say, more than once, that she was concerned about the way the Government treated black people. I did not fear any negative reaction from Dan. He and I were good pals by this time and we had both helped each other from time to time and had a lot in common.

Arming myself with a bottle of Oude Meester I set off and tapped nervously on their kitchen door. The child was in bed and Marie and Dan were sitting in the kitchen. I set the bottle down and said, 'Good evening, folks. Join me in a tot.' They were pleased to see me and made room at the table and we drank quietly for a few minutes. Taking a deep breath, I got to the point without preamble.

'Well, Marie – and Dan – I'll be leaving South Africa soon if all goes well.'

They took this with some surprise and Marie looked at me quizzically. 'Do you mean for a holiday or for good?'

Here goes, I thought, and taking a pull on my brandy I plunged right in. 'I'm afraid that once I have left I won't be able to come back again, Marie.' They both thought that I was kidding and they laughed and asked me what I had been up to. 'I'm a father,' I announced dramatically. There was a silence that seemed to last a long time.

'Didn't know you had children, man,' said Dan, looking over his glass at me.

'How many?' Marie asked and I held up a single digit. 'Oh! Is your child sick in England or something like that?' she said.

I finished my brandy and sat back and after pausing only for a few moments, said quietly, 'No, Marie, my child is perfectly well and is next-door.'

They both lowered their glasses and stared at me as if they hadn't properly heard what I had said. 'Your child is next-door. You mean in the cottage there, man?'

I nodded. 'That's right, Dan, and I want you both to listen carefully now to what I have to say before you throw me out and set Spot onto me.' They exchanged looks and were quite clearly baffled by what I had told them.

Dan hastily refilled his tumbler and mine also when I pushed it along the table towards him. He said nothing while I told them my story. To say that I had their attention was the understatement of the century. They were absolutely riveted to their seats and Marie actually blinked a couple of times and shook her head as if she couldn't believe what she was hearing.

When I finished she just sat looking at me silently for several minutes. I was touched by her reaction. Tears ran down her weatherbeaten cheeks and she put a hand over mine. 'My God, Johannes! Ek bewe van vrees vir jou man.' – My God, John! I tremble with fear for you.

I shrugged and said, 'Well, there it is, Marie. I'm glad I've told you.' I took a mouthful of brandy. 'Now you will understand why the curtains have been closed most of the time and the back door locked. I'm sorry, Marie, but I didn't want you to find out because I didn't want you to feel involved. I knew that you and Dan wouldn't drop me in it, so don't feel too badly about me having kept it to myself.'

She just looked at me and shook her head in wonder and when I had told them how long it had been going on she gasped with real surprise and said, 'You poor, poor bugger.'

Dan, who had sat dumbfounded by all this, suddenly came to life. 'Well! Let's not sit here chewing the fat. Let's go and see the baby and meet Mum.' Marie looked enquiringly at me: 'That is, if you don't mind, John.'

I stood up and walked towards the door. 'Come on. Of course I don't mind, but Cynthia will have a blue fit when you walk in.'

They laughed and said, 'Serve her right!'

Cynthia was sitting in the lounge nursing Hanna and when she saw Marie and Dan walk into the lounge behind me she actually paled beneath her normally lovely, warm coffee colour.

I walked over to her smiling reassuringly. 'It's all right, darling,' I said gently. 'Marie and Dan are not angry and they won't give us away so just relax and let them see our pride and joy.'

Marie was smashing. She said something cheerful-sounding in Afrikaans and Cynthia went red beneath her colour and laughed. Marie picked up Hanna and made a great fuss of her. 'She's a beautiful child, isn't she?' she said. Dan reached over and tickled the baby's nose. 'She certainly is, she's a real little beauty.'

They were both surprised at the lightness of Hanna's colouring and her straight, silky chestnut hair. They were also impressed by Cynthia's beauty and understood why I had fallen in love with her. Dan put it another way: 'She's worth doing hard labour for, man!'

When Marie learned that Cynthia had been cottage-bound for such a long time she said, 'Well, she can come and sit in the garden with me tomorrow if she wants to. If anyone asks questions I'll say that she used to work for me and paid me a visit to show me her baby.'

I told them our plans for the immediate future and they both agreed that we should try to obtain a passport for Cynthia as soon as possible. 'You must get the girl and the baby out of this bloody country just as fast as you possibly can,' said Dan.

'It's a miracle that you haven't been caught long before now. Don't push your luck any longer than you have to, John, man,' was Marie's motherly advice. She was wonderful with Cynthia and she put an arm around her and gave her a friendly squeeze before leaving and said, 'You're lucky, my girl. He's the one in a million that we hear about now and again,' and nudging me in the ribs she said to Dan, 'Come on, let's go and leave them in peace.'

Things were much better for Cynthia from then on while she remained in the cottage. She could keep the lounge window and curtains open but had to be careful not to be seen by Marie's little boy or his friends, while they played around the house. It was obvious that Marie and Dan were worried about Cynthia's presence for which I could hardly blame them. It would be very wrong of me to involve them in any scandal as they would still be living here after we had either left the country or gone to prison. I would have to talk to Ramona and Leonard about the problem and they would simply have to take Cynthia and Hanna into their home during the final weeks before we left South Africa – that is, if we ever managed to get away.

Marie was relieved to hear my decision but told us not to hurry about leaving. I said that I would have a serious chat with Cynthia's sister within a day or two and hoped to settle Hanna and her mum fairly quickly, then we could all breathe freely again.

Not long after revealing our secret to Marie and Dan, Cynthia and I agreed to invite Basil and Brenda to the cottage to enable them to meet Hanna. When I dropped in on the off-chance one evening at Basil and Brenda's house they were delighted at the prospect of seeing Cynthia again – and our love-baby.

'When? When?' Brenda asked excitedly.

'How about eight o'clock sharp tomorrow evening?' I suggested.

I relayed this important news to Cynthia on my return home and she went into a flap immediately. 'Oh! I must clean the place out properly,' and 'Do you think they'll like Hanna? What shall I wear?' and so on. I shook my head and grinned. She was a natural woman, that was for sure.

At eight o'clock on the dot there were three sharp knocks on the front door and as I walked along the corridor I could see their silhouettes through the frosted-glass door panel. As soon as they entered Brenda asked, 'Where is she?' Basil looked around inquisitively and said, 'So this is where it all happens, hey, you old sod?'

When we walked into the lounge Brenda was already making a fuss of baby Hanna who nestled in our visitor's arms quite contentedly. Basil kissed Cynthia on the cheek and said with a smile, 'Well done, Cynthia, she's a little cracker.' Cynthia was shy in their presence but less so than she had been when Marie and Dan had marched in.

She had cooked her own version of roast beef and Yorkshire pud and somewhere along the line had felt that a touch of garlic would add to her culinary performance. As a bit of a purist about one of my favourite meals I promised myself that I would have a little chat with her about the garlic at a later date. The meal was very tasty really and the evening passed all too quickly. It was particularly nice to see Cynthia at ease in the company of white people and I was glad to see her so happy.

As I lay awake in bed that night I thanked God for what surely must have been his help during the long, gruelling months we had spent with each other. Although I mentally cautioned myself against becoming complacent I allowed myself the luxury of beginning to think that perhaps we *might* be able to get away safely from South Africa after all.

At breakfast next morning I told Cynthia that in the evening I would be going over to speak to Ramona and Leonard about taking her and the baby. Cynthia seemed to be a bit anxious about the outcome but I pointed out that so far I had carried all the responsibility for her and Hanna, and surely her own sister could help out a little during what we hoped would be the last weeks in the Republic.

My fears were groundless. Ramona listened to my proposal and when I had finished she said that she and Leonard had been expecting my request and although it would be a tight fit they felt they could manage somehow. Ramona kept giving me what I could only describe as 'old-fashioned' looks and when I asked her if she still refused to believe that I intended taking her sister and the baby out of the Republic, she raised her eyebrows and gave a little shrug and said, 'Well! We'll soon see, won't we, man?' Len said something to her in Afrikaans and she merely shook her head and gave a rather enigmatic smile.

A few days later we were lying in bed with Hanna asleep beside me. It wasn't very late, about eleven o'clock. It suddenly occurred to me that I hadn't touched a drop of alcohol all day – I just hadn't needed it. But I felt like a cup of coffee and asked Cynthia if she would like one as well. She said, 'Yes', so I got out of bed carefully so as not to disturb the baby and padded off barefooted to the kitchen.

As I waited patiently for the kettle to boil I was surprised to feel a sort of vibration through my feet from the wooden floor. It only lasted for a few seconds but it was strange; I had never experienced such a phenomenon before. I thought it might have been due to a heavy vehicle passing along the main road which ran parallel with our road, but it would have to be a hell of a big vehicle to set up such a vibration from such a distance.

The kettle began to boil and I reached out to turn off the burner. Without any warning there came the most hair-raising sound which seemed to emanate from below the ground. It started as a low humming noise and the floor was really vibrating this time and china was rattling in time with the windows. 'What the hell's going on?' I gasped, staring around in alarm.

As the vibrations grew worse and the horrible humming sound changed to a roaring as though some manic express train from hell was thundering by under the house, I shot through to the bedroom to find Cynthia sitting up, clasping the baby in her arms and with terror on her face. 'Oh, God,

man! What is it?' she cried as the house began to shake
violently and the devilish sound increased in its intensity.

There came a loud, frantic banging at the back door, and I
heard Dan's frightened voice. 'Stay there!' I yelled to Cynthia
and I ran to the kitchen where the pendant light was swinging
alarmingly. When I opened the door to the garden Dan was
standing there wearing only his underpants. He was chalk-
white and looked terrified. He could hardly speak coherently.

'Quick, man! Get out of the house for Christ's sake! It'll
come down on you. It's a bloody earthquake!'

I felt the blood draining from my own face and my knees
seemed to turn to instant jelly. I had never experienced an
earthquake before and I realised that sitting in the comfort of
a cinema watching such a spectacle was one thing, but being
surrounded by it in reality was another matter. I had
never been as frightened as this in my entire life. The single
most terrifying thing about an earthquake, in my opinion, is
that there is nothing that one can do to escape from it. You
can't climb up a tree, or take to a lifeboat or leap out in a
parachute. You're surrounded by the thing with absolutely
nowhere to go.

Dan had fled to look after his own family and I dashed
back into the bedroom and found Cynthia cowering in bed,
terror-stricken and almost in hysterics. I realised afterwards
that the presence of the baby must have helped her to retain
a measure of self-control as she knew that Hanna was dependent on her. When she saw me she cried out again, 'Oh! God!
What is happening to us, man?'

I grabbed her by the arm and half dragged her and the baby
off the bed, acutely aware of the large water-tank situated
immediately above us in the loft. I expected it to crash through
the ceiling at any moment. 'Take the baby and get out of
the house immediately. Go down the garden away from the
building,' I yelled above the demonic noise surrounding us. I
could hear people shouting in the road outside and knew that
we daren't set foot out there.

She stopped at the bedroom door. 'What if the neighbours
see us?' she called.

'Get a move on!' I shouted angrily. 'Bugger the neighbours!'
I yelled after her. 'This is no fucking time to worry about the

neighbours or how you look. The bloody house will be on us in a minute!' At that moment my fear of the earthquake was far greater than that of the Vice Squad and I was only concerned with our survival.

The 'quake lasted for not much more than fifteen minutes, every one of which seemed at least an hour to me, while whatever it was that was passing beneath us gradually went on its fiendishly destructive and terrifying way. We went to the end of the garden to get as far away from the house as we could and after the tremors had subsided slightly I told Cynthia to remain where she was while I returned to the house to fetch a warm blanket for her and the baby. I stepped warily into the kitchen and tiptoed fearfully through the house and into the bedroom, expecting the roof and water-tank to descend on me at any moment. I didn't hang around any longer than necessary and after grabbing a couple of blankets I shot out into the garden again.

There was still a good deal of shouting and terrified yelling going on in the road beyond the house and gradually the vibrations died away and the ghastly sound from beneath the earth disappeared. After a few minutes of comparative silence, I again told Cynthia to remain where she was while I went to see if Marie and Dan had returned to their house.

I entered their cottage through the back door as they were entering through the front door, and Dan was a sight to see. Marie seemed to be made of sterner stuff but poor Dan was chalk-white and was absolutely scared stiff. We met in the centre of their lounge and as he placed a suitcase on the floor there came a slight rumble with an accompanying vibration from down below, a sort of last gasp, as it were, from the 'quake. I remembered Fred's near vertical jump-start when I absent-mindedly placed him almost into Spot's slavering jaws, but Dan's performance at this last terrestrial hiccup was spectacular. Completely forgetting his wife and small son he almost knocked them over with his remarkable take-off as he shot out of the house again.

As the slight rumble died away, he reappeared looking a bit sheepish and ashamed of what had been pure reflex action on his part. Marie glared at him and swore in Afrikaans. 'What the bloody hell's the matter with you, man? For Christ's sake stand still.' Out came the brandy in record time and after downing mine in a couple of grateful gulps I wiped my mouth on the back of my hand and thanked them: 'I'd better be off now but I'll see you both in the morning.' I didn't need to explain to them my speedy departure.

Soon Cynthia and Hanna were tucked up in a warm bed, but we slept in the other bedroom for the rest of that memorable night, just in case the water-tank decided to do something unpleasant.

'Major earth tremors bring death to the Cape' the headlines read in next morning's *Cape Argus*. An underground 'ripple' had made its way from somewhere near Port Elizabeth and had continued in a diagonal route from north to west, down through the Western Cape region, destroying many homes and some magnificent old wine farms in the Tulbagh Valley, including one I had visited earlier. It had taken the lives of eleven people during its brief but terrifying duration and I learned later that many South Africans had been convinced that it was a sign from God warning them of his displeasure at their continued ill-treatment of his coloured children. How about *that* for a national guilt complex?

The next night found me once again trundling my little family through the safety of darkness to Ramona's home. A female cousin of Ramona's living in a coloured suburb called Sunnyside had offered to take Cynthia and Hanna as she had more room in her house. I drove over to the house with Ramona and Len: by this time I was almost blasé about driving around non-white suburbs and townships at night.

The cousin and her husband turned out to be very pleasant and obviously highly respectable people, and after an hour or so of conversation we returned to Kew Town to collect Cynthia and the baby. I drove them safely back to the cousin's house, kissed Cynthia and Hanna good-night and went home more care-free than I had been for over two years.

The following evening, after dark, Leonard came over to Rondebosch to deliver the passport application which Cynthia had collected during the afternoon. I gave him a drink while I studied the form. It was straightforward enough and I typed in the information which Cynthia had already provided me with. Then I joined Len and explained that I would need to discuss the form with Cynthia and perhaps he might like to bring her over to the cottage the following evening. It would have been OK for a coloured man and woman to be seen entering my house as long as it was not too late at night and didn't happen too frequently. He didn't think that Ramona would like the idea very much, but I told him that she would when she saw the passport when Cynthia received it.

The next evening, Len and Cynthia arrived about eight forty-five, and while he sat in the lounge with a brandy listening to Springbok Radio, Cynthia and I went into the kitchen to go through the passport form in detail as I wanted there to be no mistakes. I checked it with her very carefully and reminded her that she would have to produce a copy of Hanna's birth certificate. 'You must have a copy of your own, too – and get it signed by your doctor.' I handed her the form and warned her not to lose it.

We didn't see each other for a few days which meant a few anxiety-free days for me and I owed Bob a visit. I found him back in his usual haunt at the Regency bar. 'Wotcher, cock!' was his chirpy greeting.

Ordering a round, I nodded towards the lounge and we took our drinks to our usual quiet corner table. I didn't go into too much detail but I did tell him that we were making a bit of progress now, and with luck we might obtain a passport for Cynthia and the child in the coming weeks. He was pleased but pointed out that he was going to feel a bit lonely after I had left.

'Well, Bob, just keep your mind fixed on following us out as soon as you can and we'll be sitting having a drink in a decent English pub in no time at all.'

He smiled, but it was a sad smile and I wondered whether we would ever see each other again once I had left the Republic. I did not share my thoughts with him on this point.

I asked how Beattie was. He said she was a good girl and doing all she could to help him and make sure he didn't overdo things with his weak heart. Fortunately he had not experienced any further setbacks, which I was relieved to hear.

Then we somehow got onto the subject of the Afrikaans language which Bob could find no virtue in at all. Bi-lingualism is a useful attribute for any settler wishing to progress up the ladder of success in the Republic. Bob told an amusing story about a fellow who had applied for the position of harbour master in Cape Town. According to Bob, when asked if he was bi-lingual he had replied, 'Yes, I speak fluent French as well.' Needless to say, he didn't qualify for the position.

As for me, I had never found a great need for the language during my stay in the Republic though I did make an effort to learn a few polite expressions. I found that it was usually appreciated by Afrikaner people if one made an attempt to speak a bit of Afrikaans, even if it was only to say good morning or good evening. However, there was one memorable occasion when I unwittingly dropped a very serious clanger, and although I saw the funny side of my 'howler' after the event, it was excruciatingly embarrassing at the time. It had happened during my earlier days in Cape Town and some time before I had met Cynthia.

The nursing sister whom I mentioned earlier in this book had been working in Johannesburg, and she telephoned to say that a very good Afrikaner colleague of hers would be coming down to Cape Town for a spot of leave. The young lady lived near the delightful False Bay resort of St James but had worked in Jo'burg for such a long time that she had no close friends in the Cape; the main purpose of her visit was to spend some time with her father and mother. My friend asked me if I would be a good sort and ring Janice and ask her to have supper somewhere: 'Just to cheer her up a bit, John.' I agreed and Janice, who had been told about me by my friend, was delighted and readily accepted my invitation.

I was to pick her up at her home near St James where I would be welcomed by her father and mother prior to taking Janice off to a well-known seafood restaurant not very far away. Before setting off from the cottage I inspected myself in the wardrobe mirror and was duly impressed with the immaculately attired English-looking type reflected in the glass. The RAFVR tie was absolutely gravy-less, the dark-blue blazer complete with squadron badge couldn't be faulted, and the mid-grey worsted slacks had a knife edge to them that you could have sharpened a pencil on. The suede shoes jarred a bit but one can't have everything, I suppose.

I was extremely pleased with my punctuality as I turned

into the road in which Janice and her parents lived; a quick glance at my watch showed that I was dead on time. It was a lovely evening and the sun had not yet set. Standing on the stoep with Janice were a middle-aged man and woman who could only have been her parents. I parked the car beneath the raised stoep and got out. Turning and looking up towards the little group I introduced myself and said cheerily, 'Nice to meet you, Janice: all ready for the fray?' Stunned silence from mum and dad and muffled titter from Janice. I looked down to make sure my trouser fly was fastened and that everything was as it should be, and wondered what the hell I had done.

As I walked up the steps to meet them, I saw that Janice was talking busily in Afrikaans to her father and mother who were listening and nodding, and when they finally smiled, I breathed a sigh of relief. After polite hand-shakes, I was invited in to a delightful lounge for a pre-evening drink. Janice's father and mother left the room for a moment and while they were absent I leaned towards Janice and said, 'Er . . . What was that little performance about when I first arrived? Did I do something wrong?'

Janice blushed and giggled, and said, 'Don't you realise what you said to me?'

I shook my head in puzzlement. 'All I said, as far as I can remember, was "Are you ready for the fray" – or something like that.'

She looked at me with a smile on her attractive face and whispered, 'Vrey, pronounced like your fray, is an Afrikaans word which means f-u-c-k.'

THE BID FOR FREEDOM

Cynthia received a letter from the Department of the Interior informing her that her passport had now arrived and asking her to call in as soon as she could. When she did, she was told by a pale-eyed, middle-aged Afrikaner woman that the passport could not be given to her until she was able to show them the return tickets for herself and the baby. When I heard this news I was elated and we celebrated that night with a posh meal and a bottle of wine.

Now that the passport was a reality I would have to set about selling my belongings to raise as much cash as possible, not only for the tickets but also to give us a start on arrival in the UK. I gave up my job and told everyone that I would be returning to the UK because of family problems – which was quite true.

I spent several hectic days disposing of my bits and pieces and the first thing I sold for a reasonable price was my trusty little Volkswagen. I felt quite sorry to see it go as it had never let us down. Soon I had quite a sizeable amount of money to operate with and I headed for the Union Castle building in Adderley Street to buy the tickets.

A commissionaire conducted me to a very large room with a domed, glass roof. At dozens of long tables smartly uniformed employees of the famous shipping line were busy handling passenger enquiries. I sat down in a waiting area by a circular table loaded with magazines and flicked through one nervously while waiting my turn.

'Meneer!' a voice called and I saw the commissionaire pointing in the direction of a fair-haired young lady in a pale blue uniform sitting at one of the tables. As I walked towards her she looked up at me and, guessing that I was English-speaking, invited me to sit down in a chair opposite her. 'May I help you, sir?' she asked politely. I told her that I would like to book passages on the first available boat leaving for Britain.

She nodded briskly and she began flicking through a massive sheaf of papers clipped onto a stiff board. 'The *Edinburgh Castle* will be sailing next Wednesday, sir. Would that suit you?'

I did a bit of rapid calculating in my head. It was now Friday which would give me five days in which to get everything organised; it seemed all right to me. 'Yes. Thank you, that will be fine.'

'Is it just for yourself, sir?' she asked.

'Er . . . No. The party will consist of myself and a lady and child – a baby actually.'

She ran a neatly manicured finger down a column on one of the sheets on the board and looking up at me with cool blue eyes said. 'Is the lady your wife, sir?'

I began to feel a bit sweaty. 'Er . . . No. She's a friend of my brother's family in London and I have offered to keep an eye on her during the journey as I happen to be going home myself at the same time.'

She nodded and proceeded to explain details of the cabins available. I was to share with a Catholic priest but because the baby was so small Cynthia would enjoy the luxury of a two-berth cabin to herself, and Hanna of course. This sounded admirable, as once we were beyond the three-mile limit I would be able to move in with my small family. When she told me the cost of the fares I said that I would require a single ticket for myself and return tickets for the young lady and her child. She took down my name and address and then asked me for Cynthia's name and address as well.

This stopped me in my tracks. I hadn't thought of this. In the first place I didn't know what the correct postal address was, and even if I had known, it would have revealed Cynthia's racial group straight away, and might have led to some awkward questioning. I coughed nervously. 'Oddly enough, I'm not quite sure what the lady's correct address is, but you can put them under my address if you like: after all I'm paying for the tickets.'

She began writing busily on another pad and I suddenly felt vaguely ill when I realised what I had done in associating my address with Cynthia's name. If someone at the dock noticed that a white and a non-white were both recorded at the same address it could lead to a last-minute obstruction. It was too late to retract what I had said and I tried to reassure myself that the chances of such a thing happening were very remote; nevertheless it gave me something else to worry about and I wished that the clerk would hurry up and let me get out of the building which now seemed claustrophobic. I paid for the tickets and produced my passport. Glancing at it, she handed me my ticket but when I held my hand out for Cynthia's and Hanna's she apologised and told me that she was not allowed to release them until she had seen the passenger's passport. I nodded as if understanding and walked out into sunny Adderley Street on legs made of blancmange. 'Charming!' I muttered, as I wobbled off to the nearest café to consider this latest difficulty. That's bloody well torn it, I thought as I smoked nervously. How would Cynthia be able to obtain the passport from the Department of the Interior when they wouldn't release it until they had seen the tickets? If it hadn't been so serious and worrying, it would have been farcical. The whole business was showing signs of becoming nasty and complicated.

When I contacted Cynthia and told her all this she went to see the woman at the Department of the Interior, and as I had suspected, *she* flatly refused to release the passport until she was shown the tickets. No, she would *not* accept a telephone confirmation from the clerk at the Union Castle offices; she had to see the tickets with her own disbelieving eyes. In the end it was agreed that a special messenger would walk from the Union Castle offices with Cynthia and the tickets to the Department of the Interior in the Sanlam Centre on the Foreshore. The messenger would produce the tickets for inspection by the woman who would then release the passport to Cynthia. Then the messenger, complete with tickets and Cynthia, would return to the Union Castle offices where the tickets would be officially handed over to Cynthia. This minor drama took place and when Cynthia told me about it – and showed me the tickets and passport – I burst into hysterical laughter.

A number of people around town owed me varying sums of

money and collecting kept me occupied for a couple of days, but they all coughed up and finally I withdrew my balance from the bank. Time was beginning to run out and there were still a number of things to be done. Cynthia and Hanna had their inoculations and I went off to have mine. There I found my ex-boss's wife and small daughter waiting their turn for a smallpox jab.

The mother was curious about my being there. 'Going overseas, John?' she asked politely.

Shaking my head I told her that I was going up to Jo'burg, but might have to take a short trip overseas on business and wanted to make sure that I had everything in order before leaving Cape Town.

I was left with a few items of furniture which I had collected during the years I had spent in the Republic. No great problem there.

Basil introduced me to a friend of his who dealt in furniture buying and selling and it was arranged that he would call at the cottage to have a look at my things. He was a swarthy, dark-eyed Londoner who originated from the East End. He inspected my little collection and made an offer that indicated that he might have been a frustrated burglar. I had met the type before and was not prepared to go into a deep haggling session with him, and I wasn't desperate for a few pounds, so I told him that I would shift it out to the garden and give the kid next-door a treat with a nice big bonfire. That caused his bushy eyebrows to rise and when he saw that I was quite serious he improved his offer to the sort of figure that I had in mind and the deal was done. We had a friendly drink before he loaded the stuff onto his lorry and drove away. I had another drink to celebrate and tucked the notes away with the rest of my hoard, which had now reached quite a respectable sum.

Rather a touching little incident took place about this time. Cynthia received a message from her aunt in Malmesbury telling her that the orphanage where she and her sisters had spent their childhood was anxious to contact her as they had good news for her, and Ramona and Cathy. It turned out that her father had left his few belongings to the orphanage, which had sold the possessions and invested the money on behalf of

the girls so that they would benefit when they were grown up.
Cynthia was told that her share was eighty rand – about forty
pounds in those days. It couldn't have happened at a better
time because we were almost on our way and Cynthia was
able to collect the money when she went to say goodbye to her
auntie.

Fred was causing me sleepless nights. I knew that it just
wouldn't be possible to take him with us as I didn't want him
to be stuck in a cage for six months in UK quarantine.
However, one of the young lady vets at the clinic where his
tail had been amputated had shown great affection for him
and pleaded that if I ever decided to give him away would I
let her have him as he was such a lovely animal. I remembered
this and decided to hand him over to her on the morning of
our departure. From that moment on I just couldn't look Fred
in the eye, and he seemed to know instinctively that something
awful was going to happen because he hardly let me out of his
sight after I had made this decision. He glued himself to me
and trotted around after me wherever I went in the cottage.

Although we now had the passport and tickets and had
disposed of my goods and chattels in a satisfactory way, we
were not yet out of the wood. We were still in South Africa. I
reminded myself that there was many a slip 'twixt cup and lip
and I maintained my customary caution. I even felt it might be
dangerous, if my baggage was inspected, to have 'incriminating'
photographs, and I destroyed all I had from my years in the
Cape. The day of our planned departure had to be organised
like a minor but important military operation if we were to
succeed in getting away.

I paid Basil and Brenda a visit and asked them if they would
help in the operation. It would have been very dangerous for
me to have driven Cynthia and the baby to the docks, especially
as Ramona and Cathy naturally wanted to come as well to see
their young sister and the baby off. The prospect of driving with
three attractive coloured women and a baby in my car in broad
daylight didn't appeal to me at all. My nerves would have
flatly refused to tolerate such a tense situation.

On the other hand, it would have been quite in order for a
white husband and wife to have been seen driving their female
servant to the boat, so we worked out a foolproof little scheme

that would eliminate unnecessary risks and anxiety. The *Edinburgh Castle* was scheduled to sail at 4 p.m., and I felt that the sooner we were all aboard the better it would be. I had already told Marie and Dan what I had in mind and they readily agreed to co-operate. The plan was quite simply this. On the day of departure, Cynthia and her sisters and the baby would be ready and waiting at the house in Sunnyside. I would call at Basil's studio at 12.15 p.m. and he and Brenda would follow me to Sunnyside. Basil had very kindly lent me his second car which was a Volksie Beetle like my old one. On reaching the house I would point it out, and drive on to the cottage at Rondebosch. Basil would pick up Cynthia and Cathy and Ramona and would drive straight to Duncan Dock where Cynthia and the baby would embark without any problems, amidst a large crowd of people seeing off friends and relatives.

I would leave the car on the grass verge outside the cottage for Basil to collect later, and Dan would run me down to the docks with my baggage. I would be able to embark without undue haste or panic and would be able to spend a few minutes with my friends, including Bob, before sailing. It seemed to be a reasonable plan involving no risks to anyone and it looked as though we would be able to slip quietly out of South Africa after suffering much fear and unhappiness for such a long time. I felt myself slowly unwinding as I thought about it.

It felt particularly good to know that I had one or two decent friends to call upon, for without their help I wouldn't be able to manage. I didn't want to involve myself with coloured taxi drivers as they were notoriously unreliable and I couldn't afford to take any risks at this stage.

When I broke the news to Bob that we would be leaving within a few days he tried to look pleased and happy about it but I could see that, inside, he was upset and very sad. Almost pathetically he said, 'We'll soon be joining you, mate, don't you worry about that. Beattie's got herself a nice little job on the side and we're savin' every penny we can lay our 'ands on. I reckon we'll be on the boat by Christmas.'

I didn't ask him how much he had managed to save nor did I tell him that I didn't think that we would meet again – the sixth sense was having one final fling before we left.

The poor old chap was plainly miserable at the prospect of

losing his one and only friend and I would miss him too. We had a rather mournful farewell drink in the Regency and Bob wanted to tell Reg about my impending departure, but I advised him to keep it quiet until we were out of the country.

'The old lady was asking after you the other day,' he told me, meaning Beattie's mother, of course. 'She took a real shine to you, y'know. Said Cynthia was a very lucky girl.'

I said nothing; I was thinking back on some of the adventures I had shared with Bob. That night's drinking session was a long one, and we ended up in the Ladies Bar. As we sat deep in our individual thoughts Bob interrupted them.

'Er . . . I 'aven't forgotten that money I still owe you, John.' He looked at me warily and his thin nose twitched.

I laughed and told him to forget it. 'Stick it in your going-away kitty, Bob,' I said.

He ordered another round and said, rather self-consciously, 'You've been a bloody good mate to me, John. I won't forget wot you've done to 'elp me since we've known one another, you know.'

I told him to shut up and finish his drink.

'I ain't 'arf gonna miss you, yer know.'

I told him that I would miss him too and we would have the party to end all parties when Cynthia and I met Beattie and him at Southampton when their big day arrived.

He cheered up when he heard this and promised to come to the dockside to see us off.

On the eve of our departure I gave Cynthia every penny I had managed to collect. She was to go to the bank early the following morning to change it into sterling and travellers' cheques. This would enable her to enter the UK with more than sufficient money to back her claims. I didn't care if I only had fifteen shillings in my pocket on arrival at Southampton; I couldn't be prevented from entering my own country.

A lot of little tasks still needed to be done, such as a load of ironing and some more packing. Cynthia undertook to look after that and Marie said she would keep an eye on 'the buggers across the road', because I wanted to go over to deal with some unfinished business with Ramona. I borrowed Cynthia's passport and the boat tickets for her and Hanna and drove across to Kew Town – carefully as usual.

Len opened the door and welcomed me with a smile and 'Come in, man.' Ramona, he said, was in the kitchen.

I asked him to tell her that I had important news for them and suggested that we should talk privately. He nodded in the direction of the bedroom and I went through and was playing with the baby boy when they both came into the room. Ramona was up to her elbows in flour and looked a little uneasy as she obviously wondered what the news was about.

'Is everything all right?' she asked anxiously.

'Things have never been better, love,' I replied as I pulled the passport and tickets out of a document case I had been carrying under my arm. I laid them on the bed and said, 'Well, Ramona, there they are. Cynthia's passport and ticket to freedom. We're sailing tomorrow on the *Edinburgh Castle*.'

She stared down at them and then looked up at Len and across at me, then down at the documents again. She seemed dazed by what I had just said.

'Pick them up and look at them, Ramona. They're real.'

Slowly she picked up the passport and opened it and gazed down at Cynthia's picture, then the tickets. She sank down onto the bed and stared at the floor with such a look of sadness on her face, and began to weep softly.

'I'll take good care of her, Ramona, I promise you. Don't cry, you'll see her again one day, I'm sure.'

She looked up at me through her tears and walked over to me. Suddenly she put her arms around my neck and kissed me on the cheek – a big wet kiss. She hugged me fiercely and said, 'I'm not crying because Cynthia is getting away from this bloody place; I'm crying because I didn't trust you and I would have been so much nicer to you had I known that you meant what you said about taking her away.'

I kissed her back and said, 'Don't be so daft, girl. You're a good sister and I'm looking forward to you becoming my sister-in-law.'

She was now all smiles and couldn't do enough for us. I explained that Cynthia and I had a load of chores to deal with and if she could take Hanna off our hands until the morning this would be a great help.

'Well, go and get her, don't just stand there, man.' She gave me a friendly push and I didn't need any second bidding.

We had toiled through the night, ironing and packing, and now it was almost dawn. We were both exhausted but happy and excited about this, surely our greatest day, a day we would both remember for the rest of our lives.

Cynthia had told me that she would get the early bus back to Ramona's to collect Hanna. When she walked out of the cottage I didn't care whether the Watcher saw her or not. This was the last time that she would ever leave me from the cottage. Before setting off she gave Fred a cuddle and put him down next to his beloved hedge, then she was gone.

After she had left I ran a hot bath and lay soaking in it, thinking about the last two-and-a-half years. It had been worth it, really, and I had no regrets. I recalled Ramona's face when she learned the truth. She was a happy woman now, and so was Cathy who had always had a quiet faith in me and saw her hopes for her younger sister materialise into reality. They were three very nice young women and I regretted that I had never been able to meet their parents. They must have been pretty decent people themselves no matter how humble their circumstances might have been. If Cynthia took after her mother in looks then her mother must have been a real beauty. Would she have been happy for her youngest daughter today had she been alive?

I thought about the future and wondered what it had in store for us. Happiness? Success? Health? Wealth, or would the wheel turn in the opposite direction? Only time would tell. Cynthia had presented me with a superb gift, a beautiful baby daughter, something I had never expected to have. My eyes were closing with tiredness and I forced myself to haul my weary body out of the water. I dried myself in slow, unco-ordinated movements and it dawned on me that although my eyes were open and I was able to perform functions like a zombie, my body and nervous system were fast asleep.

Fred was outside somewhere and I felt a slight touch of panic: suppose he failed to appear when I went to collect him to play with him for the last time? When I opened the front door he was there, true-blue, and he bounded happily into the house with his ever-cheerful *mreeouwl*. I picked him up and stroked his whiskery little head and he purred happily as I carried him through to the kitchen to give him his breakfast.

I felt really bad about the prospect of handing him over to the vet. After he had finished his meal and drunk some milk I played his favourite game for a while. I would roll an orange along the long corridor leading to the front door and he would skitter after it almost like a dog, rolling onto his side and punching at the orange with his paws. He grew bored with the game and sat on my knees and began washing his paws while purring contentedly. I removed his blue leather collar with the bell attached and slipped it into my pocket. It would be all that I would have to remind me of the hours of pleasure and companionship this insignificant little moggie had given to me: I still have it somewhere.

It was time to take him and when I carried him out to the car and sat him on my lap, he rubbed his head happily against my hand as he thought we were off on another long trek somewhere. When we reached the gate that led to the garden of the animal clinic he suddenly sensed that something was wrong, badly wrong, and he began to panic. I was holding him against my chest and he sank his claws in as if to cling with desperation to me. His ears flattened and he made a strange snickering sound. He was obviously terrified.

The young vet had seen me entering the front garden and she walked out of the clinic to meet me. When we stopped before each other I bent my head impulsively and kissed my little pal on the top of his head, and without speaking I managed to extricate his claws from my clothing and handed him over to the young woman. I was too choked to say anything. As she received Fred tenderly she said anxiously, 'Don't worry, Mr Carr, he will be loved and well cared for, I'm sure you know that.' I nodded and turned away and strode back to the main road but I could hardly see the car for tears.

As I returned to the cottage Marie called out from a window. I walked over to her and she told me that Dan had received an urgent message to make a call out of town and would not be able to run me to the docks. I didn't say anything but I sensed that she wasn't telling me the truth. It was no big deal as I could organise a white taxi for myself if necessary. 'Don't worry about it, Marie,' I said, hiding my disappointment with a rather forced smile. We talked about the coming trip for a few minutes and she invited me to have some coffee and cake with her before leaving. I thanked her and went back to the cottage where I assembled all the baggage in the lounge. I walked around looking into the wardrobes and cupboards; there was a stack of stuff that I couldn't take with me and I had told Len to collect some of it. There were also a couple of suits and some shirts that Bob was badly in need of.

When I said goodbye to Marie – and Spot – she kissed me and wished Cynthia and Hanna and myself all the luck in the world in our future new life together. I had already loaded the baggage into the car and as I sat down behind the wheel I hoped that it would not let me down. It was an elderly model but as soon as I turned the ignition key the motor fired at once and I trundled slowly onto the road. Giving Marie a last wave I pressed my foot down and off I went towards Cape Town and disaster.

The doors leading into Basil's studio were locked when I arrived, but I was ten minutes early and I assumed that they might have gone out for a coffee or something. Surely they wouldn't fail me, as well as Dan. I shrugged off my uneasiness and lit a cigarette while pacing around in the corridor outside. At twenty minutes to one I knew that they *had* let me down and my heart was very heavy as I went out into the brightness of the afternoon sunshine. I tried not to feel bitter about this disappointment and to put myself into their position. Perhaps I might have been tempted to do the same. Yet they would have been running no risk, I kept telling myself. Surely they didn't want to deliberately expose Cynthia and me to danger?

But I had neither the time nor the inclination to dwell on negative things at that moment. I knew now that I had a hell of a problem to deal with and I took a deep breath and made up my mind to see it through somehow. Before the end of that day, Cynthia, the baby and I would either be on that boat – or we would be in prison. It was that simple.

I drove rapidly towards Sunnyside, trying to be optimistic.

I told myself I should have no trouble in finding a coloured taxi to take the girls and the baby to Duncan Dock, though my stomach was in knots as I sped on my way. It was broad daylight and I would soon be entering an all-coloured suburb. But I was now beyond caring and as I drove past several coloured people sitting on the grass verges outside their houses I gritted my teeth and kept saying to myself, 'Don't panic, mate. It'll soon be over now, don't worry.' I parked directly outside the house and knocked on the door. I was surprised when Cathy opened it as I had expected to be greeted by Cynthia. Cathy looked worried and as I pushed the door open and followed her inside I said, 'Hello, Cathy, is Cynthia ready?'

She was decidedly ill at ease and said, 'Well, not just yet.'

'What do you mean?' I said sharply. I was very strung up at that moment and enough had gone wrong as it was. 'She is here, I take it?' I asked with rising anger. I didn't like the way things were going at all.

I walked along the corridor and found Hanna lying on a bed dressed and ready to go, in a smart, one-piece suit which Cathy had knitted for her. She wore a little matching cap and she looked lovely. I planted a gentle kiss on her funny little snub, baby nose and she slept on, unaware of the tension and drama building up around her. Cathy had followed me into the room and I turned to her impatiently. 'Look, Cathy, where the hell *is* Cynthia? She should be here now waiting for me.' I explained what had happened with Dan and Basil, and Cathy shook her head and looked at the floor; after all, what was there to say?

She told me that Cynthia had decided to do some last-minute shopping at Wynberg and had promised that she would be back by twelve-thirty at the latest. I looked down at my watch and it was now twenty minutes past one. We were still all right for time but that wasn't the point. It would have been just as bad if Basil and Brenda had turned up; they would have been far too nervous to have waited around.

My precise planning had been a complete waste of time and I hated this last-minute improvisation. It wasn't a Sunday picnic we had planned; it had been a carefully-thought-out escape operation, but for all the care anyone seemed to be taking, it might just as well have been a *braaivleis*.

The boat would sail promptly at four and the gangplanks were normally drawn away at about twenty minutes to four. We still had two hours and twenty minutes in hand, I told myself as calmly as I could, but when I tried to take a cigarette out of my packet, my shaking fingers belied the calmness of my thoughts.

'Have you got any bloody brandy in this house, Cathy?' I asked, pacing backwards and forwards along the corridor outside the room. Cathy disappeared into the kitchen and returned with a tray on which stood a bottle of Premier brandy, a glass and a plastic jug containing water. I thanked her and mixed myself a hefty tot. I couldn't afford to drink too much, though, as I would need a clear head for what lay before us.

'Surely she won't be much longer now, Cathy?' I said. It was now well past two o'clock and I was becoming very alarmed. 'Is there a telephone around anywhere?' She told me that there was a telephone next-door. 'OK!' I said. 'Nip next-door and phone for a taxi. Tell him to be here no later than half-past two. She's bound to be here by then.' I gave her a handful of loose change for the owners of the telephone and she went out quickly. She returned after about fifteen minutes looking flustered.

'I managed to book one,' she said.

'Thank God for that,' I said, relieved that something appeared to be going right. 'Did you tell him to be here at exactly two-thirty?' I asked as an afterthought.

She nodded and added, 'You mustn't rely on him to be here, though. Coloured taxi drivers turn up if they feel like it.'

I rolled my eyes heavenwards and muttered a silent prayer. It was going to be a monumental cock-up, I could see that. It was now two-thirty and we had exactly one hour and ten minutes to get on board that ship. If we missed it, we should be really in it – up to our armpits.

Cathy was quite correct in her forecast regarding the taxi driver – he didn't turn up. By now I must have looked like a madman. I was pacing furiously up and down and cursing and swearing to myself. 'What the hell is the matter with that half-wit sister of yours?' I bellowed, almost beside myself with fury and panic. 'We've dreamed of this day for very nearly three years and now she is going to ruin it at the last minute.'

Cathy didn't know what to say but she must have been pretty upset herself. She vanished into the room where Hanna, poor innocent babe, lay oblivious of the fact that her whole future lay in the hands on my watch.

At ten minutes past three Cynthia walked into the house. As soon as she saw me she giggled nervously and I strode up to her and thrusting a finger towards her face I said in a hoarse voice, 'If you laugh, I'll kill you, I swear it.' I think I must have been almost insane with anxiety and fear at the time. 'Don't stop to show Cathy your things. Don't stop to talk. Just grab the baby and get outside and into the car – and, above all, don't argue, now come *on*!'

'But I've left my thin . . .' she began.

'Forget them, it's too late now. Just get outside and into the car NOW!' I bellowed. 'We have a half-hour journey to do in twenty minutes and if we don't make it we'll be in Roeland Street tonight.'

As she was about to leave the house I yelled, 'Have you got your ticket, your passport and the money?'

She held up the handbag she was clutching. 'They're in here,' she gasped with fear, never having seen me in this state before.

The little Beetle was already fairly crammed with baggage but we managed to stuff ourselves into the car and although I could hardly change gear because of the cramped conditions, we pulled away. The neighbours were quite clearly fascinated by this development as we lurched off on our nightmare drive, and many of them were pointing at us. They were actually seeing the unbelievable taking place before their very eyes and are probably still talking about it today.

I made one last desperate attempt to find a taxi on our way through Athlone Township. I simply couldn't just drive through the gates into the docks with two coloured women and a baby without being subjected to at least ten minutes of questioning, by which time we would have missed the boat in any case.

Athlone was busy and the streets were alive with passers-by and when we reached the taxi rank there was one taxi standing there but no driver. 'Get out quick, Cathy, and see where the bloody idiot is.' She scrambled out of the car and Cynthia sat speechless clutching the baby. She had never seen her kind and loving 'husband' in this mood before; on reflection I suspect that she was watching a nervous breakdown taking place. I felt as though I was in some hellish nightmare and would wake up at any moment, and I cursed Basil and Dan to hell and back.

Cathy dashed back to the car and crawled in. 'He's drunk in the shebeen,' she said.

Silently wishing the bubonic plague on him I drove off like a maniac. We were rapidly running out of time now.

As I made that magnificent little car do things the designers had never intended it to do, I had a mad impulse to drive along the road past the cottage as it was more or less on the same route. As we turned into the road the first thing I saw was Dan's car parked outside the cottage. I screeched to a halt and told the girls to sit tight and not to panic.

When I dashed through the side-gate into their garden Dan was standing there in a safari suit sipping a brandy. He went red first, then white with shock when he saw who the insane-looking person was, standing accusingly in front of him. Dan was considerably heftier than myself but that did not deter me. I grabbed his lapels and threatened to donder him – do him up, in Afrikaans – unless he went out immediately and drove the girls to the dock. Marie said quietly, 'Do as he says, Dan, he's had enough.'

We shifted the luggage from my car to his in what must have been about thirty seconds. Several neighbours were now taking quite an interest in the two swearing and frenzied white blokes and the coloured ladies with the baby, but the drama didn't last long because we were soon on our way, and as we pulled away I leaned out and bawled to Dan, 'Don't stop for anyone. Just follow me and do what I do.'

As I pushed my foot down I caught a glimpse of Marie as she dashed out of the house yelling. She scrambled into the car with the others and slammed the door.

That was a drive I shall never forget! That little Volksie literally bounced around the corner onto the main road and a coloured workman watering the flower beds in the central division of the main highway leapt for his life as I took a swipe at his backside with my offside wing. Off I went as though the

Devil himself were after me and just managed to shoot through
the robots as they were changing to red. Casting a glance in
the rear-view mirror I saw that Dan had been caught by them.
I was glad that I was an experienced Beetle driver because the
remarkable and quite fantastic little vehicles had been known
to do funny things on bends unless one knew what one was
doing. This elderly model went round the bends on rails and
Sterling Moss would have nodded his approval had he seen
my performance that afternoon.

When I reached the main National Road, I prayed that it
would be free of traffic cops who had a tendency to lurk out
of sight along it. Dan had managed to catch up with me and
we whistled along like crazy, and soon I had turned off and
made my way into the docks without any hold-ups. I reached
the approach road to the dock where the big mail-boat was
waiting, and brought the car to a screeching halt beside
two uniformed dock officials standing beneath a portico. The
engine was running roughly and I guessed that I could have
roasted a small joint over it, but it hadn't let me down. Seeing
the baggage in the back of the car, one of the officers asked
me if I was travelling on the *Edinburgh Castle*, and when I
nodded he said, 'Well, you had better get a bloody move on
because she's due out at any moment.'

I thanked him and roared off again towards the maze of
quays watching out for the 'Mail Boat' signs. Glancing back
I saw that Dan was just pulling away from the portico and
had turned to follow me. I roared on and took the wrong
turning. Looking around, puzzled and agitated, I saw Dan
waving furiously forward in the direction that his car was
pointing. With my foot flat down I did a spectacular U-turn,
scattering coal all over a small group of coloured dock workers
who were watching my performance.

I zoomed after Dan and a few moments later saw his car
parked outside a large Customs and Immigration shed facing
the looming bulk of the *Edinburgh Castle*. I braked hard and
noticed the businesslike smoke belching from her smokestack.
As I fairly leapt out of the car a gimlet-eyed Afrikaner official
pointed a sausage-like finger in the direction of the ship and
snapped, 'Are you going on her?'

I nodded speechlessly; I was too frightened to speak.

'Then you'd better bloody well run for it. Don't worry about
your papers now, there's an officer on board the ship. He'll
sort them out when you get aboard.'

I was parked behind Dan's car and too frightened to look
in his direction in case onlookers twigged what was going on.
The Afrikaner glowered at me and stared hard in the direction
of Cynthia and Cathy. Obviously something nasty was fer-
menting in the dim recesses of his mind, but before he could
crystallise his thoughts I grabbed my bags and tore off towards
the gangplank. One had already been drawn away from the
ship's side and a small group of coloured dockworkers was
standing by the remaining one, ready to haul it away from the
ship. I learned later that the whole ship was waiting our arrival
and the solitary gangplank was there solely for our use. It was
apparent that the boat would have sailed without us if we had
been even three more minutes late.

From the corner of my eye I saw Ramona with some other
coloured people but I didn't even get a chance to say goodbye
to them. As I began to mount the gangplank, Bob came reeling
down it, his eyes glassy with alcohol. He was practically
paralytic and in a voice that must have been heard in Adderley
Street he bawled, 'Where the fuckin' 'ell 'ave you been?' For
a moment I thought he was going to fall but he recovered his
balance and his voice. 'And where the bleedin' 'ell are Cynthia
and Hanna?' I scrambled past him into the dim interior of the
ship's entrance way with Bob staggering after me.

Dozens of people were standing around and there waiting
for me with her clip-board at the ready was the same young
lady whom I had bought the tickets from. She was there to
check the passengers as they boarded the ship. Fixing me with
her clear blue eyes she gave me a little smile of recognition
and said, 'My word, Mr Carr, you nearly missed the boat,
didn't you?'

I had read on a number of occasions about characters in
novels who were unable to speak because their tongues were
stuck to the roofs of their mouths. I had always found it hard
to believe – until that day, when my own tongue seemed to be
stuck to the roof of my mouth and my throat felt as though it
were stuffed with dry cotton wool. I nodded and a sound like
'Gah!' escaped from my arid lips.

She asked me to move away from the top of the gangplank as it was going to be taken away. I remained where I was and peered anxiously down onto the quay. Two South African policemen stood at the bottom of the gangplank watching Cynthia struggling towards it with Hanna tucked under one arm, a heavy holdall in her other hand and a whole load of objects dangling from her. She looked flushed and frightened but despite the fact that a wig that I had bought for her recently was over one eye, she still managed to look outstandingly pretty.

The young shipping clerk again asked me to stand back and I managed to find enough saliva to enable me to croak, 'Not until she and the baby are on board this ship.'

She looked down at Cynthia and then at me, and with her eyebrows slightly raised she said, 'I take it that this is Miss X and baby?' When I nodded she said, 'Oh! I see,' and then, in a low voice, 'She's very pretty, I must say.' She smiled not unkindly and continued, 'It's all right, Mr Carr. You can stand back now, she and the baby will soon be with you.'

I looked down and saw that the policemen wanted to examine Cynthia's papers and question her but an official on the ship shouted something to them in Afrikaans and they shrugged and waved her up the gangplank. They gave her and me some rather searching looks but there was nothing that they could do. They could tell what was going on and I could see from the expressions on their faces that they could hardly believe what they were witnessing. As soon as I saw Cynthia step safely on board with Hanna in her arms I stood back and felt my nervous system gently collapsing inside me.

I think I would have slipped to the deck if Bob, who had been standing next to me, hadn't seen the look on my face and grabbed my arm firmly. 'Come on, mate,' he said, breathing volatile fumes into my face, 'I'll show you to yer cabin.' He led me through a labyrinth of alleyways and down numerous flights of steps and finally stopped outside a small galley. ''Ere 'e is,' he called out and from the door of the galley stepped a small, sparrow-like man who told me that 'my mate' had told 'them' all about my little jaunt. He was a kindly little man who said, 'Don't worry, mate. You're on British territory here, they can't do a thing about you now.'

I nodded but said nothing because I was furious with Bob

for telling all and sundry about my affairs, but he meant well, I knew.

He suddenly yanked a half-bottle of brandy from one of his capacious pockets and thrust it into my hand. ' 'Ere you are, John. 'Ave a swig of this.' I did and it slid down like cold tea but it seemed to put a bit of solidity into my legs once more.

From somewhere inside the vessel a bell began to clang, and another steward came down the alleyway and told Bob that he would have to go ashore as they were now ready to sail. Bob turned to me, his lined face set grim, and the silly old fellow had tears in his eyes. We shook hands firmly and I placed an arm around his shoulder because he seemed to age suddenly. I felt sorry to be leaving him and I promised that I would write to tell him what had happened to cause our delay in arriving at the dock.

'Cheer up, Bob!' I told him. 'We'll be seeing each other again soon; probably at Christmas, if you make a real effort.'

' 'Course we will!' he croaked, then with a change of expression to one of mock severity he said, 'Now you take care of that little darlin' of yours and the baby. If you don't treat 'em nice, you'll 'ave me to deal with.' I smiled and watched him make his way up the steps towards the exit.

The cheerful little sparrow-like steward said, 'Wot cabin are yer in, mate?' I handed him my ticket and he said, 'Come on, I'll take you to it.' I followed him feeling exhausted with the anticlimax of it all and he led me into a spacious cabin with a large porthole which overlooked Cape Town harbour. I dumped my hand-baggage into one of the three bunks and flopped down next to it. Now that Cynthia and Hanna were safely on board I lay back and lit a welcome cigarette and relaxed for the first time since getting up that day. I hadn't been in the cabin for more than about five or six minutes when there was a knock at the door. 'Steward, sir,' a voice called and I got up like an old, old man and tottered across the cabin and opened the door. Standing there was a short, stocky man of about forty-five years of age. He had dark, shiny hair with grey wings at the sides. His hair was parted neatly in the centre and lay flat against his skull. His deep-set eyes peered at me from beneath thick eyebrows. 'May I step inside a moment, sir?' he asked politely in a West Country accent.

When we were in the cabin he closed the door behind him and gave me a penetrating look and then said briskly, 'You're travelling with that young coloured lady with the baby, aren't you, sir?' I said nothing and he went on, 'I know what your game is.'

I was tired and irritable and annoyed by what I took at the time to be his searching and demanding manner. 'What the hell are you talking about?' I demanded angrily. 'And where did you hear such nonsense?'

He looked uncomfortable and licked his lips nervously as if he realised that he had gone a bit too far.

'Er . . . perhaps I made a mistake, sir,' he said apologetically. 'I meant no offence, I assure you, but that English friend of yours told us about you, you see, and perhaps he had been drinking too much.' He shuffled his feet. 'All I wanted to say, sir, was that it stands to reason that you ought to be with the young lady and the baby instead of being in separate cabins, like.'

I looked at him long and hard. Although Cynthia and the baby and I had got on board safely, I still didn't feel secure and I said, rather foolishly now I think back on it, 'You are not, by any chance, a police agent planted on this boat to catch people who are trying to escape from this God-forsaken country, are you?'

His bushy eyebrows rose in amazement, then a look of compassion came to his face. 'Your friend said you'd had a hard time in South Africa, sir. I'm just as English as you are and you are on my ship now and nobody is trying to catch you out, OK?' He picked up my hand-baggage and turning said, 'Now why don't you come along with me to join your pretty little wife and baby. As far as we are concerned, you are travelling as Mr and Mrs Carr and if anyone bothers you or upsets you or your wife in any way, will you promise to tell me, because we'll have great pleasure in fixing the bastards, all right, sir?' A few minutes later I was re-united with Cynthia and Hanna in her two-berth cabin.

Our kind new friend's name was Cecil and in no time he had brought in a cot for Hanna and made us feel at home. As he left, closing the door quietly after himself, I took Cynthia in my arms and kissed her and we held each other for some time. Hanna was sleeping peacefully in her cot and looking into Cynthia's beautiful brown eyes I smiled with happiness and whispered, 'I actually think we've made it, darling.'

After a few more minutes Cecil came back to tell us that we had cast off and if we wanted to wave our friends goodbye now was the time to do it. He showed us how to reach the deck and when we stepped out into the daylight among the crowd of passengers we suddenly realised that we were at last free to mingle openly with white or black people and we both grinned with the joy of it. Nevertheless we were nervous and a bit unsure of ourselves. We deliberately kept apart from each other that first time on the open deck as I didn't want to reveal our 'game' as Cecil had described it, until the ship was well outside the precincts of Cape Town harbour.

When I looked down over the rail I saw that Bob had made his presence known to Ramona and her friends, and Cathy of course, and we continued waving to each other while the boat moved slowly out of the harbour and the little group far below walked along the mole until they could walk no further.

As we slipped out into the bay I could still see them standing at the end of the mole, waving. Bob, who stood slightly away from the main group, looked desolate and I knew deep within me that we would never meet again, at least not in this world.

THE VOYAGE

After an exhausting two days and one complete night of work, followed by the insane day of departure, we were both tired out physically, mentally and spiritually, yet we found a moment to thank God for our safe departure. At six o'clock that first evening on board the *Edinburgh Castle*, Cynthia fed Hanna while I hauled myself up onto the top bunk. Cynthia joined me after making sure that Hanna was settled for the night. There wasn't a lot of room on the bunk and my nose was pressed up against the bulkhead. I was already half asleep when she lay down next to me and snuggled close. We were both still fully dressed as we intended having supper after a short nap.

Cecil told us the following day that he had knocked on our cabin door to see if we wanted any supper but he received no response. After trying again, he opened the door and saw that we were both unconscious and decided that it would be kinder of him to leave us in peace.

We woke the next morning at five-thirty to find that Hanna was letting the world know that she wanted her breakfast. The ship was vibrating gently and rolling slightly but we soon grew accustomed to it. Cynthia sent me in search of hot water for baby's feed. I found a small galley with boiling water on tap and soon Hanna was enjoying her first breakfast in a free society. Having dealt with Hanna's requirements we tucked her safely into her cot and went off to look for bathrooms. As I lay back soaking happily in the hot water I smiled and felt truly at ease for the first time in almost three years. What a wonderful moment that was for me.

However, we still had our final hurdle to face. I had read some reports in South African newspapers about non-white visitors to Britain from South Africa being refused entry into the country, despite the fact that the visitor in question had a more than adequate sum of money on him, plus his ability to provide an authentic address where he would be staying. This disturbed me and although we had got this far without being stopped it seemed to me that we wouldn't have the right to feel really safe until we had passed through immigration at Southampton. I tried not to let the subject bother me, but it did.

I said nothing to Cynthia about my fears as I wanted her to relax and enjoy her new-found freedom as a first-class citizen, for a change. I realised that we would both have some readjusting to do. Our love affair had been a secret thing until now; now it had been thrust into the open, how would we react? Would living back in my own society once more make me feel sensitive and self-conscious about having a coloured wife?

In many ways we had a lot against us and not for us. For a start there was a generation between us and we had different backgrounds and cultures. Cynthia was basically an Afrikaans-speaking South African and although she had a wide vocabulary, her English was a little weak in places and, of course, she was not white. It struck me that the recipe was not a good one for a successful and happy relationship. Only time would provide the answer to my doubts.

We had dressed and were sitting quietly in the cabin waiting for the breakfast bell. When it rang I grinned across at Cynthia and said, 'Well, love! This is where we dive straight into the deep end.' She looked at me anxiously as I continued, 'We are going to walk into a public place in which there will be several hundred white people and we are going to sit there with them and eat our very first meal together in public.' She giggled nervously and after adjusting her hair for at least the fifth time and asking me if she looked all right for at least the tenth time, we left the cabin, and closing the door carefully behind us, we set off and stepped into freedom.

A few other passengers were making their way to the dining-room and when they saw us there was much whispering and nudging. I took Cynthia by the hand and squeezed it and said, 'Be brave, darling. We have as much right to be on this boat as anyone else here. We have paid our fares so if we are stared at, just stare right back.' We found our way to the main glass doors which led into the dining-room but when we looked through them we faltered and hung around nervously outside, feeling rather foolish and self-conscious.

'Come on, darling,' I said at last, taking her arm. 'To hell with the lot of them. Let's have breakfast,' and I pushed open the door and we stepped into the large room. There were about three hundred people sitting there of whom about two-thirds were possibly South African. It was a ghastly moment. I felt as though I had just been presented to Royalty only to be told that I was indecently exposed. The room seemed to be filled with bulging eyeballs – all staring at us. I tried to assume an air of nonchalant indifference but knew it wasn't working. I cast a quick glance towards Cynthia and could see that she was scared stiff and feared that she would bolt at any moment.

I whispered to her, 'These buggers have been scaring the pants off us for the last couple of years and more. Are we going to spend the rest of our lives being afraid of them? Keep your chin up, Dad's with you.' The chief steward who had been seated behind his little desk to our left must have noticed our discomfort because he rose and walked over with a friendly smile. I told him our cabin number and he said, 'Oh, yes. Mr and Mrs Carr, I believe. I've been looking forward to meeting you.'

He told us that our table was situated on the other side of the room but added kindly, 'But we don't want you running the gauntlet every time you eat, do we?' and to our relief he walked us to a table for two not far from the entrance. We could have kissed him.

He served us himself and asked if the baby was all right. When Cynthia asked if the ship had similar baby-food to what she was giving Hanna, he said, 'Bless you, my dear, come along with me for a minute.' He took her and showed her a large cupboard filled with all types of baby foods and said, 'Help yourself to whatever you need from this little lot and if you need more, just ask me, OK?' He was a very decent fellow of the old school and he really looked after us during our journey.

We quite enjoyed our first breakfast aboard and after

checking to make sure that Hanna was still fast asleep, we went on a short exploration of the ship.

After the first few days we soon settled down and felt at ease and enjoyed some deck games such as quoits, table-tennis and so on. Cynthia had some rather stunning clothes and she always looked outstandingly beautiful and I was extremely proud of her. I had the impression that many of the other passengers would like to have spoken to us but were probably as shy as we were. However, after we had been aboard about five days a few cracks began to appear in the reserve of some of the passengers who were obviously dying to hear our story.

Actually little Hanna was responsible. Even at three months, she was gloriously lovely like her mother and people just couldn't prevent themselves from making a fuss of her. Because of this we got to know quite a few people during the voyage and we had become welcome in a number of groups – including groups of South Africans.

The cabin that I had been put into when I had first boarded the ship was to have been shared by myself and a Roman Catholic priest. The day after we set sail I returned to the cabin to collect a couple of things which had been left there after I had moved in with Cynthia. I found the priest sitting on one of the bunks and we got into conversation. He was a plump, jolly fellow with receding white hair. He introduced himself and told me that he had been given to understand that he would be sharing the cabin with another person.

'I was a bit worried, you know,' he said with a twinkle in his eye. 'When I found myself alone here I thought you might have fallen overboard. What a blessed relief that you are all right.'

We got talking and I told him about Cynthia and myself and gave him a brief outline of what we had been through. He listened with obvious interest and as I finished I said, 'Well, there you are. You can form your own conclusions.'

He peered at me over his rimless glasses and asked, 'Do *you* feel that you have done the right thing?'

I said, 'Without a shadow of doubt. I am not what could be described as a religious person by any means but I do have

300

what could be loosely described as a working relationship with God and I don't think that he despises me for doing what I think is right.'

He dwelt on this philosophical outburst for a while and looking at me with a gentle smile, said, 'It's more than likely that you might have bent some of the rules a bit but I am sure that God, in his wisdom, has more than a shrewd idea of your true feelings and I don't think that you need fear too much. However, I do suggest that you tidy things up a bit as soon as you are able to do so, if you follow my meaning – and join me for a drink in the bar later on.' I told him that I would look forward to doing so and as I left he called out, 'And bring your lady along as well.'

Soon we were nearing our journey's end. We stopped at Las Palmas for a few hours and enjoyed a performance from a visiting troup of Spanish dancers. We also bought a couple of umbrellas and a smart poncho for Cynthia.

Not long after we sailed we experienced cooler weather and we were soon rolling gently across the Bay of Biscay towards Britain. In the early hours of the morning we arrived at Southampton and we awoke to hear dock-side sounds that told us that we had berthed. I went out and found a porthole and peered out of it across Southampton Water. It looked grey and flat and across the water I saw a number of typical English houses with red tiled roofs. I called to Cynthia to come and see and when she looked out she shivered and said, 'It looks cold out there.' I hugged her and laughed and told her that she would find it a bit cooler than what she had been used to in Cape Town.

It was time for passengers to prepare for disembarkation and we said our farewells to Cecil and his colleagues and the chief steward, and thanked them for all that they had done to make our voyage a happy and memorable one. They wished us good luck and we made our way upstairs to the main lounge where immigration officers had set up a long table and were scrutinising passports and papers and wielding rubber stamps with brisk efficiency.

I paused at the door and said, 'Now be careful, Cynthia. Don't look at me or wave to me or anything like that. Just stick to your story and show them your letters and money.

Don't deviate in any way otherwise we might end up on our way back to sunny South Africa.'

She giggled nervously and took her turn in the queue. I waited and watched as she moved slowly along towards the table. At last it was her turn and she stepped forward as one of the officers beckoned to her. Other passengers seemed to be dealt with quite quickly and when the officer drew a chair over and asked Cynthia to sit down my stomach began churning away and I thought, Oh, Christ! Here we go again. Will it ever end?

I began perspiring despite the chilly atmosphere and as I sweated away in my own little hell she took out the letters and handed them across to the officer who took them and began to read through them. When he had finished he asked her more questions and kept looking down at the letter in his hand with a doubtful expression on his face. She then held out the travellers' cheques for him to examine, and her return tickets. He studied them with great care and carried on talking. God! Would the man talk for ever, I thought.

He opened her passport and began writing in it. Reaching out for a rubber stamp, he paused for a moment before thumping it firmly down onto the document, and handing it back to her, along with the other pieces of paper. She stood up, looking uncertain where to go, and he said something and smiled and pointed towards the main hall of the ship – and FREEDOM.

EPILOGUE

The author married Cynthia not long after they had established themselves in the UK where another baby daughter arrived – an almost identical replica of Hanna. Basil and Brenda Keller visited them while on their way to a new life in North America. They apologised for their failure to appear during the final, dreadful day of departure from the Republic.

Bob wrote regularly from Cape Town and a year after John and Cynthia arrived in Britain they received a cheerful and optimistic letter informing them that he and Beattie intended joining them in the UK in time to celebrate the coming Christmas.

This was to be the last letter that the author would receive from his old friend. A few days after its arrival a cable arrived with the following message: Sorry to inform you that poor Bob collapsed and died of a heart attack in the flat. Letter to follow, love, Beattie.

Early in the following year, John returned to Africa – this time West Africa – to take up a position as general manager and creative director of an old-established advertising agency. Cynthia and the children followed shortly afterwards. If this had been a novel the story might have had a happier ending but their marriage went wrong and Cynthia decided that she wanted to make a new life for herself elsewhere – on her own.

John and the girls, who were then both very young, stayed in West Africa for some time until he finally settled in the Isle of Man after spending almost nine years in what was once known as 'the white man's grave'. However, his days as an expat were not yet over and he spent another four-and-a-half years working overseas, this time in Saudi Arabia.

In Saudi Arabia, after many lonely years, he first made

contact with his present wife, a beautiful young Filipina nursing sister who was working as the senior theatre-sister in an open-heart surgical unit. They courted for a long period, mainly by correspondence, and eventually fell in love and married in the Isle of Man.

They live happily in their small cottage with their four-year-old son – John – and Sarie, John's younger daughter.

Hanna lives with Cynthia and her new husband somewhere in Europe.